Reforming International Institutions

Reforming International Institutions

Another World is Possible

Edited by the
UBUNTU Forum Secretariat

This book has been prepared and proofread at the Secretariat of the UBUNTU Forum by Vicky Nebot under the supervision of Josep Xercavins and Marta Garrich and with the collaboration of Alba Mengual.

First published by Earthscan in the UK and USA in 2009

For a full list of publications please contact:

Earthscan
2 Park Square, Milton Park, Abingdon, Oxfordshire OX14 4RN
711 Third Avenue, New York, NY 10017

First issued in paperback 2014

Earthscan is an imprint of the Taylor & Francis Group, an informa business

Copyright © UBUNTU Foundation 2009. Published by Taylor & Francis.

ISBN 13: 978-1-84407-811-0 (hbk)
ISBN 13: 978-0-415-85027-8 (pbk)

Typeset by 4word Ltd, Bristol, UK
Cover design by Susanne Harris

A catalogue record for this book is available from the British Library

Library of Congress Cataloging-in-Publication Data has been applied for.

Contents

Part 4   The Proposals – Arranged by Themes

List of Figures

List of Contributors

Luis Alfonso de Alba

Mexican diplomat since 1983, he was appointed Ambassador on December 2001, and since 2004 he has been the Permanent Representative of Mexico to the United Nations and other International Organisations in Geneva. On 19 May 2006, he was elected first President of the United Nations Human Rights Council, a mandate he held from 19 June 2006 to 18 June 2007. Previously, he was Chairman of the Council of the International Organization for Migrations (IOM) from November 2004 to November 2005. Ambassador de Alba was also Chairman of the Disarmament and International Security Committee (First Committee) of the General Assembly during its 59th Session (2004).

Samir Amin

Born in Cairo, from 1957 to 1960 he was Research Officer at the government Institution for Economic Management. After that he became advisor in the Ministry of Planning in Bamako (Mali) from 1960 to 1963. In 1963 he was offered a fellowship at the Institut Africain de Développement Économique et de Planification (IDEP). Until 1970 he worked there as well as Professor at the University of Poitiers, Dakar and Paris (of Paris VIII, Vincennes). In 1970 he became Director of the IDEP, which he managed until 1980. In 1980 he left the IDEP and became Director of the Third World Forum in Dakar, an international association formed by intellectuals from Africa, Asia and Latin America aiming to strengthen ties among third world countries.

Renata Bloem

A Swiss national born in Germany, she completed her studies in Medicine, Languages and Literature at the Universities of Bonn, Munich and New York, and started her academic career by teaching at international schools and cultural institutions worldwide. Since 1985 she engaged in NGO work as a strong advocate for human rights. Elected CONGO President at the General Assembly in November 2000 and re-elected in December 2003–2007, she led CONGO delegations to the World Conference against Racism, to the World Summit on Sustainable Development and organized

Civil Society Fora in Asia, Latin America and Africa. Together with her CONGO Team she has been at the forefront of guiding, supporting and coordinating civil society in the process of the World Summit of the Information Society (Geneva and Tunis). Today she serves CIVICUS at the UN in Geneva.

Boutros Boutros Ghali
Born in Cairo, he became the sixth Secretary-General of the United Nations on 1992, when he began a five-year term. At the time of his appointment by the General Assembly on 3 December 1991, he had been Deputy Prime Minister for Foreign Affairs of Egypt since May 1991 and had served as Minister of State for Foreign Affairs from October 1977 until 1991. He was a member of the International Law Commission from 1979 until 1991, and is a former member of the International Commission of Jurists. He has many professional and academic associations related to his background in law, international affairs and political science, among them, his membership in the Institute of International Law, the International Institute of Human Rights and the African Society of Political Studies. He is currently the President of the Egyptian National Council for Human Rights.

Aldo Caliari
Born in Argentina, since 2000 Aldo has worked at the Center of Concern where he was at first responsible for advocacy and coalition-building activities around the International Conference on Financing for Development (Monterrey, Mexico, 2002) and its follow-up, as well as bringing a human rights approach to the work of the Rethinking Bretton Woods Project. Aldo has done considerable writing and public speaking on issues of global economic governance, debt and international financial architecture. In the last few years he has focused on linkages between trade and finance and policy 'coherence' between financial and trade institutions. He routinely acts as a consultant on these topics for international organizations, foundations, media and civil society groups and networks.

Martha Chouchena-Rojas
A Colombian and French national, she has been deeply involved in international policy, especially in her position as Head of the Global Policy Unit of the International Union for Conservation of Nature (IUCN), where she coordinated the Union's policy work on biodiversity, climate change and trade, as well as its contributions to the United Nations and other key processes. Prior to joining IUCN in 1994, she served as the Director of the National Parks Department and as a negotiator for Colombia, and as

Program Coordinator for the FAO Tropical Forestry Action Plan, among others. She taught at the Universidad de los Andes of Bogota and the University of Geneva. She currently works as an independent consultant on environment and sustainable development, with emphasis on climate change policy.

Birgitta Dahl

Born in Sweden, she served the Swedish Parliament as a member for 33 years (1969–2002), and was its Speaker from 1994 to 2002. She has held government positions as Minister of Energy (1982–1986), Minister of Environment and Energy (1986–1990) and Minister of Environment (1990–1991). Among her international engagements, she has served the UN Secretary General's-High Level Advisory Board on Sustainable Development as its Vice-chair from 1993 to 1996 and as its Chair from 1996 to 1998. She has been a senior advisor to the GEF (Global Environmental Facility) since 1997 and she was a member of the Panel of Eminent Persons on United Nations-Civil Society Relations 2003–2005. The Panel finalized its work with a report to the Secretary General in 2005.

Juan Eduardo Eguiguren

Chilean diplomat, appointed Ambassador on 2007. Director of Multilateral Affairs in the Chilean Ministry of Foreign Affairs since January 2009. Chairperson of the United Nations Commission on Science and Technology for Development (2008–2009). Director of Special Policies International Security and Disarmament (2007–2009). Vice-chairman of the Diplomatic Conference for the International Convention on Cluster Munitions (Dublin, May 2008). Deputy Permanent Representative of Chile to the International Organizations in Geneva (2003–2007). Counsellor in the Mission of Chile to the United Nations in New York (1998–2000) and Alternate Representative of Chile to the UN Security Council (1996–1997).

Richard Falk

American Professor Emeritus of International Law at Princeton University. Currently teaching at the University of California – Santa Barbara, writer, speaker, activist on world affairs, and an appointee to two United Nations positions on the Palestinian territories. In 2001 he served on a United Nations High Commissioner for Human Rights (OHCHR) Inquiry Commission for the Palestinian territories. On 26 March 2008, the United Nations Human Rights Council (UNHRC) appointed him to a three-year term as a United Nations Special Rapporteur on Occupied Palestine. Author of Achieving Human Rights (2009).

John Foster
Born in Canada, he became Principal Researcher (Civil Society/ Governance) at the North-South Institute in 2000. His previous career includes 17 years as a social justice policy officer with the United Church of Canada and more than seven years as Chief Executive Officer of OXFAM-Canada. John Foster served as an NGO representative on the Canadian delegations to the Copenhagen Summit on Social Development (1995) and the Geneva 2000 General Assembly review of that Summit. He addressed the UN NGO Millennium Forum and the World Civil Society Conference. He is a former Executive member of the Canadian Council for International Cooperation, former Chair of the International Coordinating Committee of the Social Watch, and a member and former Vice-chair of the Commonwealth Foundation Civil Society Advisory Committee.

Marta Garrich
Born in Barcelona, she has been a member of the Secretariat of the World Campaign for In-depth Reform of the System of International Institutions and the World Forum of Civil Society Networks – UBUNTU since 2005. She holds a bachelor's degree in Political Science and an MA in European Studies from King's College, London. Before joining the Secretariat of the UBUNTU Forum she worked as an external relations specialist at Sabadell town council. She has also fulfilled various roles within the network of voluntary associations in the city of Barcelona.

Edoardo Greppi
Professor of International Law at the Faculty of Law, University of Turin, where he also teaches International Institutional Law and European Union Law. He is Director of the Master of Laws in International Crime and Justice, jointly organized by the Faculty of Law, University of Turin, and the United Nations Interregional Crime and Justice Research Institute (Unicri). In 2006 he was elected a member of the Council of the Italian Society of International Law (SIDI-ISIL). He is also a full member of the International Institute of Humanitarian Law (Sanremo), Associate Senior Research Fellow at Istituto per gli Studi di Politica Internazionale (ISPI), Milan, and a member of the Scientific Committee of the World Political Forum.

Heidi Hautala
She was the leader of the Finnish Green Party in 1987–1991, and a presidential candidate in 2000 and 2006. She was a member of the national parliament from 1991 to 1995. After Finland joined the European Union (EU) in 1995, she was elected to the European Parliament. She returned to the national Parliament in the elections of 2003. She currently continues to

work closely with EU affairs as a deputy member of the Grand Committee. In addition, she has chaired the Green parliamentary group and currently she is the Chair of the Legal Affairs Committee in the Finnish Parliament. Also she is a member of the Parliament's Speaker's Council. She advocates environmental responsibility, openness in politics, and global justice.

Tomas Magnusson
A well-known figure in the Nordic peace world. He was elected President of the International Peace Bureau (IPB) at the Triennial Assembly of the organization held in Helsinki in September 2006. He has a background in journalism and was for several years Chairperson of the Swedish Peace and Arbitration Society. He currently directs the Gothenburg Initiative, a locally-based agency dealing with development aid and migrants.

Federico Mayor Zaragoza
Spanish scholar and politician. He has held the following political posts, among others: Undersecretary of Education and Science in the Spanish government (1974–1975), member of the Spanish Congress of Deputies (1977–1978), advisor to the Spanish Prime Minister (1977–1978), Minister of Education and Science (1981–82) and member of the European Parliament (1987). In 1978 he became Deputy Director-General of UNESCO. In 1987 he was elected Director-General of UNESCO, a post he held until 1999, when he created the Foundation for a Culture of Peace. In 2001 he also became the President of the UBUNTU Foundation. In 2005 he was named Co-chair of the High-Level Group for the Alliance of Civilizations, a post he held until November 2006 when the Group presented its final report.

Asha-Rose Migiro
Dr. Asha-Rose Migiro of Tanzania took office as Deputy Secretary-General of the United Nations on 1 February 2007. She is the third Deputy Secretary-General to be appointed since the post was established in 1997. Dr. Migiro served as Minister of Foreign Affairs and International Cooperation from 2006 to 2007 – the first woman in the United Republic of Tanzania to hold that position since its independence in 1961. Before that, she was Minister for Community Development, Gender and Children for five years. Prior to Government service, Dr. Migiro pursued a career in academia. She was a member of the Faculty of Law at the University of Dar-es-Salaam, where she rose to the rank of Senior Lecturer. She headed the Department of Constitutional and Administrative Law (1992–1994), and the Department of Civil and Criminal Law (1994–1997). Her work was published widely in local and international journals.

Lluís Miret
Born in Barcelona, he is an industrial engineer with an MA in NGO Management from ESADE in Barcelona and another in Business Management from the IE Business School in Madrid. He has also studied the creation of scenarios for the future under Mihaljo Mesarovic and Josep Xercavins. He was a member of the Secretariat of the World Forum of Civil Society Networks – UBUNTU from its foundation up until the year 2009.

Núria Molina
Núria joined Eurodad in July 2006 as Policy and Advocacy Officer. She works on aid and poverty issues with a particular focus on World Bank and IMF. Before joining Eurodad, Núria worked as Policy and Development Officer at the European Anti-Poverty Network – EAPN. She has also been Executive Officer at the World Forum of Civil Society Networks – UBUNTU in Barcelona for four years. Other jobs have included consultancy for the World Federalist Movement and the UN Financing for Development Office in New York and lecturing at the Communications faculty of the Fairleigh Dickinson University in Barcelona.

Jorge Nieto Montesinos
Born in Arequipa, Peru, he is the President of the Instituto Internacional para la Cultura Democrática (the International Institute for Democratic Culture), based in Mexico City. He has lectured at FLACSO, the Latin American Faculty of Social Sciences, and run UNESCO's Global Governance Unit. He organized the first regional summit on political development and democratic principles in Brasilia in 1997. There he presented the report 'Governing Globalization, The Policy of Inclusion: Changing Over to Shared Responsibility'. His main arguments were then adopted by various Latin American governments. He has written books which have been produced by the Mexican publishing house Fondo de Cultura Económica, among others, as well as essays and articles in various journals and periodicals around the world. He is a consultant to the United Nations and regularly lectures at different universities in Europe and the Americas.

William R. Pace
Since 1994 he has been the Executive Director of the World Federalist Movement – Institute for Global Policy in New York. He has been a life-long civil and human rights activist, environmentalist and peace-advocate. In 1999, he served as the Secretary-General for the Hague Appeal for Peace civil society conference, a monumental gathering for peace in the city of The Hague, Netherlands. In 2001, Mr. Pace was awarded the William J. Butler Human Rights Medal from the Urban Morgan Institute for Human

Rights for being one of the 'cardinal figures in the creation of a Permanent International Criminal Court'. He is author of numerous articles and reports on international affairs and UN issues, multilateral treaty processes, and NGO participation in international decision-making.

Antonio Papisca
Professor of International Relations, Jean Monnet Professor *ad honorem*, Chairholder of the UNESCO Chair in Human Rights, Democracy and Peace at the University of Padua. He is the Director of the quarterly 'Pace diritti umani/Peace human rights' edited by the Human Rights Centre of the University of Padua. From 1990 to 2002 he was a member of the European University Council for the Action Jean Monnet, Brussels; from 2002 to 2004 he was the President of the European Community Studies Association, ECSA-World. He was the founder in 1997 of the European Master degree in Human Rights and Democratisation based in Venice. He is the author of numerous works on international relations, intercultural dialogue, human rights and peace, the international role of local governments and 'city diplomacy'.

Poul Nyrup Rasmussen
Born in Denmark, he holds a Master of Science in Economics from University of Copenhagen. He was Prime Minister of Denmark from January 1993 to November 2001. He is currently a member of the European Parliament for the Danish Social Democrats, member of the Bureau of the PES Group, member of the Foreign Affairs Committee and substitute-member of the Economic and Monetary Affairs Committee. He is also the President of the Party of European Socialists, PES and founder and former President (2003–2007) of the Global Progressive Forum.

Sergi Rovira
Born in Barcelona, he is a member of Secretariat of the World Campaign for In-depth Reform of the System of International Institutions and the World Forum of Civil Society Networks – UBUNTU and is responsible for the Environmental Governance project. He was in charge of the Sustainability area at the UNESCO centre of Catalonia and has attended several United Nations conferences on the environment and sustainability as a representative of civil society. He regularly publishes articles in different journals.

Lene Schumacher
She was at the Danish UN Association when she started working on the UN Conference on Financing for Development (Monterrey, 2002) as an intern

at the WFUNA office in New York. She was then writing her thesis for a Master degree on 'The role of Civil Society in the UN system' and worked with WFUNA until the end of April 2002, when she joined the World Federalist Movement. In the New York offices of the World Federalist Movement – Institute for Global Policy, she worked as the Director of Programmes until the end of 2007. She currently works at the Ministry of Foreign Affairs of Denmark.

Salil Shetty

He joined the United Nations in October 2003 as Director of the United Nations Millennium Campaign after two decades as a recognized civil society leader. In the last three years, Mr. Shetty has played a pivotal role in building up the global advocacy campaign for the achievement of the Millennium Development Goals in over 50 countries. Prior to joining the United Nations, he was the Chief Executive of ActionAid. He serves on the Boards of The Overseas Development Institute, London, the Agence France-Presse Foundation, Paris, and the Global Call to Action Against Poverty (GCAP) Foundation, The Hague.

Andrew Strauss

Professor of International Law at the Widener University School of Law. He earned his bachelor of Arts from Princeton University's Woodrow Wilson School of Public and International Affairs and his Juris Doctorate from New York University School of Law. In the fall of 2008 he and two colleagues became the first faculty members at Widener to be awarded the title of Distinguished Professor of Law. Professor Strauss is co-author (with Burns Weston, Richard Falk and Hilary Charlesworth) of the recently published fourth edition of International Law and World Order, a leading international law textbook.

Yash Tandon

Born in Uganda, Dr. Yash Tandon was the Executive Director of the South Centre until February 2009, and is presently Senior Advisor to the Centre. Dr. Tandon's long career in national and international development spans as a policymaker, a political activist, a professor and a public intellectual. He has written over a hundred scholarly articles and has authored and edited books on wide ranging subjects including on African politics, Peace and Security, International Economics, South – South Cooperation and Human Rights. Prior to the South Centre, he served as the Founding Director of the Southern and Eastern African Trade Information and Negotiations Institute (SEATINI). He has also served on several advisory committees.

Chico Whitaker

Chico Whitaker (Francisco Whitaker Ferreira) today represents the Brazilian Justice and Peace Commission at the International Council of the World Social Forum, of which he was one of the founders. Born in 1931 and trained in architecture, he was Director of Planning for agrarian reform until the Brazilian military coup of 1964. From 1967 onwards he lived in exile for 15 years. In France he worked for the Catholic Committee against Hunger and for Development and coordinated the Secretariat of the International Conference for a Society Overcoming Denominations. In Chile he worked for the United Nations (CEPAL). Back in Brazil he has been an advisor to the Cardinal Archbishop of São Paulo, Paulo Evaristo Arns, served as a Workers' Party representative on São Paulo city council and acted as Secretary of the Brazilian Justice and Peace Commission. In 2006 he received the Right Livelihood Award.

Josep Xercavins

Born in Barcelona, in 1999 he was awarded his Doctorate in Science at the Technical University of Catalonia (UPC). In 1996 he became the UPC's UNESCO Chair in Technology, Sustainable Development, Imbalances and Global Change, having acted as its Coordinating Professor until June 2002. He was the first academic director of the Master degree in Sustainability at the UPC, and also created the Interdepartmental Doctorate Programme in Sustainability, Technology and Humanism. From 2000 until 2009 he became the Coordinator and chief organizer of the Ad Hoc Secretariat of the UBUNTU – World Forum of Civil Society Networks.

Preface

This book departs from convention in many ways and this preface seeks to highlight one of them: this is a book on a project, a process, a movement, a campaign, a proposal for the future; hence its unconventional macrostructure, which reflects the evolution of that wide-ranging process over time.

This work has five parts presenting a broad overview of the fruits of that process from a historical standpoint, showing how the discourse and political action was built up and developed, how it was gradually strung together, elaborated and implemented in political terms over these last five years of intensive work. The documents are presented in chronological order everywhere except in Part 4, where some concessions were made, these being pointed out as they arise.

To guide readers, the editorial team behind this book – the Secretariat of the UBUNTU Forum and the World Campaign – sought to set the documents in their context, and that is the purpose of the grey boxes dotted around these pages: they tell readers what they need to know to understand the work and to place each document in its historical setting. They cover everything from the time of writing to notes on the context behind the documents, together with brief supplementary explanations when these were felt to be essential for full understanding.

Generally speaking, the original version of the various documents was preserved so as to respect the authors' intentions and the plurality of the book.

Lastly, it only remains to stress that this is a plural book, taking in different and sometimes even contradictory points of view, and dealing with differing scenarios. For indeed the In-depth Reform of the System of International Institutions which will no doubt finally be achieved can only be the result of an amalgam of needs, visions, ideals, proposals and correlations of forces.

Josep Xercavins, Marta Garrich, Lluís Miret and Sergi Rovira
Secretariat of the World Campaign for In-depth Reform of the
System of International Institutions and the World Forum of
Civil Society Networks – UBUNTU

Prologue

Federico Mayor Zaragoza

Federico Mayor Zaragoza is the President of the UBUNTU Foundation (the legal entity covering the legal activity of the Secretariat of the UBUNTU Forum), the Chairman of the Culture for Peace Foundation, and he is an ex-Director General of the United Nations Educational, Scientific and Cultural Organization (UNESCO).

Featuring now among his many occupations after his long and fruitful period heading the UNESCO is the mission of enlightening and stimulating the UBUNTU Forum and its Campaign for In-depth Reform of the System of International Institutions. He has contributed a great deal to it, and so no more appropriate foreword could be found for this book than the following document, written in late 2004 with great far-sightedness.

Reforming the United Nations

Uncommon unanimity has been reached: the United Nations (UN) is indispensable and needs to be reformed in depth and urgently such that its functions, attributes, resources and composition – considering not only States and associations of the latter, but also elected members and representatives of 'civil' society – reflect the current state of the world and allow it to successfully meet its challenges.

The UN and other specialized institutions of the system, the international courts and specific tribunals ... all of them provide valuable contributions, but they do not have the support and respect due them, especially from the 'major' Member States. Nonetheless, treaties and agreements of great importance continue to be irreplaceable points of reference on a global level, for instance: the non-proliferation of nuclear weapons; the prohibition on production and use of chemical weapons... More recently, a significant series of summits and resolutions passed by the

United Nations General Assembly (UNGA) have laid out standards for Education (1990), the Environment (1992), Social Development (1995), the Role of Women (1995), the Culture of Peace (1999), the Declaration of the Millennium Development Goals (2000), etc.

However, these guidelines, protocols, declarations and recommendations are generally not binding for States and everything depends on the States' will to incorporate them into their national legal systems.

Many studies, reports and projects for reforming the United Nations have been successively put forth over the years, on initiative of the UN system itself as well as of various other institutions. I recall those that were sponsored by the then-Secretary-Generals, Javier Pérez de Cuéllar and Boutros Boutros Ghali in the late 1980s and early 1990s, respectively. The truth is that the United Nations system as a whole gradually deteriorated, endogenous development aid (the promised 0.7 per cent of the gross domestic product (GDP)) being substituted by loans granted under draconian conditions and, what is much worse, universal ethical principles were substituted by the law of the market. After the major wars of the 20th century, the United States put forth a new world order based on multilateralism, shared development, justice and peace. Yet at the end of the Cold War in 1989, on the other hand, it inclined towards oligarchy, economic globalization and the circumstantial use of the United Nations. The US moved from inclusion to exclusion and hegemony. The marginalized and needy do not know who to turn to, because their principal international intermediary is going through a period of severe crisis. The United Nations has been assigned inappropriate humanitarian aid functions. The World Bank ('from reconstruction to development', don't forget!) and the International Monetary Fund impassibly continue to do the opposite of what their own reports state they should do.

To reach the unanimous conviction I referred to at the beginning, it has unfortunately been necessary to reach the current state of chaos and confusion in so many dimensions: social asymmetries and unsustainable economic policies, radicalization, resentment, humiliation, hunger (thousands of deaths from starvation every day!), shameful and ignominious migratory flows, violent acts, etc. 'Remedy resolutions' are 'wrenched' out of the Security Council to heal the major wounds of credibility and moral authority originated by the 'preventive war' on Iraq and the detestable management of the military victory, while the essential issue is not being remedied: the Middle East. It is there that the United Nations should act immediately, with the clear and explicit support of the European Union, the United States, Russia and the Arabic countries. Suicide terrorists and selective assassination will never bring an end to the conflict. Under these circumstances, it is essential not to become 'distracted' by the all-embracing power of the media. Attempting now, for instance, to call attention to Sudan, after years and years of ignoring so many calls, constitutes a stratagem that would be even more despicable if it were not for the human tragedy involved in any case.

It is likewise important to mention the practical disappearance at the UN of 'memberships', both ideological and group (such as the Non-Aligned Countries, '77+ China', etc.), it being therefore of the essence to go back to the start, such that all peoples count to the appropriate proportions. All dissidence has been silenced: citizens' movements, trade union movements, 'progressive' religious groups... And what about the voice of universities, the scientific community and academia in general? With few exceptions, there is silence. Silence in the face of injustices and the social rupture they cause; silence in the face of cultural uniformity and the progressive indifference of youth; and silence, above all, in the face of the trivialization of universal values...

NGOs assume the highly dignified role of assistance and solidarity that does not usually adopt attitudes of protest. It is essential to know the reality of the present situation, because nothing can change if it is not understood in depth. In whose hands does power really lie? And energy sources? To whom does Africa belong? And the mass media? And the industrial/armaments complex? The world has experienced drastic changes over the past few years in many spheres: population; pandemics; new 'actors' on the international arena, that is, large private corporations; internal conflicts in which the United Nations – and only the United Nations – should intervene in cases of genocide, mass violation of human rights or the absence of government; information technology, which brings knowledge in real time of the terrible conditions in which so many people live and allows us to sympathize; a confusion of value and price...

Today it is clear – and therein lie some prospects, though tenuous, of change – that the present paths, so dark, cannot be redirected if the present continues to prevail over the future, force over the word, economy over politics and arbitrariness over citizens' voices. Making the other world that many of us wish for possible requires several things: a new social contract (immediately tackling the problems of hunger and AIDS, which kill thousands of human beings every day in their 'silent warfare'); a new environmental contract (with 'alliances' that would allow the technical and specialized human resources of several neighbouring countries to convene in a matter of hours in cases of natural disaster – such as forest fires, plagues, floods, etc. – or man-made disasters, such as cleaning of oil tankers on the high seas); and new cultural and moral contracts as well.

As I said at the beginning, there are many organizations of all types that have chosen the reform of the United Nations as the priority of their activities. The 'network of networks' – UBUNTU, World Forum of Civil Society Networks, which was founded in 2000 at the Polytechnic University of Catalonia – has carried out studies and concrete proposals, with the cooperation of several NGOs and personalities, to adapt the international institutions to meet present-day challenges. The objectives are: (a) global democratic governance; (b) knowledge and observance of human rights throughout the world; (c) peace and security based on justice and freedom; and (d) sustainable human development.

Let's not fool ourselves: the reform required is not a 'technical' matter. It should be based on the same democratic principles that the lucid founders of the United Nations system rendered in the fantastic preamble to the UNESCO Constitution: Justice, liberty, equality and solidarity. 'Intellectual and moral solidarity', they added. Only thus can we transform fear, pain and outrage into personal action, into the daily resolve to strengthen democracy; that is, citizen participation, understanding, dialogue and maintaining an attitude of constant inquiry, with the confidence brought by the capacity to create, invent and innovate that distinguishes the human condition.

Frequently and with the best intentions, many individuals give a hand to those in need. This is very good, but global policies regulated by the United Nations are called for, because what the needy hope for – and deserve – is justice, to count, to be taken into consideration. Only a strong and well-coordinated United Nations system could establish the security of peace throughout the world. The peace of security is silence, fear, suspicion and mistrust. For the security of peace, it is urgent to have the best armies under the blue flag of the United Nations when military action is inevitable. And the most advanced intelligence services to enforce compliance with international regulations through the appropriate punitive mechanisms. Each organization within the system must comply with its original missions. It must lend its ear to the peoples. It must have the best advice in order to anticipate and prevent. This would be a step of extraordinary importance in the history of humankind. And in that of the United States. It would fulfil the dreams of Presidents Wilson and Roosevelt. And more importantly, those of hundreds upon thousands of human beings.

List of Acronyms and Abbreviations

AMR	ECOSOC Annual Ministerial Review
ATTAC	Association for the Taxation of Financial Transaction for the Aid of Citizens
BWIs	Bretton Woods Institutions
CAMDUN	Campaign For A More Democratic UN
CDF	Comprehensive Development Framework
CEPR	Centre for Economic Policy Research
CICC	Coalition for an International Criminal Court
CONGDE	Spanish NGOs for Development Liaison Service
CONGO	Conference of NGOs in Consultative Relationship with the United Nations
CoPs	Conference of the Parties
CSD	Commission on Sustainable Development
CSO	Civil Society Organization
CTT	Currency Transaction Tax
DAC	Development Assistance Committee
DCF	Development Cooperation Forum
DPI	Department of Public Information
ECOSOC	Economic and Social Council
FAO	Food and Agriculture Organization
FDI	Foreign Direct Investment
FfD	Financing for Development
FONDAD	Forum on Debt and Development
GATT	General Agreement on Tariffs and Trade
GDP	gross domestic product
GEF	Global Environment Facility
GEI	Global Economic Institutions
GGRP	Global Governance Reform Project
GNI	gross natural income
GPF	Global Progressive Forum
HIPC	Heavily Indebted Poor Countries
HLS	ECOSOC High-level Segment
ICC	International Criminal Court

ICJ	International Court of Justice
ICTs	Information and Communication Technologies
IDA	International Development Association
IDRC	International Development Research Centre
IFF	Intermediate Financing Facility
IFG	International NGO Facilitating Group on Financing for Development
IFIs	International Financial Institutions
ILO	International Labour Organization
IMF	International Monetary Fund
INFUSA	International Network For a UN Second Assembly
IPB	International Peace Bureau
IPU	Inter-Parliamentary Union
IUCN	International Union for Conservation of Nature
IULA	International Union of Local Authorities
LSE	London School of Economics
MDG	Millennium Development Goal
MERCOSUR	Southern Common Market
MSF	Doctors Without Borders
NATO	North Atlantic Treaty Organization
nFfD	New and Innovative Mechanisms in Financing for Development
NGO	non-governmental organization
NIGD	Network Institute for Global Democratization
OCEP	Office of Constituency Engagement and Partnerships
ODA	Official Development Assistance
OECD	Organisation for Economic Co-operation and Development
PAIGC	African Party for the Independence of Guinea and Cape Verde
R2P	Responsibility to Protect
SDR	Special Drawing Rights
TNCs	Transnational Corporations
TRIPS	Agreement on Trade-Related Aspects of Intellectual Property Rights
UN	United Nations
UNCTAD	United Nations Conference on Trade and Development
UNDCP	United Nations Development Capital Programme
UNDP	United Nations Development Programme
UNECLAC	United Nations Economic Commission for Latin America and the Caribbean
UNEF	United Nations Emergency Force

UNEO	United Nations Environmental Organization
UNEP	United Nations Environment Programme
UNESCO	United Nations Educational, Scientific and Cultural Organization
UNGA	United Nations General Assembly
UNICEF	United Nations Children's Fund
UNITAID	International Drug Purchase Facility
UNOG	United Nations Office at Geneva
UNSC	United Nations Security Council
UPC	Polytechnic University of Catalonia
UPF	Pompeu Fabra University
WB	World Bank
WEED	World Economy, Ecology and Development
WEF	World Economic Forum
WFM	World Federalist Movement
WHO	World Health Organization
WPF	World Political Forum
WTO	World Trade Organization

Part 1

The World Campaign: Context and Stages

By Way of Introduction: The World Forum of Civil Society Networks – UBUNTU, Democratic Worldwide Governance and the World Campaign for In-depth Reform of the System of International Institutions

Secretariat of the World Campaign and of the UBUNTU Forum

After his tenure as Director General of the United Nations Educational, Scientific and Cultural Organization (UNESCO), Federico Mayor Zaragoza came back to live in Spain (Madrid), and created the Fundación Cultura de Paz (Culture of Peace Foundation) in 2000, which he has chaired ever since, with Ana Isabel Prera as its Director. Among his first projects is the role of enlightening and leading what was to become the UBUNTU Forum.

In that same year of 2000, he was awarded an honorary Doctorate by the Polytechnic University of Catalonia (Universitat Politècnica de Catalunya – UPC). Both the rector of that University, Dr. Jaume Pagès Fita, and the then Director of the UNESCO Centre in Catalonia, Mr Fèlix Martí Ambel, advised Federico Mayor to entrust the definition, implementation and coordination of the new project to Professor Josep Xercavins i Valls, who was then busy coordinating the UNESCO Chair in Technology, Sustainable Development, Imbalances and Global Change at the UPC. For that reason, the headquarters of what was to be and now is the international Secretariat of the UBUNTU Forum is located in the northern campus (Campus Nord) of the UPC, in Barcelona, the capital city of Catalonia.

That was how the Secretariat of the UBUNTU Forum came into being, and its initial core group – comprising Manuel Manonelles, Lluís Miret, Núria Molina and Josep Xercavins himself as coordinator – proceeded to lay the methodological and conceptual foundations of the process that was to lead to the two plenary meetings that respectively started up and concluded the founding of that project (the first of those meetings having been held in the first half of 2001, and the second at the beginning of March 2002 in the Parliament of Catalonia).

The first and main result of that founding process was the creation of the World Forum of Civil Society Networks – UBUNTU, the founding document of which is given in the section on 'The founding document of the UBUNTU Forum' below. The part specifying the ultimate objectives, vision and mission of the new UBUNTU Forum includes these words:

> *The ultimate aim of the UBUNTU initiative is, given the particular serious-ness of the current problems, to promote the construction of a world that is more human, just, peaceful, diverse and sustainable, thus contributing to bring about a transition from a culture based on force and imposition towards a culture of peace, dialogue, justice, equity and solidarity.*

And continues:

> *In order to achieve this, it will be necessary to be equipped with new pro-cedures and institutions of democratic worldwide governance on every scale (reforming what exists and/or creating new forms) which, with other actors, and always taking into account the active participation of civil society.*

Looking back now it could be said that in order to change the world, to build a better world, which is the ultimate objective, the UBUNTU Forum sees moving forward towards true global democratic governance as funda-mental, and for that purpose, as already noted in that book, reforming our international institutions is essential. And that can only happen with the active participation of civil society.

In the context of the discussions that arose during the founding of the Forum, and given that the participants in the UBUNTU Forum were mainly networks of international civil society organizations of widely differing kinds and with diverse aims (championing human rights for all, empowering women, seeking peace through disarmament or working for environment-friendly development, among others), it could be said that one of the projects that would be of real interest to them all would be the building of global democratic governance. Through that project, the policies required in various fields for 'changing and improving' the world for the benefit of the vast majority of humanity could be defined and implemented.

The founding document of the UBUNTU Forum

Presentation

At the end of 2000, Federico Mayor made a call to the different actors in civil society around the world:

> *The 21st century is faced with a process of 'globalization' in which agreements, mergers and joint endeavour in the international networks of the big financial, industrial and service industries enormously influence the whole world. This situation has made it necessary for another actor on the world scene, the so-called 'civil society', to establish worldwide links so as to be able to influence the issues on the world agenda that affect it each day to an extraordinary degree. Thus, as many voices as possible should unite to attain sufficient magnitude to be heard and to bring about an interaction that would favour the presence of a 'more human sense' in political, social, economic and cultural actions on a worldwide scale. The main objective is to join forces, to construct bridges of dialogue and communication between personalities and intellectuals, international organizations and institutions, people from the university and media spheres etc., who are primarily concerned with working for peace, democracy, sustainable development, human dignity and human rights and who, working together to defend these great principles, might open up a favourable dialogue with other actors in the international arena so that this debate might eventually have an important part to play on the world stage.*

The aim is to create a network of networks, a movement of movements in which, united yet diverse, all these elements can jointly weave structures and forums of opinion and encounters that make it possible to work for the values and principles that sustain life in a democracy, thereby attaining true human development on a worldwide scale that ensures both harmony with nature and cultural diversity.

This call has led to the scheduling of two constitutive meetings (April 2001 and March 2002), covering a period that has been particularly rich in events concerning civil society. At the first meeting it was decided to create the World Forum of Civil Society Networks – UBUNTU. **UBUNTU is an age-old African term for humaneness – for caring, sharing and being in harmony with all creation. As an ideal it promotes cooperation between individuals, cultures and nations.** This decision was confirmed at the second meeting and the project has gone ahead at different institutional and operative levels. The desire that the Forum should be a proactive (prospective and propositive) voice for placing the human being at the centre of all political, economic and social decisions has also been accentuated.

Ultimate aims: Vision and mission

The ultimate aim of the UBUNTU initiative is, given the particular seriousness of the current problems, to promote the construction of a world that is more human, just, peaceful, diverse and sustainable, thus contributing to bring about a transition from a culture based on force and imposition towards a culture of peace, dialogue, justice, equity and solidarity. In order to achieve this, it will be necessary to be equipped with new procedures and institutions of democratic worldwide governance on every scale (reforming what exists and/or creating new forms) which, with other actors, and always taking into account the active participation of civil society, would guarantee:

- more representative, participatory and democratic processes of decision-making that guarantee the legitimacy of political decisions;
- limited and responsible exercise of power on regional, national and worldwide scales;
- coherence between policies in the macroeconomic, commercial, cooperation and environmental spheres that will enable a truly social human and environmentally sustainable development throughout the planet oriented by the principles established in the Universal Declaration of Human Rights;
- public conception and management of global common goods and of the scientific and technological knowledge and powers of humanity, the development of which should be in accordance with the general interests of society;
- preservation and development of cultural diversity in opposition to globalization with tendencies towards homogenization;
- promotion of a development model based on education and health, incorporating the viewpoint of gender, in defence of life, and against violence and the proliferation of arms.

Functional aims: Priorities

- To find spaces and ways of working together so that different networks, people and organizations of global civil society might unite their voices, work together on proposals, organize specific joint actions and increase their mutual knowledge and relations.

- To influence, through this joint work, the drawing up and implementation of policies which promote the inalienable exercise of individual and collective human rights at all possible levels.
- To strengthen the voice of civil society and reinforce the role of existing organizations. The UBUNTU initiative therefore aims at:
  - having a holistic and global outlook rather than a specific, issue-related or local one. To take into account specific and local issues and their inter-relation with, and complementing of, global issues;
  - making the strengths of civil society more visible and effective throughout the world;
  - working together to identify the main challenges facing humanity and proposing common strategies and plans of action based on those already in existence.

Starting with the reality of each moment and taking up the previous work as an example to follow, take up again and develop. Especially the United Nations' major declarations and international treaties – from its Charter to, for example, the 'Declaration and Plan of Action for a Culture of Peace'; the declarations and programmes of action resulting from international summits – official and parallel – of the 1990s; and the programmatic activity which has directly led to the organization of civil society in recent years – the 'Hague Appeal for Peace', the 'Manifesto for a Culture of Peace', the 'Final Declaration and Plan of Action of the United Nations Millennium Forum', the 'Earth Charter', etc.

- To work on new common proposals concerning the world's problems, their possible solutions and management (procedures and institutions, the effective presence, along with other actors, of civil society, etc.).
- To engage in common activities – statements, campaigns, etc. – among the organizations participating in the initiative, as an action that will offer permanent information to citizens concerning the major issues on the world agenda.
- To create capacity for dialogue, political pressure and influence of civil society with regard to governments, international organizations, economic power and the mass media.

Functioning

A forum of debate and action (permanent in its virtual form and periodical in its physical manifestations) is being fostered so as to favour coordinated work while articulating the participants in the forum, bearing in mind and extending plurality and diversity, their strengths and conceptual and thematic richness.

- Participants in the forum are all those organizations and/or people who, on the basis of this foundational process, accept the essence of this document and wish to participate. The sovereignty of the UBUNTU Forum resides in its participants.
- The UBUNTU Forum will function in accordance with the following procedures:
    - The Meeting of the forum: this will be held every one or two years. The agenda and main documents are to be debated in a prior participatory process. The virtual Meeting of the forum is that which permits the permanent forum and will be carried out in the forum's virtual space which guarantees full access to all participants, and mostly at a distance by means of communication technologies.
    - The Coordinating Committee (and where necessary, the working groups): this is the body of work and general motor which guarantees appropriate functioning, procedures and activities of the forum.
    - The Ad Hoc Secretariat: this constitutes the professional management of the forum, an entity with its headquarters at the Polytechnic University of Catalonia (UPC), Barcelona, which is coordinated by Professor Josep Xercavins i Valls.
    - Decisions are taken by consensus whenever possible, and otherwise by simple majority of the participants. The decisions taken are never binding for a minority opinion. Any decision and/or public manifestation of the initiative must be accompanied by a list consisting exclusively of the participants who have voted in favour or expressed their support for it.

April 2001/June 2002

The Global Democratic Governance and the reforms in some international institutions by Jorge Nieto Montesinos; and the decision to launch the campaign

While we stressed above that the founding document of the UBUNTU Forum already mentioned the ambition to move towards what was to become its main project – the World Campaign – it is worth noting here that this did not come about by chance.

In the period between the two initial plenary meetings (2001–2002), the first meeting of what was to become the Coordinating Commission of the UBUNTU Forum was held. The Commission, taking its cue from the discussions in the first of those plenary meetings, commissioned a working document from Jorge Nieto Montesinos for the second plenary meeting. Jorge Nieto Montesinos is the Director of the International Centre for a Democratic Culture (Centro Internacional para una Cultura Democrática), and, in conjunction with Adam Jones, Farid Kahhat and Verónica Zebadúa, he drew up the report 'Global Democratic Governance and the Reform of some International Institutions'.

The document, reprinted hereunder, was passionately and brilliantly presented by Jorge Nieto at the second plenary meeting, and it made a decisive contribution to that meeting's success, not only in concluding the foundation of the UBUNTU Forum, but also in simultaneously taking the formal decision to launch the UBUNTU Forum's first great project: which was later to be called the World Campaign for In-depth Reform of the System of International Institutions, though back then it was just a title, an idea.

Introduction

The present world panorama is grim and uncertain. The climate of optimism established at the end of the Cold War and increased on the eve of the new century has now been utterly dispelled.[1] The new millennium was heralded in by terror and war, and by horrifying images of people driven to desperation by the social consequences of an unjust world economy dominated by the multinationals. There is a logical thread linking the events of September 11 in New York and Washington, the images of the war in Afghanistan and economic disaster in Argentina: globalization without rules. This is the context in which we explore the problem of building global democratic governance, a complex problem of inevitably technical dimensions, highly specialized in many aspects. At its core, however, is an age-old issue: power struggle and the legitimate institutions that can regulate it.[2] This is, by its very nature, an eminently political question, for which reason a number of ethical decisions must inevitably be taken with regard to our evaluation, theories and proposals regarding global democratic governance.

This is not the first time that the problems of world governance have been posed in their planetary dimensions. As long ago as 1795, in its most illustrious predecessor,[3] immediately after the signing of the Basle peace treaty, Kant linked the chance of world peace – perpetual, no less – to the establishment of a government of governments, cosmopolitan law and world citizenship. It is true that Kant conceived not the institutional system of democratic governance we now propose, but a world government formed by a federation of states to create effective conditions for peace.[4] But it could not have been otherwise, thinking, as he did, from within the system of sovereign states whose absolute legal power was consecrated in the 1648 Peace of Westphalia, which brought into being what is known by the experts as the Westphalian order or system.

What were the main pillars of this order?[5] One, that nation-states were the only sovereign bodies. Two, that this sovereignty was exercised over a geographical territory through the establishment of physical frontiers. Three, that the nation-states' central governments were the agents with the greatest power in the world. Four, that no law could exist above that of the nation-state, and that international law was that deriving from treaties signed by sovereign states, consecrating the inalienable right of non-inter-ference. Finally, five, as a corollary of the above, that, in the absence of supranational law, war between sovereign states was legitimized as a means of resolving disputes. Hence the subsequent efforts to 'civilize' war.

This order, now nearly 300 years old, is now being questioned by the transformations accelerated or created by the globalization process.[6] This crisis constitutes the hub of our concern about global democratic gover-nance since, without rules, ungoverned globalization becomes an important source of world instability, disorder and ungovernability.[7] What are the changes which make the present situation new? Firstly, that nation-state governments are no longer the sole source of legal sovereignty. Degrees of sovereign power have been transferred to other instances – supranational, sub-state or non-state. Secondly, systems of authority based on the idea of geographical territory are under question, and power, often faceless,[8] is exercised beyond and despite frontiers. Thirdly, national states are no longer alone on the international scene: other political forces have emerged which take part, often with even greater force, in international power struggles.[9] Fourthly, many elements forming the bases of a supranational law have appeared in recent decades – protection of human rights, of the environment, of humanitarian law – curtailing states' absolute sovereignty. And, fifthly, despite the present conditions, international opinion is clearly turning against war, at least in its Westphalian interpretation as a legitimate and 'natural' resource. Having said this, we must immediately state the proviso that, since the globalization process is uneven and asym-metrical, although all the nation-states were affected by these trends, some have been more affected than others. It is no doubt the states in the countries of the South that have most seen their relative power curtailed.

And the situation prior to this was already considerably asymmetrical and hierarchical.

The creation of the United Nations Organization in 1945 was marked by the compromise between the logic of the Westphalian international legal system and the logic of a legal system based on the broader international community, even if the latter played a subordinate role. The factors contributing to this compromise were the horrific experience of two world wars, the emergence in reaction to it of a humanist consciousness led by a generation of visionaries and, we should not forget, the incipient conflict of the Cold War between two systems, two ideologies and two nuclear superpowers who, in their dispute, opened up a space for this compromise.

Since then, these two logics – that of states and that of the broader international community – have systematically clashed in successive efforts to establish the institutions for global democratic governance.[10] And different power groups or alliances have formed around them which not always – in fact, hardly ever – express a diaphanous conflict between states as unique, privileged actors in a system of international relations in crisis, and the organizations, activists and intellectuals of cosmopolitan citizenship. In any case, if it had, all the developments which have occurred in spite of all would probably not have come about. Governments, without an international body formally charged with thinking about the problem of global democratic governance, might well have reduced the debate to the often insipid, banal language of tawdry diplomatic compromise. Intellectual bodies, for its part, despite their interesting and coherent formulations, have often failed to take into account the conditions necessary for making proposals for institutional change possible. Let us look now at some of these processes for building global democratic governance.

The logic of United Nations reform

Those who propose UN reform tend to work from one of two viewpoints: they either see an organization which is costly to run and which, if conserved,[11] should become a figurehead of such values as honesty and effectiveness, or they see it, and particularly the Security Council, as an undemocratic organization which does not attend to the needs of the world's people.

It is no surprise that this first line of criticism tends to be supported by the powerful developed countries that dominate such important institutions as the Security Council and specialized economic agencies such as the World Bank (WB) and the International Monetary Fund (IMF). Neither is it surprising that concerns about democracy and the position of the poorest UN members tend to be taken up by representatives from developing

countries or non-governmental organizations (NGOs) concerned princi-
pally with issues of peace, justice and development.[12]

Democracy and development: These issues lie at the core of criticism and reform proposals put forward by South representatives and
many NGOs.

Bureaucracy and administration: This area includes proposals to
decrease the number of UN officials, particularly those working in the
Secretariat, to eradicate corruption, to reduce costs and duplication of
administrative functions and to use the new communication technologies to improve coordination.

The Security Council: Should this UN deliberative and executive
body be enlarged to give greater representation to non-western countries? Should the right of veto be extended to the most representative
developing countries? What are the greatest obstacles to Security
Council reform?

Peacekeeping: UN peacekeeping activities began in the late 1980s
and early 1990s with missions in Central America, the Balkans, south-
east Asia and other places. But serious questions have been posed
about UN action, particularly in Somalia, former Yugoslavia and
Rwanda.

A communication of this type can hardly do justice to the broad range of
UN reform initiatives put forward. For example, calls for better communications between NGOs and the world body are but briefly touched on.[13]
Other issues not dealt with in detail are the International Penal Court initiative, female representation in UN structure and decision-taking processes
and proposals for funds for the eradication of world poverty and for the
preservation of the world habitat, put forward by the 2000 Millennium
Forum.

Some conclusions and possibilities for action

The above analysis suggests that obstacles to the large-scale reform of the
United Nations' institutions and prospects and of international financial
institutions (IFIs) reside, more than anything, in the mixed nature of the
organization, in the compromise between two logics in which one is pre-
eminent: the logic of states. Formed by delegates from sovereign states, the
United Nations has been hamstrung from the first by the disparities and

rivalries inherent in the system of states. The struggle for reform has revealed, more than anything else, the mutually irreconcilable visions which exist with regard to the UN's role. Simplifying greatly, the developed countries view that the organization should serve as an extension of the foreign policy of the most powerful nations, and the developing countries stress on greater democracy in decision-taking and the development goals of the poor countries. Reform will therefore require a decrease in the great powers' international influence and commitment on the part of developing countries in their dealings with the rich countries, as well as active engagement and intellectual daring on the part of individuals and organizations on the side of the logic of global democracy. In many cases, it is from the organizations that the greatest impetus has come for the construction of a global system of governance, in association with committed workers from the organizations themselves and groups of countries from the South and, on occasion, the North.

The crucial missing ingredient here is the necessary political will: 'We have the sobering paradox that while the objective need for the United Nations is even greater now than it was when it was created, there is little evidence of the enlightened political will and vision that gave rise to the creation of the UN and Bretton Woods Institutions (BWIs) in the aftermath of World War II. Without a revitalization of enlightened political will inspired by a transcending vision of the risk and opportunities that confront the human community as we move into the 21st century, there is little likelihood of effecting the fundamental changes required in these institutions to enable them to respond effectively to these needs.'[14] This statement is valid not only for UN reform processes but also for all processes of building global democratic governance. As she says for the specific case of the World Trade Organization (WTO), but which is valid for the whole process, reform leaders and activists should 'keep up the mobilization and pressure, and mount an offensive of counter-proposals with the ultimate objective of building genuine international democracy'. Thus, rightly, says Susan George, adding that 'this will call for a sustained collective effort, for discussion and action. It cannot be planned in every detail at this time.'[15]

Can the political will necessary to achieve global democratic governance conceivably be built? A unilateral outlook will probably continue to dominate the foreign policy of the most powerful state in the world, making this will extremely difficult to muster. But there exists the possibility that a coalition of Third World states seeking to broaden their margins of autonomy, along with allies found among the more progressive nations in the developed world and the effective initiative of international civil society, might arise to counter the United States' unilateral tendencies and press for meaningful reform. In many areas, such moves would encounter resistance from the only superpower. But even unilateral powers can be persuaded by the use of concerted action to modify or reverse their course. Although enormously difficult, it is possible that such a force might be able to nudge world politics in a more positive direction. Any attempt to build such a coalition would, no doubt, first have to overcome internal difficulties and disagreements. This is perhaps the most important political challenge in the present situation, the Gordian knot in the construction of global democratic governance. It is difficult to see, if such an initiative is not forthcoming, how attempts to reform the United Nations can be transformed from being merely cosmetic or elitist into visionary movements in tune with the needs of humanity.[16]

In the process of building global democratic governance, the two logics which co-exist on the ever-shifting and changing international scene multiply as in a kaleidoscope. A network like this one might act wisely to build the necessary political will without which such a difficult situation as the present one cannot be tackled. The essence of building global democratic governance is political in nature. This network, halfway between the Club of Athens and the Porto Alegre World Social Forum, may find its mission in liaising between the expressiveness of those who won the streets long ago and the instrumental capacity of those with experience in building a world order. Fostering fresh dialogue between North and South, returning issues of development – and sustainable development – to the international agenda. Regionalizing and decentralizing initiatives and spaces for encounters to build democracy. Showing those who believe there is no alternative to the present situation the error of their ways. And, above all, speaking clearly: we must avoid a new silence being added to the old one of those who have been silenced and the new one of those who prefer to remain silent,[17] the silence of those who speak.

The World Campaign for In-depth Reform of the System of International Institutions

Secretariat of the World Campaign and of the UBUNTU Forum

First phase of the World Campaign (2002–2005)

Presentation and aims of the World Campaign in 2003

Why this campaign?
Humanity is facing particularly grave problems and challenges at present: we still have not achieved peace and security based on justice and freedom in the world; huge numbers of our planet's inhabitants live in deplorable conditions of poverty; the rich countries continue to be shackled to a model of economic growth whose impact on the environment jeopardizes the sustainability of life for future generations; loss of cultural diversity is impoverishing, perhaps irreversibly, one of humanity's most important characteristics.

The globalization process intensifies interrelations and interdependence among world's problems and challenges. As a result, what happens on a global scale has a decisive influence locally, on what affects the life of all the citizens in the world. Moreover, globalization is leading to a weakening of political authority: while markets are becoming global, the influence of political institutions required for their democratic, equitable and efficient functioning decreases every day. In this state of affairs, people all over the world are beginning to claim their democratic entitlement to participate in decisions that affect their lives so directly. Global civil society should play a key role in promoting the democratization of the system of international institutions.

In such a context, the break-down of the international system for peace and security which became evident in the recent war in Iraq and the unilateral course of action embarked upon by the world's leading power have caused widespread turmoil with serious consequences for the system of international institutions, particularly the United Nations. Unilateral action in the field of peace and security has become part of the global equation, making in-depth reform of the world institutional system even more necessary and urgent.

This campaign intends to encourage a series of reforms of international institutions towards a global system of democratic governance through representative procedures involving the participation of all the actors of the world scene. Its key objective is to contribute to establishing a consistent, transparent, responsible and effective global architecture based on developing international legislation whose democratic value and legitimacy is widely accepted. At the heart of this system would be a stronger, more democratic United Nations organization, with effective control over all its bodies and agencies and over global multilateral organizations. Such an institutional system would be empowered to contribute to building a fairer, more equitable, diverse, sustainable and peaceful world.

Campaign objectives

To launch a process for in-depth reform of the system of international institutions. To involve all actors of the world scene: international institutions, different levels of government and civil society in its broadest sense. To draw up agreements among civil society over the conceptual and methodological guidelines for such reform. To this end, key lines of action include:

- An Internet gateway on the reform of international institutions that, among other things, provides a forum for debate on reform issues: **www.reformwatch.net**
- Raising world public opinion about the need and importance of in-depth reform of the system of international institutions to move towards world democratic governance.
- Initiatives aimed at obtaining the support of world public opinion, employing the usual mechanisms as well as setting up a first experiment in 'world citizen legislative initiative' by Internet, collecting as many signatures as possible in support of the campaign as diverse and representative as possible.
- Channelling the pressure of world public opinion towards the international powers (international organizations, different levels of government, world economic actors, etc.) to impress on them the importance and need for such in-depth reform.

- Furthering the definition and establishment of a World Panel on Global Democratic Governance that can be given the mission of drawing up a proposal for the reform of the system of international institutions through representative procedures involving all actors of the world scene.

The World Campaign Manifesto

The campaign is organized around a Manifesto that describes the reasons behind and proposals for in-depth reform of the system of international institutions, inviting the world's citizens to pledge their support to it:

> **We, citizens of the world, determined to safeguard future generations from war, poverty, injustice, cultural uniformization and environmental degradation,**
>
> **DECLARE** the particular seriousness of the problems and challenges facing humanity and, in particular, that:

- The globalization process is increasing the interdependence and complexity of world problems and widening the gap between rich and poor people. While markets become increasingly global, the influence of political institutions required for their democratic, equitable and effective functioning decreases every day. We witness the expansion of policies applied by world economic institutions which favour the market and the large corporations, to the detriment of those promoting sustainable human development, as set out in UN summits of the 1990s and the millennium.
- The weakening and marginalization of the system of international institutions as regards peace and security issues has led to unilateral use of force in recent armed conflicts (Iraq...). This fact reinforces the use of military superiority to impose the interests of the world's leading power rather than promoting conflict resolution collectively and in accordance with processes and protocols established through the UN.

In this state of affairs, we citizens proclaim that a fairer world is possible, and we reclaim our democratic entitlement to participate in global decisions that affect our lives every day. To this end, we

> **PROPOSE in-depth reform of the system of international institutions to guarantee:**

- Democratic governance of globalization to contribute to resolving the grave problems and challenges that face our world. This would mean placing human beings and the well-being of the planet instead of trade and economic interests at the centre of the priorities of international institutions. In other words, to give priority to human rights above all other international legislation.
- The eradication of poverty and the promotion of more equitable development and respect for cultural, natural and gender diversity. To achieve this, it is necessary to put into practice institutional mechanisms that would reduce social and environmental imbalance worldwide and guarantee a more ethical functioning of the world's economy. Part of these mechanisms should include the establishment of taxes on international financial transactions and the regulation of transnational corporate activity.
- World peace and security, embracing human and environmental security, based on justice and freedom. This requires a system of international institutions based on democratic principles, which respects and promotes a culture of peace and collective interests and values, and which is provided with mechanisms and means to ensure respect for international rules and agreements. In this sense, a universal system of international justice is essential.
- The establishment of mechanisms to enable the world's citizens and civil society organizations to achieve direct representation and participation in global decision-making processes within the framework of the international system.

The pursuit of these goals requires a stronger, more democratic UN, placed at the centre of a consistent, democratic, responsible, effective system of international institutions. More specifically, we need to democratize the composition and decision-making procedures of UN bodies and agencies to ensure that they are effective and democratic. And we need to reform and integrate within the UN all other global multilateral organizations (IMF, WB, WTO, etc.). To achieve these objectives, we seek to

FOSTER a process of:

- Reflection and analysis by world civil society about ideas and proposals for the reform of international institutions.
- Mobilization of world's citizenry to promote and participate actively in the reform process.
- Promotion of multi-stakeholder dialogue at world scale on the need for and nature of this reform.

- A world citizen legislative initiative, based on the support for this manifesto pledged by citizens and organizations worldwide. The manifesto will then be submitted to the UNGA, calling for the organization, with the participation of all actors on the world scene, of a World Conference on Reform of the System of International Institutions.

Second phase of the World Campaign (2006–2009)

Presentation and key political messages on the second phase of the Campaign

After all the developments in the world of International Institutions in recent years, especially in 2005 – when most of the 'extraordinary' general meetings of such international institutions as the WTO, the BWIs and the UN did not live up to expectations – and, according to the Organizing Committee assembled in Barcelona on 10 and 11 February, if this Campaign did not already exist, it would be absolutely essential to launch it. **The Campaign therefore continues, and it is our aim to extend and increase its impact by taking current political realities into account** (with substantial differences, at different levels, from 2002 and 2003, when it was designed and first launched) **and by re-launching it with new political and working goals in a second phase covering the 2006–2009 period** (benefiting from the knowledge and experience accumulated over the initial phase, from 2002 to 2005, particularly the know-how acquired from our growth and impact, at not only a conceptual and documentary level but also at a practical level).

Key political messages on the second phase of the Campaign
Four levels can be highlighted:

- With regard to the major challenges facing humanity – both in the field of peace, security, human rights and justice, and that of sustainable human development, beginning with the immediate need to improve basic living conditions among most of the world's population – we need, among many other things, but as an essential element, to change world policies as they stand at present. This requires, once more without doubt as an essential element, the in-depth reform of the system of international institutions; that is, to repeat the call 'TO MAKE ANOTHER WORLD POSSIBLE: REFORM INTERNATIONAL INSTITUTIONS'.

- Continuing to insist on the need to reform the system in order to: (a) render effective the central position of a strengthened, democratized UN; and (b) reform world financial, economic and trade organizations (IMF, WB and WTO), bringing them under the umbrella of the UN. That is to say, reiterating, with even greater emphasis, the key points in the CAMPAIGN MANIFESTO, among others, meeting the need for mechanisms enabling the citizens and civil society organizations around the world to be directly represented and to participate in global decision-making processes. In short, the call for WORLD DEMOCRATIC GOVERNANCE to help solve the serious problems and huge challenges that face the world today.
- Drawing up proposals concerning the reforms needed. In this regard, we shall continue encouraging and promoting open discussion – that is to say, not putting forward closed proposals, but fostering debate and exploring ideas in depth – as regards the document PROPOSALS TO REFORM THE SYSTEM OF INTERNATIONAL INSTITUTIONS. FUTURE SCENARIOS and, particularly the 'LONDON DECLARATION', a more succinct version of this document.
- Conceiving the second phase of the World Campaign as a framework-campaign, with the goal of producing results in the medium term and comprising the above-mentioned levels by promoting concrete, specific campaigns (in some cases, with objectives that can be achieved in a relatively short time) or taking part in movements and campaigns of a similar or complementary nature.

Objectives and guidelines

- To ensure that a process of in-depth reform of the system of international institutions gets under way; to generate concrete and specific reform processes that are effective for themselves and that, within a coherent framework, contribute to the in-depth reform process.
- To involve the maximum possible number of actors in the global arena in this process: international institutions, different levels of government and civil society in its broadest sense. To involve key actors in the current political momentum in the World Campaign: the world of parliamentarians and their international organizations; the world of local authorities and their international organizations; governmental groups and regional and sub-regional groups linked to them; sub-state political bodies; related media; other branches of international civil society (i.e. the Corporate Social Responsibility Movement), etc.
- To continue to draw up proposals within civil society (and/or jointly with other actors) based on the conceptual, intentional and methodological foundations of the reform.

- To contribute to the construction of an international social and political movement capable of generating the process or processes of reform.

Guidelines
In order to achieve all of these objectives, the Campaign will focus on:

- **Raising awareness among public opinion** of the need and importance of an in-depth reform of the system of international institutions in order to move towards global democratic governance and in this way to contribute to solving the serious problems and challenges facing the world.
- **Carrying out activities and obtaining the support of global public opinion** using the usual mechanisms. Continuing to implement tools on the Internet in order to collect signatures in support of the Campaign that are as diverse, representative and numerous as possible. Directing actions intended to gain the global public support not only of individual citizens, but also, and very importantly, to gain the broadest and most diverse support possible from civil society organizations throughout the world, in order to have them as part of the Campaign.
- **Setting up committees and/or groups of focal points to promote the Campaign** at all possible levels (regional, state, sub-state, local, sectorial, etc.) that contribute in a more active way to attaining the objectives of the Campaign and that are representative of it, not only as instrumental means, but also as explicit objectives of the Campaign, since their existence will really mould a World Campaign.
- **Channelling the pressure of global public opinion to the international powers** (international organizations, different levels of government, participants in the global economic scene, etc.) in terms of the importance and the need for in-depth reform.
- **Carrying out all types of events (meetings, consultations, debates and activities in general) aimed at the presentation, dissemination, extension, debate and increase of support for the Campaign, at drawing up proposals** and, in general, at achieving each and every one of the Campaign objectives.

In addition to these things, efforts will be made within the agenda of the Campaign to begin processes intended to:

- Create a World Commission for In-depth Reform of the System of International Institutions that, linked clearly and explicitly to the Campaign, would assume and exercise the role of 'lobbyist' for the Campaign. To this end, contacts would be made and developed with the intention of establishing a dialogue with the United Nations system, other international organizations, different levels of government and other important groups in the world sphere.

- Establish points of contact with the media in order to strengthen the dissemination and all other aspects of the Campaign. In addition to this, where possible, the Campaign should develop its own instruments of communication.

- Channel the dynamics of the Campaign, wherever possible and at different territorial levels, towards debates and the adoption of favourable and explicit positions on the part of parliaments, city councils, different levels of governments, social movements and organizations, etc.

- Use the existing possibilities to promote explicit 'internal' debates on the issue within the International Institutions themselves (i.e. promoting an annual meeting of the Department of Public Information (DPI)-NGO that focuses on this point; working to introduce these themes as points on the agenda firstly at the Economic and Social Council (ECOSOC) meetings and then at ECOSOC meetings with the Bretton Woods Institutions and the WTO, etc.).

- **Work on ensuring that the Campaign's conclusions be presented to the UN General Assembly and on preparing a petition to convene a world conference on the in-depth reform of the system of international institutions.**

The World Social Forum and 'To make another world possible ... reform the International Institutions'

Chico Whitaker

The process of creating and forming the UBUNTU Forum and its World Campaign for In-Depth Reform of the System of International Institutions ran virtually in parallel with the forming of the World Social Forum. Manuel Manonelles, a member of the Secretariat of the UBUNTU Forum from the outset until 2006, frequently represented the Secretariat at International Council of that World Social Forum.

The UBUNTU Forum and its World Campaign for In-depth Reform of the System of International Institutions have always been there at the World Social Forum meetings over the years (Porto Alegre 2001, 2002 and 2003; Mumbai 2004; Porto Alegre 2005; Bamako 2006; Nairobi 2007). Our stance at that important arena has always been essentially to assert that 'To make another world possible ... many things need to be done ... but among them it will also be essential ... to reform our international institutions.'

> The author of the following text – undeniably leader in the World Social Forum process – reflects, from a historical perspective in this case, on that presence of ours in the Forum and on the relationship of mutual influence linking their work and ours.

Just when the World Forum of Civil Society Networks – UBUNTU was being created, the first World Social Forum was held in Porto Alegre (Brazil) in 2001, and it gradually turned into a planet-wide process with radical objectives: to help those who wish to change the world by moving on from neoliberalism.

This talk of 'changing the world' may seem extravagant, but that is indeed the general intention of those who have had the benefit since then of the facilities for meetings and articulation created by the World Social Forum. In working to supersede neoliberalism, they are proposing to build something radically different from the world we see around us – what they call 'the other world that is possible'.

As we all know, neoliberalism – the term applied recently to capitalism in its globalized phase – is the dominant economic system today all over the Earth. With the State at its service in the long-standing capitalist countries and in the ex-socialist ones, and with that system being imposed in China (the last great socialist country), neoliberalism now controls raw materials, the production of goods and services, and the minds and hearts of all humanity. The insatiable quest for gain, the accumulation and concentration of wealth, and competition and profit as the driving forces behind human activities, are the characteristic features of capitalism, and they are the prime forces behind what is happening in the world today, along with their natural consequences such as wars and putting the future of life on the planet at risk.

Yet it has become clear in the 21st century that moving on from neoliberalism means bringing about deeper and more wide-ranging changes than was originally envisaged when capitalism first began to be systematically criticized back in the 19th century, and doing more than was done in 20th-century experiments with new economic and political systems. It is not enough to change the decision-making system for production, planning it with society's needs in mind, and it is not enough to put an end to the dictatorship of private ownership of the resources and means of production, or to take the State and place it in the service of society as a whole. Still less can all means be deemed acceptable for bringing about change, since the results may be shaped by the means used to attain them.

What is emerging more clearly now is that no real change is possible without cultural change in the various political and economic actors – a full-blown cultural revolution – so that the entire political and economic system may switch to operating on a different basis: a basis of sharing, cooperation, mutual help, solidarity, responsible self-management, the social responsibility of individuals, companies and governments, citizens as subjects, radical and real democracy, peace and dialogue for settling conflicts, 'being' rather than 'having', and respect for nature, all viewed from **the perspective of the meaning of the word UBUNTU: 'humanity for all' or 'I am what I am thanks to what we all are'**.

Moreover, political parties ceased to be the sole instrument for political action towards the end of the 20th century. A new political actor took to the stage: civil society, meaning groups of citizens organized in various ways, acting independently of governments and parties though seeking to monitor and lobby them and acting in a very wide array of situations and levels. A good example of this process is in fact the creation of the UBUNTU Network.

And the World Social Forum came into being in order to serve civil society as a new political actor, to reinforce it, and to make it ever more cohesive without losing its plurality, enabling it to build its united front while respecting its diversity. Without presenting itself as a new institution or drawing up its own political programmes, and without seeking to represent anyone or to become organized as a network, the World Social Forum has asserted itself gradually as a multiplicity of facilities for the various civil society organizations to get together and to recognize each other, overcoming prejudices, barriers and artificial divisions, identifying common ground, and launching new initiatives, even planet-wide ones.

However, since the cultural changes needed are very far-reaching, the Forum's progress obviously involves many tensions, since the people organizing the forums also have to forget the habits, methods and strategies for political action that in many cases they have devoted a great deal of their lives to back in the 20th century.

Yet all this is a matter for discussion, exchanges of views, practice and learning in the organized gatherings. And the horizontal, diversity respecting nature of those gatherings is gradually making it possible to build a new political culture, more in line with 'the other world that is possible'.

UBUNTU is one of the actors in this adventure. Acting as a network – an innovative form of social organization, better suited to the nature of the civil society that emerged at the same time as it – UBUNTU is focusing on one of the essential fields in civil society's struggle: the absolute necessity of reforming our international institutions, in view of the absolute control governments exercise over them and the almost absolute lack of control exercised over them by society. Among those institutions, the ones that are most resistant to reform are precisely the ones brought into being by the

Bretton Woods agreements to ensure world domination for capital – the very situation that those who wish to 'change the world' seek to supersede.

Welcome, UBUNTU, to all the forums of the World Social Forum, at all levels. If UBUNTU's proposals for action are to gain ever wider support and new links, and if we are to become increasingly aware that the task of changing the world demands that action be taken on many fronts, we must forge bonds of solidarity far beyond our own particular struggles.

PART 2

ANALYSIS

3

Analysis of the Evolution of the Proposals for the Reform of the System of International Institutions

Núria Molina

The decision to launch the Campaign was taken at the second plenary meeting of the UBUNTU Forum, but the idea was certainly not to start from scratch: rather, work was to proceed following the constructive, additive line taken by the UBUNTU Forum. By 'additive' we mean that our aim was not to work in a wholly new direction, but to reinforce and encourage the people who were already working on a challenge that was preoccupying many, and to try to succeed in dealing with it. It is said that there has been talk of the need to reform our international institutions ever since they were first created. Without going back as far as that, the author of this book – a member of the Secretariat of the World Campaign and of the UBUNTU Forum since its beginnings until 2004 – set out to bring together the most significant reform proposals that had appeared before 2002, which is when the book was published (hence it does not include Kofi Annan's 2005 initiative, among others).

The proposals presented here are classified chiefly by where they came from in political terms: from within the United Nations itself, internationally organized civil society, and so on.

Proposals from international organizations

United Nations initiatives

Boutros Boutros Ghali: 'Democracy: A Newly Recognized Imperative', Global Governance 1, 1995.

Democracy in the international community of states remains at a very rudimentary stage. It is generally accepted but still largely unapplied.

Sovereignty rather than democracy has been the guiding principle in the history of the international system of states. However, the norms, practices and values of democracy should be extended to the international arena because it is beyond the capacity of any one state acting on its own and providing all the services and protection that its citizens require. The question that arises is: Could action taken by the international community extend democracy beyond the frontiers of the sovereign state to cover those actors and forces that are, at present, beyond the bounds of democratic accountability? The time has come to move forward to democratize the international system at all levels of state and non-state involvement.

Kofi Annan: 'Renewing the United Nations: a Programme for Reform', Report of the Secretary-General, 14 July 1997. Resolution adopted by the General Assembly on 14 November 1997.

Strengthening leadership capacity in the Secretariat: establishment of the position of Deputy Secretary-General; establishment of a Senior Management Group. Enhancing strategic direction from the General Assembly. Increasing administrative effectiveness and efficiencies. Reaching out to civil society. Assuring financial solvency. Promoting sustainable development as a central priority of the United Nations. Addressing the need for fundamental change through: refocusing the work of the General Assembly on issues of highest priority; establishment of a ministerial level commission to examine the need for fundamental change through review of the Charter of the United Nations; 'Millennium Assembly' and 'People's Assembly' to be held in the year 2001.

United Nations Development Programme (UNDP): 'Human Development Report', 1999. Chapter 5 – 'Reinventing global governance for humanity and equity'.

Reinventing global governance is not an option: it is an imperative. Key priorities: putting human concerns and human rights at the centre of international policy and action; protecting human security; narrowing the extremes of inequality between and within countries; increasing equity in negotiation and structures of international governance; building a new global architecture for the 21st century.

• A more coherent set of international principles: economic, social and cultural rights as well as political and civil ones; the goals and commitments of the global conferences of the 1990s; democratic and equitable

governance, globally and nationally; the WB and IMF need to explore how these principles are brought into their policies/operations.
- Develop a global code of conduct for multinational corporations and a global forum for their monitoring.
- Reducing financial insecurity and preventing future financial crisis: removing the requirements that countries liberalize capital accounts as a condition for borrowing; incorporating standstill provisions into the rules for borrowing from the international financial institutions.
- Protecting people.
- Controlling global crime.
- Promoting public-private partnerships.
- Narrowing global gaps: there should also be redistribution at the international level through development cooperation.

The United Nations and Inter-Parliamentary Union (IPU) in 2000 convened a 'Conference of Presiding Officers of National Parliaments' at UN Headquarters immediately before the Millennium Summit.

This could be an important step in integrating the voices of parliamentarians into UN processes. A UN Parliamentary Assembly would be modelled on the European Parliament, so the peoples would be represented in it as supporters of democratic political parties. Initially, at least, the delegates would be appointed or elected by the parliaments. The long-term objective is directly elected representation as in the European Parliament.

United Nations Development Programme (UNDP): 'Human Development Report 2002'.

The Report highlights a number of reforms that could address some of the more obvious imbalances in global decision-making. These include: eliminating the UN Security Council veto, reforming the selection process for the heads of the IMF and World Bank (currently controlled by Europe and the United States) and new programmes to help the poorest countries better represent their interests at the WTO.

Kofi Annan: 'Strengthening of the United Nations: an Agenda for Further Change', Report of the Secretary-General, 9 September 2002.

Need for a strong multilateral institution acutely felt in the era of globalization. Much has already been achieved: reforms begun in 1997 led to the Millennium Declaration (time-bound development goals), to greater coherence and fruitful partnerships with non-State actors. But more changes are needed: intergovernmental organs must also change. The General Assembly and the Economic and Social Council need to adapt and the Security Council reform needs new impetus (Open-ended Working Group to examine the reform of the Security Council). A need for a stronger General Assembly. Strengthening of the Economic and Social Council: annual dialogue with the BW institutions and the WTO. Doing what matters: integrating human rights throughout the United Nations system; the United Nations High Commissioner for Human Rights will be strengthened. Working better together: establishment of a high-level panel to make recommendations to find better ways to organize UN and civil society relationship. Global Compact.

Initiatives from the Bretton Woods Institutions

James Wolfensohn, 'Strategic Compact', 1997:
This programme is aimed at making the World Bank a quicker and less bureaucratic institution, which is more able to respond continuously to changing client demands and global development opportunities, and is more effective and efficient in achieving its main mission, which is reducing poverty.

James Wolfensohn, 'Comprehensive Development Framework' (CDF), 1998:
In 1998, Mr. Wolfensohn suggested the need for a more integrated approach to development based on a framework articulated and 'owned' by the country itself. That vision builds on these ideas: The CDF principles were widely and explicitly accepted by the international community as a basis for achieving greater poverty reduction and sustainable development. A network of CDF focal points within multilateral, bilateral and UN agencies has been meeting regularly on various aspects of implementation. The World Bank's President outlined a vision of the World Bank as an institution committed to forging closer partnerships with other actors to enhance development effectiveness: representatives from governments, bilateral donor agencies, multilateral financial institutions, academia, NGOs and other civil society organizations as well as the private sector.

Inter-governmental and governmental initiatives

South Centre: 'For a Strong and Democratic United Nations. A South Perspective on UN Reform'. Geneva, 1996.
    South Centre is an intergovernmental organization composed of developing countries intended to coordinate participation in international forums.

- UN finance: A thorough review should be carried out of the system of financing the UN by means of voluntary contributions, with the goal of gradually reducing its role until it is phased out; new means of financing the UN, including international levies and taxation, should be established to supplement and eventually supplant the core assessment system.
- General Assembly: to enable the General Assembly to take its intended central place in global policy-making and to ensure that there is more democratic participation in deliberations and decision-making procedures.
- Security Council: Enhancing the representativeness of the Security Council; ending the power of veto; abolishing permanent seats.
- The economic role of the UN: The UN role must be strengthened so that the necessary integrated and holistic approaches can be developed to deal with the increasingly complex set of socioeconomic issues, and so that gradually the necessary coordination of macro-economic policy at the global level can be achieved. In particular, ECOSOC and the United Nations Conference on Trade and Development (UNCTAD) require protection against forced erosion.
- Reforming the Bretton Woods Institutions: to place their work and policy within the broader context and framework for development policy established through the work of the UN and its various mechanisms. This will also involve democratizing the governance of the Bretton Woods Institutions and improving transparency at all levels. To deal with these concerns, a major and comprehensive intergovernmental process should be launched at the political level.

General Assembly/9228:
Assembly President proposes increase in Security Council membership to 24, adding five permanent, four non-permanent members (20 March 1997).

Ministerial Declaration of the Group of 77: 'Principles on UN Reform', 26 September 1997.

- The reform process must strengthen the UN's ability to fulfil its role and functions in the development field, with the General Assembly providing the leadership to ensure the fulfilment of the social and economic goals enunciated in the United Nations Charter.
- The reform process should not be motivated by the aims of downsizing the United Nations and to achieve savings.
- The developmental tasks of the United Nations are of fundamental importance and may not be treated as secondary to its peacekeeping,

human rights and humanitarian functions. Managerial measures to reduce overlap of functions, eliminate redundancies and minimize fragmentation are exceedingly important, but must be subservient to the larger goals of the reform process.

- The United Nations must carry out its mandated, comprehensive role in the economic and social areas.
- The United Nations General Assembly's role in the area of macro-economic policy formulation and coordination has to be strengthened.
- The United Nations, by virtue of its universal membership, is the most credible organization for performing developmental tasks. Assumption of some of these tasks, especially economic policy formulation and coordination, by limited groups outside the UN system or by organizations within the UN system with 'weighted' means of decision-making, is not the best way of ensuring equitable economic growth and development.
- All reform proposals must aim at giving greater effect to the principles of transparency, pluralism and democracy which are the unique strengths of the United Nations.
- The decision-making process of the Bretton Woods Institutions should be reformed to allow for greater democracy, universality and transparency.
- The reform of the Secretariat should proceed with the objective of enhancing the effective implementation of the objectives of the Charter; emphasize the prerogative of the General Assembly in the creation, transfer and abolition.
- Financing for the United Nations: Member States must fulfil their legal obligations to pay their contributions promptly.

International Financial Institution Advisory Commission:
In 1999 the US Congress established a bipartisan International Institutions Advisory Committee to consider the future of the IMF, the World Bank and the other multilateral development banks. The Committee, which was chaired by Professor Allan Meltzer, reported in March 2000.

The Meltzer Report:
The report states that the International Monetary Fund (IMF) and World Bank Group are largely failing in their mission to address world poverty and economic stability, and need major overhaul. Unanimously, the Commission supported a proposal maintaining that the IMF restrict its efforts to short-term crises assistance and recommended that the IMF, the World Bank and the various regional development banks forgive their loan claims held against the heavily indebted poor countries (HIPC). Structural recommendations for the IMF and the multilateral development banks call

for 'far-reaching changes to improve the effectiveness, accountability and transparency of the financial institutions and to eliminate overlapping responsibilities' (Allan Meltzer, 'IFIAC Report', March 1999). It also recommends that the World Bank and regional development banks especially should limit their activities to technical assistance and administering poverty alleviation grants.

Proposals from ad hoc groups

Stockholm Initiative: 'Stockholm Initiative Aims for Stronger World Government', 1991.

The 28 proposals concurred upon below represent a shot-across-the bow of George Bush's New World Order. The following are the ones we would like to highlight:

- That the United Nations takes on a broadened mandate at the Security Council level, following the wider understanding of security which has developed, and that its composition and the use of the veto be reviewed.
- That the Secretary-General be given a stronger position and the means to exercise authority, and that the method of appointment of the Secretary-General and of higher-level staff be reviewed.
- That the system-wide responsibilities and authority of the Secretary-General concerning inter-agency coordination and cooperation should be firmly established.
- That the financing system of the United Nations be reviewed, and that countries who do not adhere to the financial rules be deprived of the right to vote.
- That the activities of the United Nations in the economic and social fields be strengthened and rationalized.
- That the International Monetary Fund and the World Bank be coordinated, among themselves and with the United Nations system and the General Agreement on Tariffs and Trade (GATT), with the aim of clearer division of labour, better harmony and full universality in their work.
- That a World Summit on Global Governance be called, similar to the meetings in San Francisco and at Bretton Woods in the 1940s.
- As a matter of priority, the establishment of an Independent International Commission on Global Governance.

Commission on Global Governance: 'Our global neighbourhood', 1994.

A panel of 28 eminent personalities, chaired by Ingvar Carlsson of Sweden and Sridath Ramphal of Guyana, that began to meet in 1992 and completed its report – 'Our Global Neighbourhood' – in 1994. The report includes proposals to:

- Reform the Security Council, so that it becomes more representative and maintains its legitimacy and credibility.
- Set up an Economic Security Council to have more effective – and more democratic – oversight of the world economy.
- Establish a United Nations Volunteer Force so that the Security Council can act more quickly in emergencies.
- Vest the custody of the global commons in the Trusteeship Council, which has completed its original work.
- Treat the security of people and of the planet as being as important as the security of states.
- Strengthen the rule of law worldwide.
- Give civil society a greater voice in governance.
- Explore ways to raise new funds for global purposes, e.g. a tax on foreign currency movements, and charges for using flight lanes, sea-lanes and other common global resources.

Erskine Childers and Brian Urquhart: 'Renewing The United Nations System', Dag Hammarskjöld Foundation, 1994.

The Dag Hammarskjöld Foundation and the Ford Foundation jointly published this report in 1994. Written by Erskine Childers and Brian Urquhart, two very keen and articulate former UN officials, it is widely considered the best overall statement on UN reform.

This report proposes to reform the overall UN system during the 50th anniversary of the United Nations by:

- Re-empowering the UN to formulate global macroeconomic policies (reciprocal representation between the UN and its specialized agencies – WB and IMF; need for a non-commercial bank to respond to needs of developing countries; to negotiate global strategies for WTO work at the UN).
- Reforming of the three 'missing' specialized agencies in order to create an equitably governed low-interest lending facility, monetary fund and world trade organization, following policies established by the General Assembly, with direction from the ECOSOC.
- Consolidate all UN development funds in a single UN development authority.
- Establishing an International Human Rights Court under the World Court.

- Improving the functioning of the General Assembly.
- Creating a peoples' world assembly which is democratic, has a genuinely useful role in the UN's intergovernmental process, and has legal status as a UN body.
- Creating additional funds through levies on arms sales, transnational currency transactions, international trade, international air or sea travel, an annual UN lottery.

Independent Working Group on the Future of the United Nations: 'The United Nations in Its Second Half Century', 1995.

The Working Group was convened by the Ford Foundation at the request of Secretary-General Boutros Boutros Ghali in late 1993. This initiative, funded by the Ford Foundation and based at Yale University, was co-chaired by Moeen Qureshi of Pakistan and Richard von Weizsäcker of Germany. Yale Professors Paul Kennedy and Bruce Russet served as Directors. The report was issued in 1995.

The central recommendation of this Report calls for three related Councils: a new Economic Council, a new Social Council, and the existing but enhanced Security Council, all three serviced by a common Secretariat and working together on behalf of human security and sustainable development. The Economic Council and the Social Council would coordinate policy and programmes through a Global Alliance for Sustainable Development, comprised of state representatives of the highest level. The Organization needs to eliminate redundancy by transforming, rationalizing or abolishing certain units. The three-Council arrangement recommended here would provide such an opportunity.

The Secretary-General should convene a committee of permanent representatives and senior staff to consider reforms. The financial crisis of the Organization needs to be addressed securing the commitment of Member States to pay their assessments. An expert group should examine the options for other public sources of revenue, such as designated levies on global commons.

High Level Expert Panel on Financing for Development (FfD): Report by the High Level Expert Panel on Financing for Development, 2001.

On 15 December 2000, UN Secretary-General Kofi Annan appointed a High-Level Expert Panel of eminent persons, chaired by the former Mexican president Zedillo.

Need for a world system to manage economic issues at global scale. We make our own the proposal put forward by the Commission on Global Governance, 'Our Global Neighbourhood':

- To create a World Council at the highest political level to play a leading role in managing world public affairs. Non-binding decisions. Draw up strategic frame for long-term policies to promote development.
- Organization of a Summit on Globalization to speed up reform processes already under way and to launch others that are urgently needed to make the potential offered by the globalization process a reality:
- Support for multilateralism.
- Rapid reform of international financial architecture.
- Reform and strengthening of the WTO, which should launch a round in favour of development.
- Institutional response to environmental and employment issues.
- New sources of finance: tax on monetary transactions (Tobin tax); carbon tax; revive use of Special Drawing Rights (SDR) created by the IMF.
- International Tax Organization.
- Migration policies.

Global Financial Governance Initiative to make international financial system more stable, equitable and attuned to needs of developing countries. It is a joint project of institutions and experts in international finance, including the Forum on Debt and Development (FONDAD), the North-South Institute, Oxford University, the International Development Research Centre (IDRC) and the United Nations Economic Commission for Latin America and the Caribbean (UNECLAC).

Aims: debating reform of the international financial architecture and broadening the scope of the debate and highlighting developing country perspectives.

On 2002 and 2001 the Working Group III on Institutional Governance, coordinated by Ngaire Woods from Oxford University, has held three meetings and generated a draft reform agenda in terms of the core functions of global financial institutions (research and expertise, emergency financing, and conditionality) as well as the structure and organization of existing institutions (and possible new institutions).

This Working Group suggests: Reforming the IMF and the World Bank:

- New institutional roles in crisis management and standstills.
- More focused developing country bargaining and advocacy.
- Enhancing ownership and long-term effectiveness in developing lending and emergency financing.
- Applying corporate governance principles to the governance of the IMF and the World Bank.

- Reviewing voting rights and voice in the IMF and the World Bank.
- Ensuring better representation of developing countries on the Executive Boards.
- Enhancing the capacity of developing countries to contribute.
- Use the G-24 and existing institutions better.

Civil society initiatives

Reforming the United Nations

International Network For a UN Second Assembly (INFUSA), 1985.
UN Second Assembly. The number of seats allocated to each participating country would be proportionately related to population size. The delegates in the Second Assembly would be non-governmental and non-party, and would be directly and/or indirectly elected. They would represent the peoples of the United Nations as global inhabitants and members of civil society, while the delegates in the General Assembly would continue to represent us as national citizens.

Campaign For A More Democratic United Nations (CAMDUN)
http://www.camdun-online.gn.apc.org
   CAMDUN was established in 1989 as a project of the International Network For a UN Second Assembly (INFUSA), which was formed in 1983. CAMDUN's main objective remains that of INFUSA – the establishment of an organ of the UN to represent the world's citizens as members of civil society (a UN peoples' assembly), linked with the UN General Assembly (in which the governments represent the citizens as subjects of the member states). Such bicameral global representation could lead to the UN becoming a 'United Nations and Peoples' for permanent peace. CAMDUN also seeks democratization of other elements of the UN system, in support of individual and collective human rights, sustainable development and equitable international relations. Cooperating for a more democratic UN: Action for UN Renewal, Association of World Citizens, Campaign for a More Democratic United Nations, Communications Coordination Committee for the United Nations, NZ Forum for UN Renewal, Operation Peace Through Unity, UNGA-Link UK, World Civil Society Forum – UK Support Group.
   'CAMDUN Second International Conference on a More Democratic United Nations', Vienna 1991:

- Instituting a UN duty on international trade, including financial movements between member states, to provide the core funding of the Organization.
- Enlarging the Security Council to 18 members.
- Abolishing the Security Council 'veto', by instituting non-discriminatory voting powers, or failing this, by providing for a non-concurring vote of permanent members to be overridden by a concurring vote of the non-permanent members.
- Renaming the Security Council as 'The Peace and Security Council' if under a revised Charter it continues to have 'primary responsibility for the maintenance of international peace and security'.

Campaign for UN Reform (United States), 1992.
The 14-point programme to reform and restructure the UN System:

1. Create International Disarmament Organization.
2. Improve UN Peacekeeping Capabilities.
3. Strengthen UN Environmental and Conservation Programs.
4. The UN Human Rights Machinery.
5. Establish Special International Criminal Court.
6. Increase Use of International Court of Justice (ICJ).
7. Provide Better Dispute Settlement Mechanisms.
8. Improve General Assembly Decision-Making.
9. Modify Veto in Security Council.
10. Provide Adequate Stable UN Revenues.
11. Reform UN Administrative System.
12. Restructure World Trade and Monetary Systems.
13. Consolidate UN Development Programs.
14. Create UN Authorities for Areas not under National Control.

World Federalist Movement
'UN Parliamentary Assembly', 1992. This would be modelled on the European Parliament, so the peoples would be represented in it as supporters of democratic political parties. Initially, at least, the delegates would be appointed or elected by the parliaments. The long-term objective is directly-elected representation as in the European Parliament.

'Empowering the UN'
Proposals: a more representative and democratic Security Council with more transparent decision-making procedures; UN financing: Currency Transaction Tax (CTT) and how to implement this new global levy;

central position of the General Assembly as the chief deliberative, policy-making and representative organ of the United Nations.

Charter 99

The current world government is not to be found at the United Nations. Global policies are discussed and decided behind closed doors by exclusive groups, such as the G8, the Organization for Economic Cooperation and Development (OECD), the Bank of International Settlements, the World Bank, the International Monetary Fund, the World Trade Organization and others.

These agencies are reinforced by informal networks of high officials and powerful alliances. Together they have created what can be seen as dominant and exclusive institutions of world government. All too often they are influenced by transnational corporations (TNCs) which pursue their own world strategies. These agencies of actual world government must be made accountable. If there are to be global policies, let the policymakers be answerable to the peoples of the world. We call on you, therefore, to initiate the process of democratic global governance following fundamental principles: openness and accountability; environmental sustainability; security and peace; equality and justice.

Toda Institute for Global Peace and Policy Research, based in Tokyo, Japan, and Honolulu, Hawaii; the School of Social Sciences of La Trobe University, Melbourne, Australia; and Focus on the Global South, an institute based in Thailand and dedicated to regional and global policy analysis, micro-macro issue-linking and advocacy work, are collaborating on a project titled the 'Global Governance Reform Project (GGRP)'. Spotlighting issues of global concern, the project sponsors commissioned studies in three areas: 'globalization and global governance', 'global financial flows', and 'global peace and security'.

Study results to date have been compiled in Democratizing Global Governance (2002), edited by Esref Aksu, GGRP coordinator and research associate at La Trobe University, Melbourne, Australia, and Joseph A. Camilleri, professor of international relations at La Trobe University, published by Palgrave Macmillan, UK. Joseph A. Camilleri is the author of the last chapter, 'Reimagining the Future', which tackles issues related to Major Structural Reform: General Assembly, People's Assembly, Consultative Assembly, Security Council, Economic and Social Security Council, Secretary-General/Secretariat, Financial arrangements, Regional organizations, Emerging global civil society.

Economic democracy: reforming international trade and finance institutions

The Halifax Initiative

Currency Transaction Tax. With the support of the Association for the Taxation of Financial Transaction for the Aid of Citizens (ATTAC), Tobin Tax Initiative, War on Want.

A global citizen's movement has emerged in support of the currency transactions tax, or 'Tobin' tax as it is often called. The tax is a means to reassert national economic sovereignty, help prevent financial crises and generate billions of dollars for global social development and environmental protection. It should be collected and redistributed in a fully transparent and accountable manner through the United Nations.

Bretton Woods Project

A thorough review of the policies, functions, governance and structures of the multilateral financial institutions is essential. A review should be transparent and involve developing country governments and other stakeholders such as NGOs and civil society organizations, academics and parliamentarians. It would be very inappropriate if it is orchestrated by the G7 and therefore it must be led by an independent, representative body elected through a transparent process. The review should also examine what aspects of the global architecture are still missing and take forward the stalled reform efforts initiated in response to the financial crises of 1997 and 1998.

'50 years is enough'

Assessment of Institutions' Future: 'We demand that the future existence, structure and policies of multilateral institutions such as the World Bank Group and the IMF be submitted to a reevaluation conducted through a democratic, participatory and transparent process building on the findings of a neutral and credible Truth Commission. The process must accord full participation to the peoples most affected by the policies and practices of the institutions, and include a significant and influential role for all parts of civil society, including farmers' associations, trade unions, women's organizations, NGOs, faith-based groups and student/youth organizations.'

World Economy, Ecology and Development (WEED)

At the heart of the reform agenda proposed by WEED lie the calls for institutional reform of the Fund itself, including the democratization of the Fund's decision-making structures. The report joins an existing chorus of voices calling for restructuring of voting patterns within the Fund which grants the US 17.8 per cent of voting rights and other industrialized nations substantially more power than the debtor nations. However, the report rejects proposals for a one-country-one-vote system, preferring a decision-making structure based on a country's population, economic potential and its ranking in UNDP's Human Development Index.

Jubilee

The 'Jubilee Framework' (January 2002) is a step towards democratizing international capital markets. The existence of a framework, enabling any indebted nation to file for a standstill on debt payments, or for her creditors to declare her insolvent, will be a form of regulation of international capital flows; and will discipline both lax lenders and reckless borrowers. Fundamental to the 'Jubilee Framework' is public participation in the proceedings of the court and in the resolution of crises involving public money.

Oxfam Great Britain

Jacob Werksman: 'Institutional Reform of the WTO', 2002:

- Greater transparency and participation, particularly from developing country members, but also from representatives of civil society.
- Adoption of more specific special and differential treatment with regard to the timing of filings and the implementation of rulings involving developing countries and provision of more technical assistance for developing countries, and particularly least-developed countries, in bringing and defending WTO disputes.
- Improve the external transparency of the WTO.
- Reforming the WTO mandate to make explicit that trade is not an end in itself.
- More effective coordination between the WTO and other international institutions.
- Establishing mechanisms to improve understanding of the linkages between international trade policy and equally important non-trade objectives.
- Establishing mechanisms to monitor the poverty impact of WTO sanctions.

International justice

Coalition for an International Criminal Court (CICC)

The CICC is a network of well over 1,000 NGOs advocating for a fair, effective and independent International Criminal Court (ICC). The International Criminal Court is a permanent court capable of investigating and trying individuals accused of the most serious violations of international humanitarian and human rights law, namely war crimes, crimes against humanity and genocide. Unlike the International Court of Justice, whose jurisdiction is restricted to states, the ICC considers cases against individuals; and unlike the Tribunals for Rwanda and the Former Yugoslavia, created to address crimes committed during these conflicts, its jurisdiction is not situation-specific and is not retroactive.

Amnesty International

Amnesty International is campaigning for an end to impunity at the international level. To achieve this, the organization, together with thousands of NGOs and civil society groups worldwide, is lobbying all governments to take steps to establish an international system of justice, complemented by national systems to bring perpetrators to justice. In particular, Amnesty International is calling on all states to:

- Ratify the Rome Statute of the International Criminal Court and enact effective implementing legislation to cooperate fully with the Court.
- Enact and use universal jurisdiction legislation for the crimes of genocide, crimes against humanity, war crimes, torture, extra-judicial executions and 'disappearances', in order that their national courts can investigate and, if there is sufficient admissible evidence, prosecute anyone who enters its territory suspected of these crimes, regardless of where the crime was committed or the nationality of the accused or the victim.

Some of the principles on the Effective Exercise of Universal Jurisdiction (abstract):

- Crimes of universal jurisdiction.
- No immunity for persons in official capacity.
- No immunity for past crimes.
- No statutes of limitation.
- No political interference.
- Grave crimes under international law must be investigated and prosecuted without waiting for complaints of victims or others with a sufficient interest.
- Internationally recognized guarantees for fair trials.
- Public trials in the presence of international monitors.
- No death penalty or other cruel, inhuman or degrading punishment.

Proposals from the academic world

Held, David et al.: 'Cosmopolitan Democracy: An Agenda for a New World Order', 1995.

In this book the authors argue that the form of international regulation that dominated the world for the last 40 years no longer exists and that a new world order must be developed based upon the principles of legality and democracy.

The book looks at the development of international organizations and suggests that they need reforming so as to be made more accountable, and this includes the United Nations. There also has to be a new balance between decisions taken at a local, national, regional and international level. This together forms a new model of cosmopolitan democracy. This idea should also be combined with a new concept of civic participation and citizenship that reflects the redistribution of power at regional and global levels.

Woods, Ngaire: 'Governance in International Organizations: The case for reform in the Bretton Woods Institutions', 1998.

If the IMF and the World Bank are to achieve the standard of good governance they themselves have defined for borrowing members, some reform of the constitutional rules, as well as the decision-making procedure and practices within both institutions, is required. More specifically, in order to enhance their own accountability, transparency and members' participation, the institutions need to consider:

- Redrawing quotas.
- Revitalizing basic votes.
- Ensuring that operational decisions are made in an open and recorded way (i.e. not by the practice of consensus on the Board).
- Ensuring that clear and impartial rules govern the use of special majorities.
- Introducing double majorities where particular stakes or stakeholders need safe-guarding.

Rodrik, Dani: 'Governing the Global Economy: Does One Architectural Style Fit All?', JFK School of Government, University of Harvard, 1999.

What kind of an international architecture: Need for a global set of institutions that provide regulatory, lender-of-last resort and safety-net functions. This set of institutions should provide three functions: regulating market behaviour, stabilizing aggregate demand and redistributing the risk and rewards of market outcomes.

Global Economic Institutions (GEI)
The 'Global Economic Institutions (GEI) Research Programme' is a research programme funded by the Economic and Social Research Council of Great Britain. The purpose of the programme is to study how existing global economic institutions and regimes operate, how they might be improved and whether new institutions are needed. Ten projects began work in 1994, a further six began in 1996 and activities include a number of workshops and conferences. The programme will run until 1999. Networking services are provided for the programme by the Centre for Economic Policy Research (CEPR).

C. L. Gilbert and D. Vines, eds.: 'The World Bank: Structure and Policies', Cambridge, Cambridge University Press, July 2000.
The World Bank is dedicated to the promotion of sustainable economic development and to poverty reduction throughout the developing world. It faces new challenges as capital shortages are replaced by large but volatile capital flows. The contributors to this volume argue that the Bank's greatest asset is its accumulated knowledge and experience of the development process, and propose that it organizes itself around the concept of Knowledge Bank. They propose a shift in priority, away from lending with conditionality imposed on borrowing governments, towards assistance to governments in devising good development strategies. Part I examines the existing structure of the Bank and considers the World Bank as an institution. In Part II the effectiveness of World Bank assistance is evaluated.

Centre for Global Studies: 'Rethinking Governance', 2000. University of Victoria.
The problem is that we do not have a global government and we need a substitute for it – global governance. Better global governance is unquestionably needed. Governance must provide needed public goods. But this cannot be the exclusive purview of governments. Governance is not synonymous with governments. There are many more actors involved today in governance – civil society, regional supranational institutions, international organizations, etc. Governments need to see non-state actors as groups that have power and legitimacy, albeit a legitimacy different from governments and varying according to organizations and issues. In addition, power is seen as unfairly distributed, with developing countries lacking the scope to argue their case effectively. This effort is not dedicated to those who want to freeze or diminish the role of international organizations. The appropriate route is to improve the governance of the international system. There is an impressive array of good practices and ideas to emulate and adapt in

order to improve procedures enhancing participation, transparency and accountability. We should govern at the international level more flexibly, more sensitively, more democratically: all these are points where it is easier to agree on the faults in the way existing institutions operate than it is to find agreement on new structures. It seems unlikely that one model will fit all circumstances. Learning from experiment and experience with different options may be the most promising way forward.

Transnational Institute. Annual Report 2000.

- Global Economic Justice Programme.
- An Alternative Global Economic System:
  - Genuine international cooperation based on loose global economic integration.
  - Cancel Third World debt.
  - Subject transnational corporations to international law.
  - Close tax havens.
  - Impose an international tax on financial transactions to alleviate poverty and redress environmental damage.
  - Institute a universal welfare threshold for all as a right.
  - Subject international financial institutions, such as the World Bank, regional development banks and the IMF, to democratic control.
  - Alternative Financial Architecture.
  - Reorient finance from speculation to long-term investment in the real economy.
  - Reduce instability and volatility in global financial markets.
  - Allow maximum space for national governments to set exchange rate policy, regulate capital movements and eliminate speculative activity.
  - Democratization Programme.
  - Globalization and Democratization.
  - Aid for Civil Society Building.
  - Civil Society as Global Actor.
  - Towards Substantive, Participatory Democracy.

World Institute for Development Economics Research/United Nations University. Deepak Nayyar (ed.): 'New Roles and Functions for the UN and the Bretton Woods Institutions', 2001. With the collaboration of Amit Bhaduri, Lance Taylos, Yilmaz Akyüz, Richard Falk, Jong-Il You, Joseph Stiglitz, Shrirang Shukla, José Antonio Ocampo, Devesh Kapur.

- Reforming the UN: Security Council reforms such as enlarging membership and circumventing the veto; full or partial independent UN financing through some version of the Tobin tax on international foreign exchange transactions or stock market transactions and some charges on the use of the global commons; Global Peoples Assembly; Economic Security Council; Volunteer Peace Force.
- Reforming the IMF and the World Bank: the IMF needs to improve accountability and seek the general interest of peoples and governments and the collective interest of the world economy; the World Bank needs to be transformed into an institution more concerned with development and to restructure its voting system.
- Making the World Trade Organization more democratic.
- A new financial architecture to manage global macroeconomics, including inflation control, restoring full employment and stimulating investment, and which is designed first of all to deal with crisis management and crisis prevention. It should also support the integration of developing countries into the world economy in a manner that promotes development.
- A system of governance for transnational corporations.

Stiglitz, Joseph: 'Globalization and Its Discontents', New York and London: W. W. Norton & Company, 2002.

Stiglitz states that institutional reforms must be undertaken restricting the financial sphere:

- Standstills on debt repayment when financial crises occur, giving otherwise healthy firms an opportunity to recover from financial crises.
- Special bankruptcy provisions that kick in when exceptional macroeconomic disturbances break out, providing management with a chance to restructure ailing companies.
- Greater reluctance by the IMF to lend billions in bail out packages.
- Improved regulation of banking, including, for example, restrictions on speculative real estate lending.
- The use of short-term capital controls and 'exit taxes' to protect countries against 'the ravages of speculators'.
- Granting more seats at the IMF to countries from poor regions in the global economy.
- More open discourse at the IMF, the World Trade Organization and other international agencies.
- A narrowing of focus at the IMF to managing crises, leaving policies of development and transition to other institutions such as the World Bank.
- The developed countries and international financial institutions should

provide loans enabling developing countries to buy insurance against fluctuations in the international capital markets.
- Improved safety nets.
- Debt relief and a more balanced trade agenda.

Yadav, Vikash: 'Reforming the Governance of the IMF', 2002:

- Democratizing the governance structure of the IMF will significantly improve the institution and thus enhance the operation of the global economy.
- The legitimacy of international rule making organizations can be improved if decisions are achieved through a more democratic framework.
- The implementation of a democratic framework for rule making requires a reform of the Fund's 'quota regime', as it is the quota regime that mediates the distribution of voting power at the IMF. The distribution of power within the Fund's quota regime must adapt to better represent the increasing weight (and vulnerability) of developing and particularly emerging market countries in an increasingly integrated world economy.

4

World Democratic Governance

Josep Xercavins

On the one hand this document is an analysis of the precedents and context in which the World Campaign started out in life, and on the other it is also a personal political reading of the Manifesto by the Secretariat's Coordinator.

The Washington Consensus, the fall of the Berlin Wall and other precedents for the world political situation

Some essential defining characteristics of the world political situation

I shall begin this paper, which, in any case, has an essentially ideological and political character, rather than academic, by describing what are for me the essential, defining characteristics of the present world political situation.

The worsening state of the world; at many levels, affecting both humanity and the planet itself, most importantly:

- increase in absolute terms (which might be logical, in view of rising population), but also of the relative number (and, therefore, a very important indicator) of citizens all over the world living in conditions we consider unacceptable: below poverty thresholds; in short, unable to satisfy their basic needs to any appreciable extent;
- increasing imbalances between the rising numbers described above of citizens all over the world living in conditions we consider unacceptable (however it is measured: almost always more than half, often considerably more, of total world population) and the population that, generally speaking, enjoys an improving standard of living, at least economically, in the 'North';

- a quantitative and qualitative increase in violence and conflicts between people, which is, in my opinion, very much linked to the situation described above in a process of cause and effect, though, naturally, this is not the only cause;
- increasing, serious negative impacts of human activity on the planet Earth (environmental unsustainability), of which we form an inextricable part and on which we logically depend absolutely, at least in the short and medium term.

On the veracity of this assessment, I refer here only to UN Secretary-General Kofi Annan's Report, published in January 2002, on the preparatory process for the Johannesburg Summit,[1] under the highly revealing title of: 'Agenda 21 and Sustainable Development – Good Plan, Weak Implementation'. I quote here, practically verbatim, some of the key statements in the press summary accompanying the report:

- Soil degradation affects at least two thirds of the world's agricultural land.
- Freshwater is becoming scarcer in many countries due to agriculture, which consumes 70 per cent.
- About a quarter of the world's fisheries are over-fished and half are fully utilized.
- More than 11,000 species are now considered threatened and more than 800 species have already become extinct.
- There has been a net loss of 4 per cent of the world's forest in the last decade.
- Global consumption of fossil fuels increased by 10 per cent from 1992 to 1999.

The report makes these points after speaking of population and poverty, in terms both well known to all and worrying, having begun by discussing the economy in the following terms:

- Most countries enjoyed economic growth during the first half of the 1990s. Not all countries benefited, however: the gap in the standard of living between Africa and other regions widened. Economic and social conditions in the transition economies also deteriorated.
- Globalization also proved to have an extremely volatile side. Financial crises in Mexico and East Asia.
- Official development assistance (ODA) flows fell during the 1990s.
- Foreign Direct Investment (FDI) flows to developing countries grew steadily, reaching a peak in 1994 before falling sharply until 1998, after which they slightly rebounded once more.

- Government subsidies have increased in all countries.

Consolidation of a new world techno–socio–economic situation that has become known, rightly in my opinion, as globalization,[2] and with differentiating characteristics compared to the past, and which is taking shape and changing at unprecedented speed, causing a dramatically increased sensation and reality of complexity, uncertainty and changing models:

- made possible, basically, by new technological possibilities, particularly in communications and information, but also in the field of production and the way the economy functions;
- leaving behind a period in which political players, the historic subjects, were very clear and, among them, the nation-state was fundamental. State frontiers have ceased to exist for many basic flows in our times: environmental, financial, information, etc.;
- that has even helped to bring into being an important social movement, one more or less cohesive and structured, known as anti-globalization, though there are attempts from within the movement itself to change this name to 'alternative globalization'.

The world's leading superpower has become even more so (powerful and leading), although only comparatively, and has, at least at present, opted to act as such in a totally egocentric and, therefore, unilateral, way.[3]

- The most serious manifestation of this policy to date is, without doubt, the decision, in view of the impossibility of reaching agreement within the UN Security Council, to start a war – the Iraq War – which was therefore, and quite justly, qualified as illegal. Events following this war have only served to drive home just how illegitimate it was!
- The present US administration's knee-jerk reaction to the terrible events of 11 September 2001 lead one to suspect that the attacks are being used to impose an 'Orwellian' world both at home and abroad.
- All the evidence supports claims that the present situation is – or at least this is the intention – ruled by imperialism.

A kind of 'undeclared' bipolarization affects the system of international multilateral institutions.

- The international multilateral institutions (more or less multilateral, needless to say) play different roles in each of the essential characteristics described above. This is the result of different considerations that I aim to discuss in the first section of this paper.

- But what my heading really seeks to affirm is that, in my view, we have witnessed this kind of undeclared bipolarization take shape between, on the one hand, the UN system proper and, on the other, the world financial, economic and trade institutions (Bretton Woods, IMF, WB and WTO). The UN system proper produces large and, I believe, good programme results, the fruit, fundamentally, of its world summits, but is now saddled with what has become known as the 'implementation gap' and what we could almost call the absence of implementation. Meanwhile, the world financial, economic and trade institutions (Bretton Woods, IMF, WB and WTO) have quietly gone about the work of deciding and, above all, establishing the neoliberalism that has reigned in the world for the last 20 years or more.

Developments in the international political situation during the 1990s; the somewhat divergent effects of the Washington Consensus and the fall of the Berlin Wall

With the help of Figure 4.2, compiled from various sources and revised and updated for this paper, I shall attempt to situate and compare the absolute and relative contexts of the summits in Rio (early 1990s: 1992; the first of a series of highly characteristic UN summits) and Johannesburg (10 years later: 2002). This seems to me to be an indispensable exercise, one that gives considerable help in clarifying matters.

Rio 92 took place, among other things, at a moment in history that, in spite of everything (the first Gulf War, for example), was without doubt quite exceptional. The fall of real communism and the bilateral world; what was undoubtedly the most important process of international distension in decades; what we might call lack of definition regarding the future of politics and the international situation that surely helped the United Nations system to play a stronger role than ever before in terms of deploying its internal resources (more characteristic and progressive programmes, more important officials, etc.). In short, they 'permitted' the UN to do this.

Not knowing of any assessments that have reached conclusions to the contrary, I, at least, cannot but acknowledge the quantity, quality and importance of the agreements reached at Rio.

But, moreover, this is true, not only because of Rio in itself, but also because Rio was a stone thrown into a pond whose ripples spread until practically the end of the 1990s, the decade of UN progressive summits: Vienna and Human Rights; Cairo and Population; Copenhagen and Social

Development; Beijing and Women, etc. All delivered important, progressive declarations and action plans, whose only though definitive drawback was in their application, as some were completely or partially left unimplemented!

And this last clearly fundamental fact has also caused the UN as we can see at present and occurred again even at Johannesburg to fall from one of its only upturns, one of the most important revivals of fortune since the Cold War, into one of its deepest troughs as regards the role many of us no doubt wish and hope it could and would play. UN member states do not comply with the measures they approve within the organization.

But why did this happen, why is it still happening? Because the world's rich and powerful long turned off onto a different route. Reagan and Thatcher started a great conservative, neoliberal revolution which had much to do with the fall of real communism, but which did not fully show its face until well into the 1990s.

The instruments they used to implement the more international aspects of their policy which formed the majority, in fact did not include the UN status quo of the bilateral world or multilateral revival after the end of real communism but other 'old' institutions, the Bretton Woods Institutions, reincarnated in this case, however, to play a leading role. Fundamentally, the International Monetary Fund (IMF), with its structural adjustment, privatization and deregulation policies, making its loans to developing countries conditional on their agreeing to slim down their public sectors and policies. And, to a lesser degree, the World Bank (WB), laying down the guidelines for international cooperation based more on the private sector and on Foreign Direct Investment (FDI) than on the public sector, on Official Development Aid (ODA). As is well known, these institutions are completely controlled by the rich and powerful nations (their decision-making is, basically, proportional to member countries' GDP) and they were, moreover, complemented a few years after these events, by the most controversial and, despite its importance, undefined of international organizations: the World Trade Organization (WTO), established, in fact, in 1994 as an instrument to promote liberalization in international trade.

The issues the WTO is concerned with are complex because: (a) they are many and by no means restricted to trade; and (b) in the current neoliberal international scenario, they are becoming (largely according to plan) those that drive all other developments. But not only trade seems to be the driving factor, but also UN member states (in this context, the UN can be considered the 'world public system') seem to be failing to meet their responsibilities as regards aid to developing countries (both Official Development Aid and Direct Foreign Investment have been falling in the developing countries over the last decade). Furthermore, they are requiring (through world financial and economic institutions such as the International Monetary Fund and the World Bank) that states wishing to receive their aid should reduce their public deficits through neoliberaliza-tion, through privatization and abolishing protectionist measures in as many economic sectors as possible. It is in this context that the great transnational corporations, which end up managing as they take over these local economic sectors, will demand maximum commercial liberalization of goods and services from the world. It is no coincidence that the WTO was founded in 1994, during the most expansive period in the economic global-ization process.

The result of these policies is the type of economic globalization we have seen, and which the development of Information and Communication Technologies (ICTs) have facilitated enormously, defining a context extraordinarily different for Johannesburg and for Rio.

To put it in the simple but easily understood terms of 'European lan-guage': all over the world in the 1990s, a neoliberal framework, which began to take shape in the 1980s, led by the Bretton Woods Institutions (IMF and WB), was implacably put into place, rather than the more social-democratic or Keynesian framework formulated but not implemented by the UN. And although the results, particularly at macroworld level, are truly alarming (larger absolute and relative imbalances than ever; more poverty than ever; more environmental problems than ever), we continue to witness the continuing expansion and domination of this neoliberal economic model in which the market and trade have ceased to be a tool for human development to become an end in themselves.

Although certain disagreement exists regarding the paternity and exact date when the term was coined, this entire neoliberal phase is also known as the 'Washington Consensus'. Briefly, for one salient reason: because it was a phase that clearly obeyed the dictates of the Bretton Woods Institutions (IMF and WB) and which, as is well known, have their headquarters in Washington!

Moreover, an extract from one of the sources attributed with first coin-ing and providing an explicit, public definition of the 'Washington Consensus' is reproduced in Figure 4.1.

This is, in my view, at least a key element in a more in-depth explanation as to why the UN's progressive programmes of the 1990s, and which, in the above-mentioned language, featured a large component of 'social democ-racy', were not worth the paper they were written on.[4] Returning to 'European language': instead of shaping a more balanced world in all senses using cohesion funds policies the option chosen was, in effect, to allow the rich and powerful countries in the world (the minority) to continue accu-mulating wealth despite the further impoverishment of the world's poor

FISCAL DISCIPLINE

Large and sustained fiscal deficits contribute to inflation and capital flight. Therefore, governments should keep them to a minimum.

PUBLIC EXPENDITURE PRIORITIE

Subsidies need to be reduced or eliminated. Government spending should be redirected toward education, health, and infrastructure development.

TAX REFORM

The tax base "should be broad" and marginal tax rates "should be moderate."

INTEREST RATES

Domestic financial markets should determine a country's interest rates. Positive real interest rates discourage capital flight and increase savings.

EXCHANGE RATES

Developing countries must adopt a "competitive" exchange rate that will bolster exports by making them cheaper abroad.

TRADE LIBERALIZATION

Tariffs should be minimized and should never be applied toward intermediate goods needed to produce exports.

FOREIGN DIRECT INVESTMENT

Foreign investment can bring needed capital and skills and, therefore, should be encouraged.

PRIVATIZATION

Private industry operates more efficiently because managers either have a "direct personal stake in the profits of an enterprise or are accountable to those who do." State-owned enterprises ought to be privatized.

DEREGULATION

Excessive government regulation can promote corruption and discriminate against smaller enterprises that have minimal access to the higher reaches of the bureaucracy. Governments have to deregulate the economy.

PROPERTY RIGHTS

Property rights must be enforced. Weak laws and poor judicial systems reduce incentives to save and accumulate wealth.

Source: "What Washington Means by Policy Reform", in John Williamson, ed., *Latin American Adjustment: How Much Has Happened?* (Washington: Institute for International Economics, 1990).

Figure 4.1 *The original 1989 Washington Consensus*

countries (the majority) and the serious impact on the global environment that this caused.

Johannesburg was, then, viewed in this way, neither a success nor a failure, although there has been considerable discussion as to whether it was one or the other. However, it was another victory, for the moment, as I shall go on to explain, of the 'world neoliberal framework, world dominance and private management and market deregulation' over another possible model, the 'world social-democratic framework, world dominance and public management and market regulation' that, in principle, should be more respectful towards humanity and the planet that shelters us. At world level, the basic public actor under the second model would be (we have no alternative at present) the UN. For this reason, I shall refer to it, on occasion, as I do in Figure 4.2, as the 'UN framework'.

The Millennium Development Goals (MDGs) set out by the General Assembly of the Millennium United Nations, the Resolutions of the WTO Ministerial Conference in Doha: the Development or Millennium Round, the Monterrey Consensus of the 'United Nations Conference on Financing for Development' and the 'Type 2 partnership agreements' from the 'United Nations World Summit on Sustainable Development in Johannesburg': the recent and the latest broad programme type keys to international institutions.

I should like to complete my description of the present world political situation by continuing in the vein of the previous section, glancing once more at Figure 4.2 (this time, more specifically, at the bottom rows).

By the turn of the new millennium, broadly speaking, all the Summits + 5, to review those we have mentioned previously, considering them the most progressive summits in UN history, have taken place. Generally speaking, each and every one was a disappointment. We saw at times complete failure to implement action plans and approve declarations (such as, for example, the case of the Summit on Social Development in Copenhagen) and even, as the 1990s came to a close, U-turns (a case in point is the Beijing + 5 Summit on Women in New York).

At the same time, globalization and the realization that the promised benefits completely fail to arrive for the developing world; on the contrary, it is becoming clearly established as the new world socio-economic stage par excellence. From the environmental viewpoint, the failure to ratify[5] and/or comply with the Kyoto agreements provide further indication of the way things are going.

	"UN framework"	"Neoliberal framework"		Parallel key events
1980s		Reagan and Tatcher		Reagan and Tatcher
1982			Launch of structural	International debt crisis
1989			adjustment policies,	Fall of the Berlin Wall
1990			privatisation,	Gulf War
			deregulation, IMF,	
1991			WB; etc	
1992	Río - Earth Summet		G	
1993	Viena - Human Rights		L	
1994	Cairo - Population	WTO founded	O	Chiapas Mexican financial crisis
1995	Copenhague-Social		B	Internet - WEB world
	Pekín - Women		A	
1996	Estambul - Habitat		L	
1997	Kyoto / Río + 5		I	Asian financial crisis
1998			S	Russian financial crisis
			A	
1999		Seattle - WTO	T	
2000	Millenium Summit; MDGs		I	Millenium Forum
2001	Durban - Racism		O N	Porto Alegre / Genoa
11-09-01	11-09-01	11-09-01		11-09-01
2001		Doha - WTO		Financial crisis in Argentina
2002	Monterrey - Financing			Porto Alegre
	Johannesburg - Sust. Development			Lula
2003				Porto Alegre
15-02-03 Iraqi War	15-02-03 Iraqi War	15-02-03 Iraqi War		15-02-03 Iraqi War
2003		Cancún - WTO		

Figure 4.2 *Evolution of the international political situation*

One might say that, in this regard, the 20th century ended in Seattle with the failure of the WTO meeting there, linked to the 'official' birth of the 'anti-globalization' movement. Both things, though, have older origins including, in 1994, the establishment of the WTO and the uprising in Chiapas.

2000 was the year of good intentions. And the UN had its own! Watered-down, but still … In its declaration, the UN Extraordinary General Assembly, the Millennium Summit, approved the well-known Millennium Development Goals, or MDGs. These are, in any case, no more than objectives, overly modest for some – myself included – and, as could be no different given the context in which we find ourselves and this is, in my view, always the most serious aspect, I shall continue to argue in this section without identifying or specifying the means and paths (economic, institutional, etc.) needed to achieve them.

Let me now refer you to Figure 4.3.

Entire books will be needed for years to come if we are to begin to assimilate the year 2001. From the explosion of the so-called social movements (the first Porto Alegre forum under the slogan 'Another World is Possible', the events of Genoa, among others, linked to the 'anti-globalization' movement, etc.) to the most explicitly important failure of a UN Summit, the Durban Summit on Racism (to which we must add the as-yet unevaluated but none the less important rupture within the NGO movement), ending with the world-shaking, tragic events of September 11 in the USA.

But, just a few weeks after those events, so important in so many ways (among other things for their demobilization effect on society), in Doha, a city in the United Arab Emirates pretty well isolated from the rest of the world, ministers from the WTO member states reached the agreement they had failed to achieve in Seattle. The Agreements of the WTO Ministerial Conference in Doha are, precisely, an agreement to reopen a more liberalizing world trade round, the most important ever launched. Apart from goods trade, moreover, this round of negotiations includes practically everything (ranging from agriculture to such essential services as education and health, as well as such fundamental economic areas as financial investment and the access of transnational corporations to all state public tenders). The new negotiations are known as the Millennium Round but, above all, the 'Development Round'! To gain a quick idea of the range of these talks, see Figure 4.4, below, which contains the contents of the Doha Declaration work programme for the round.

The Doha Agreements themselves are not very well known, yet are those most quoted in the texts of official UN summits held subsequently! According to Doha, the intensification of the world trade liberalization process is the cornerstone behind the new direction to be taken by world

1 Eradicate extreme poverty and hunger	Reduce by half the proportion of people living on less than a dollar a day. Reduce by half the proportion of people who suffer from hunger
2 Achieve universal primary education	Ensure that all boys and girls complete a full course of primary schooling
3 Promote gender equalit and empower women	Eliminate gender disparity in primary and secondary education preferably by 2005, and at all levels by 2015
4 Reduce child mortality	Reduce by two thirds the mortality rate among children under five
5 Improve maternal health	Reduce by three quarters the maternal mortality ratio
6 Combat HIV/AIDS, malaria and other diseases	Halt and begin to reverse the spread of HIV/AIDS Halt and begin to reverse the incidence of malaria and other major diseases
7 Ensure environmental sustainability	Integrate the principles of sustainable development into country policies and programmes; reverse loss of environmental resources Reduce by half the proportion of people without sustainable access to safe drinking water Achieve significant improvement in lives of at least 100 million slum dwellers, by 2020
8 Develop a global partnership for development	Develop further an open trading and financial system that is rule-based, predictable and non-discriminatory. Includes a commitment to good governance, development and poverty reductiónnationally and internationally Address the least developed countriesí special needs. This includes tariff- and quota-free access for their exports; enhanced debt relief for heavily indebted poor countries; cancellation of official bilateral debt; and more generous official development assistance for countries committed to poverty reduction Address the special needs of landlocked and small island developing States Deal comprehensively with developing countriesí debt problems through national and international measures to make debt sustainable in the long term In cooperation with the developing countries, develop decent and productive work for youth In cooperation with pharmaceutical companies, provide access to affordable essential drugs in developing countries In cooperation with the private sector, make available the benefits of new technologiesóespecially information and communications technologies Source: http://www.un.org/millenniumgoals

Figure 4.3 *Millennium Development Goals*

```
• Implementation              • Dispute settlement
• Agriculture                 • Trade and environment
• Services                    • Electronic commerce
• Market access               • Small economies
• TRIPS                       • Trade, debt and finance
• Trade and investment        • Trade and transfer of technology
• Trade and competition policy • Technical cooperation
• Government procurement       • Least-developed countries
• Trade facilitation           • Special and differential treatment
• WTO rules                    • Organisation and management of the work programme


Source: http://www.wto.org/english/thewto_e/minist_e/min01_e/mindecl_e.htm
```

Figure 4.4 *Work programme for the Doha Declaration, which opens the development round*

economic policy. The market, more deregulated than ever at present, will be the frame in which the world's problems (poverty, the environment, development, cultural diversity, etc.) will be resolved.

Five months before the end of a mythical decade, Rio-Johannesburg, the last preparatory step in the UN context, took place: the World Summit on Financing for Development in Monterrey, which produced or, perhaps, better, tried to produce the so-called Monterrey Consensus.

The Monterrey Summit was, in fact, a mandate for the Millennium Summit precisely to specify the resources, instruments and ways to finance development. What I have often stressed is, in short, the basic question: How to implement? How to achieve? In this case, the MDGs (Millennium Development Goals). And what is this so-called, or alleged, consensus (which rose up from the ashes of September 11 and the Doha trade concerns)? The headings of the main sections in the final summit document make this pretty clear:

- Mobilizing international financial resources for development: foreign direct investment (FDI) and other private flows.
- International trade as an engine for development (that is to say, full speed ahead on the Doha liberalization path).
- Increasing official development assistance (ODA) to 0.7 per cent of GDP of the developed countries. (Doesn't this sound rather familiar? Although it is obviously indispensable and no doubt still completely insufficient!)

Apart from the use of a slightly more progressive language on debt issues, the so-called Monterrey Consensus is, in fact, the ratification of the international neoliberal model. The third heading above is, today, pure rhetoric from the past. And the other two principal points are nothing more than the adaptation of development cooperation issues to the neoliberal model, making them subsidiary to the Doha Round, that is to say, to the intensification of trade liberalization.

Exactly the same thing happened soon after Johannesburg. What, then, is the main criticism that we can and should make of the Monterrey action or implementation plan and after Johannesburg? Well, precisely that it is not what they say it is!

We find ourselves time and again, and particularly in the case of Johannesburg, before a long list of objectives, always long-term (10–15 years, over which so many things happen that many can be considered excuses should the goals not finally be met, even though the true reason may have been that no efforts were really made to achieve them), practically always with no quantification of objectives and always, above all, with absolutely no clear and explicitly financial and institutional commitment.

What the Johannesburg action plan does once more is to pass onto the market with no intention of regulating it, what is more the responsibility for solving the world's main social and environmental problems! The states, particularly the rich and powerful states, evade all financial or institutional commitments within the UN system, while the international economic and financial institutions, the World Trade Organization above all, and private resources become, practically exclusively, the only framework for tackling challenges.

Aware as I am of just how strong my accusations in the previous paragraph sound, we should perhaps go a little deeper into the subject. Perhaps, here, the subject of the Type 2 Partnership Agreements may prove helpful. It is probable that in the future even the terminology used to refer to this subject will be different: as it stands at present, it is much too revealing to be allowed to pass down into history. Type 1 agreements at a summit are those approved as such by the summit: the political declaration, the action plan, etc. Type 2 agreements are summit agreements, listed and considered outcomes from the summit, but not explicitly approved by it, that is to say, by the corresponding extraordinary UN General Assembly plenary session.

Some 300 partnership proposals were presented at Johannesburg as part of the official summit programme, and we can still find these on the summit's official website, explicitly listed as outcomes from it! As the fine word itself suggests, these are agreements between partners, usually but not necessarily all together, governments, companies, international organizations, universities, NGOs, etc. to submit projects in the general direction of the summit, in this case on sustainable development.

Sounds wonderful, doesn't it? And the answer would certainly be 'yes' if not for ... if not for the fact that they do not form part of Type 1 agreements, that is to say, it is not made clear anywhere what the relation is nor whether there should even be such a relation between the goals (political declaration and action plan) approved at the summit and the goals these Type 2 Partnership Agreements pursue. If not for the fact that they are answerable to no one, neither at the beginning (so, why this project and not another, perhaps with a higher priority but perhaps not so beneficial to certain partners) nor at the end (whether goals have really been met, any collateral impact, etc.). If not for the fact that, when the action plan says that additional funding should be found, the following possibility is, de facto, being posited: the possibility of sinking such funding into these partnership agreements rather than in funds subject to public institutional 'control' of any kind. Too much, in my view, not to be clearly seen as the opening up of a new path for the neoliberal option as practically the only reference framework for international policy these days. A new step, let there be no doubt about it, towards privatizing 'international cooperation for sustainable development'.

Is the WTO's 'Development Round', which embraces a clear political and ideological identification with the Washington Consensus, the right way to achieve the 'United Nations Millennium Development Goals (MDGs)'?

In 2002, then, we witnessed another step towards the hegemony of what we call here the international neoliberal model. Taking its lead from Doha, between Monterrey and Johannesburg, the UN, the only current existing body of global problem management system, allowed this step to be taken. Not only do we not have a new consensus as was claimed at Monterrey, but the Washington Consensus has become consolidated and is being imposed paradoxically, in my view with ever growing force.

We have given enough consideration to the above claim and need not insist more on this point. However, as it stands or is explained here, one might reach the conclusion that the UN itself was responsible for this situation and that is not the case.

The UN is an international organization and, under the present state of affairs, its member states enjoy absolute sovereignty! The results of a UN summit are the fruit of long, complex negotiations among these states. It is clear, however, that not all states are equal or have the same muscle. Recently, it has been usual to see three-sided negotiations within the UN, between the US, the EU and the G77, occasionally with the active participation of such countries as the Scandinavian nations, Switzerland, Canada, Australia, etc., and though simplification always leaves something out, little more. But, in fact, the European Union (EU) ends up playing a truly minor role, the result, according to the experts, of the Community's well-known lack of unity as regards foreign policy. In practice, therefore, the real negotiations take place between the US (and, among other things, its active unilateralism) and the regrouped but weak and contradictory G77 (which brings together more than 120 developing countries) plus China. And, though I will not say that the G77's negotiating position expresses, generally speaking, its explicit objections to moving forward within the neoliberal framework, I will say that it expresses, generally speaking and in a fairly 'elementary' way, its urge to escape from the predicament it is trapped in, and from which the group's members see no release if the international political situation continues its present course of development.

In short, I believe that there can be little doubt, at present, of the continuing hegemony of the US (which also, indirectly, favours the EU's more economic and financial interests) and its positions regarding international policy, based, primarily, on consolidating it as the sole world power. The US promotes international structural reforms necessary to further the interests of its economic and financial sectors, which need to expand continuously in order to continue reaping profits. In other words, they need an ever bigger market, particularly for their products and investments, which can also thereby benefit from less strictly controlled social, environmental and fiscal conditions and, therefore, enjoy larger profit margins.

Now, a more or less clearly hegemonic framework notwithstanding, reality is still reality. And another characteristic trend in the global world is that, despite all, such an intervisible and interdependent world as ours cannot renounce, nor renounce the attempt to meet, the Millennium Development Goals. The MDGs express, at the very least, the international community's response to the inhuman conditions in which over half the world's population is forced to live.

We can summarize the analysis we have made up to this point by saying that the UN is well able to define these goals but has not, to date, been able to take into its hands the keys needed to meet them. The world's rich and powerful nations have steered the last two summits, those in Monterrey and Johannesburg, to leave the UN bereft of operational results. The world's rich and powerful nations continue to ratify and to impose the Washington Consensus. At present, they plan to continue imposing it through the latest round of negotiations opened up by the WTO: the Development Round.

The key question is, then: Is the WTO's Development Round, which is and remains clearly in tune politically and ideologically with the Washington Consensus, the right way to achieve the MDGs?

Although, at this point in this paper it no longer even needs saying, clearly, in my view the answer is: NO! Because of all the arguments listed here, but also one in particular: how, after nearly 20 years of a policy that has led to a world whose problems make it absolutely essential to draw up the MDGs described in Figure 4.3, can we expect the same policy that has caused many of these problems to now solve them? It is obvious that the same need that drove us to establish the new goals should make us change our policy in order to achieve them. Surely, it cannot be the same policy that has generated the problems we now seek to resolve?

Democratic worldwide governance

Democratic worldwide governance: basis and features

The fact is that there are few possible summaries of the by no means short first part of this paper, except as follows: a system of international institutions resulting from a particular period in the history of humanity that following the great wars of the 20th century attempts to face very different situations, possibilities and circumstances such as those arising in the 1980s and 1990s and, particularly, in the early years of the 21st century. For a host of different reasons, it is not up to the job and ends up 'permitting', among other things, the following well-documented states of affairs:

- that much of humanity lives in conditions that do not satisfy even their basic needs;
- that violence among people forms part of the daily bread in many parts of the world;
- that we are beginning to pay a high price for our mistreatment of the planet we form an inextricable part of;
- that the gap between rich and poor, powerful and weak, grows wider every day, not due to any natural phenomenon, but as the result of policies applied;
- that a small group of the world's most rich and powerful are exercising more and more power and dominance over the rest, and with more and more impunity and in ever more arbitrary fashion.

And since, in fact, the way these few rich and powerful rich have steered the planet's fortunes and, particularly, the way they have managed the new context we have come to know as globalization having decided, basically, to use it to deregulate, privatize, etc., allowing the injustices we describe here to increase, leaves only one possible alternative or path (if we except, needless to say, that of turning back (?), something history has always shown to be impossible). This alternative is, precisely, that of ensuring the democratic governance of globalization. Such a measure is, clearly, intimately linked to the need for in-depth reform of our present system of international institutions, basically, so that this system can articulate, formulate, 'rehabilitate' this democratic governance, radically reversing the current trends and circumstances described here, and which are causing so much damage.

What we need, then, to respond to policies that seek to transfer wholesale to the market from the institutions themselves (but, remember, from certain institutions more than from others) the responsibility for resolving and managing the world's problems is to restore to these institutions, once they have been suitably reformed (some, again, more than others), the responsibility, according to generally accepted ethical principles, to draw up policies to govern world social, trade, economic, financial, etc., dynamics. Then human beings (the most intrinsically and least instrumentally human) can take up a central place once more, becoming the real subject of such policies. Year after year, day after day, the need for market regulation is becoming an ever more unquestionable need if we want truly to advance towards a fair, more equitable, diverse, free, peaceful world.

This is the view of a new initiative which is beginning to emerge in civil society: the World Forum of Civil Society Networks – UBUNTU. Having become firmly established, this movement is now channelling its energies precisely into a World Campaign for In-depth Reform of the System of International Institutions.

Concerning the World Campaign Manifesto

To speak of reform in the terms we speak of it here is not, in principle, particularly original. However, a glance at the depth behind the analyses, principles and objectives that drive this campaign soon shows the quantity and quality of differences between what is proposed by the campaign and other current initiatives for reform of the international institutions.

Well, if I had to sum up, in one or two reasonably short sentences from the manifesto, the core thinking behind the campaign and that which makes it, as I have said and always in my opinion profoundly original, apart from, needless to say, more necessary than ever, I would choose these two:

• The first can be seen as a summary of the entire campaign manifesto:

The pursuit of these goals requires a stronger, more democratic UN, placed at the centre of a consistent, democratic, responsible, effective system of international institutions. More specifically, we need to democratize the composition and decision-making procedures of UN bodies; to strengthen the UN General Assembly, placing all its bodies and agencies, as well as world multilateral

organizations (IMF, WB, WTO, etc.) under its effective, democratic control.

I would emphasize: 'NO to only UN reform'; 'YES to reform of the system of international institutions'.

If the undeclared bipolarization that affects the system of multilateral international institutions, a situation described in the first section of this document, is one of the most important problems facing the UN, then reform limited only to the UN would be a serious mistake. Such restricted reform could only lead, in present circumstances, to further weakening of the UN, turning it into 'merely' a humanitarian agency.

Any reform proposed and, above all, effectively put into practice, should aim to radically remedy the UN's inability to wield a democratizing influence on global financial, economic and trade policies. In other words, as the paragraph from the campaign manifesto that we highlight here insists, the key reform is that which places world economic, financial and trade institutions under the real political control of the UN which should itself also be reformed, of course. Only in this way can we build a system of international institutions in which there is not a divorce, not to say conflict, between political programmes and their implementation.

- The second summarizing sentence, also reflected in many other campaign texts and approaches, is as follows:

We propose in-depth reform of the system of international institutions towards an authentic system of global democratic governance that guarantees the existence and effective functioning of mechanisms, enabling the world's citizens and civil society organizations to be directly represented and to take part in global decision-making processes within the framework of the international system.

And I would emphasize: 'NO to suprastructural reform conducted solely and exclusively by States'; 'YES to reform in which all players currently present on the world scene take part'.

There are certain indispensable points we must make here:

- To date, the subject of reform of the international institutions has only been considered, or at least only in-depth, within the organizations themselves. With certain honourable exceptions and completely understandably if we take into account what were the leading, practically only, political actors on the world stage until quite recently: the nation-states. Here, we must remember, moreover, that the international institutions were designed and structured largely for this purpose: to deal with international questions, that is to say, relations between states. Finally, it is clear that very few real reforms have been possible over the course of history as the result only of the position adopted and participation of actors from within, in this case, the nation-states.

- In the age of globalization, however, there exist fundamental flows, activities and situations that go far beyond the states, making them insufficient and even inadequate for managing the new subjects on the world agenda. As has occurred so often in history as regards, for example, the economic situation, a change scale (from state to transnational) that we have still not been able to digest and that, in fact, clearly points, once more, to the imperious need for global democratic governance has happened. Our worst environmental problems at present are also at a planetary scale leading to the same conclusion.

- However, another consideration has emerged, one that, moreover, bears close and intimate relation to the previous point: the appearance (though some are still at the emerging stage of new political actors or subjects) of the transnational corporations themselves; the megalopolizes, etc.; and the world or global citizenry we shall talk about later on.

- As a result, it is as logical as it is inevitable and indispensable that future proposals to reform the system of international institutions should not only take these new actors into account, but that these new actors should play a leading role, at times the leading role, in reform processes and, needless to say, in the structural results produced by reform.

- Only a strategy, therefore, that involves all actors and creates in this case more than ever a state of world opinion and public participation favourable to such a reform as that proposed can, in the current situation, lead to a satisfactory outcome, in which the path to achieve it will, as always, be as important as the goals themselves.

What reform, what system of Democratic Worldwide Governance, are we thinking about?

The path of the campaign I have described here helps to take us forward. We soon learned that we cannot stay at the level of formulating the ideas, even though I at least continue to think that reaching a first consensus at this level is indispensable and forms a first, important step forward. However, the road to global democratic governance requires more specific operational proposals to be constructed to give better shape and form to the general ideas already outlined.

Here, however, we must gauge our methods very carefully, and each actor must find their own. One cannot say at the moment that civil society has developed and reached consensus over its proposals. Proposals exist, more and more, but not all coincide, even in the basic principles. There is a wealth here, then, but therein also lies a challenge. In order even to achieve consensus at a level of broad principles, however, we need to be able to visualize specific aspects of proposals. To do so at present, in the opinion of the UBUNTU Forum, requires placing on the table a range of possible scenarios allowing us to open up a broad, plural debate that, rather than generating opposing positions, enables us to begin identifying points of consensus that, from the level of concretion, also serves to consolidate it at the level of principles and basic ideas.

However, personally, I should not like to leave out of this paper a description of certain specific proposals that, in my view, illustrate, in the form of a possible, concrete scenario, the general ideas presented here. My goal here is not so much to defend this scenario but to stimulate debate about it. The scenario is outlined below, in Figure 4.5.

From globalization to world citizenship and cosmopolitan democracy

From globalization to world citizenship; the global demonstration of 15 February 2003

After analysing the present world political situation in the above section on 'The Washington Consensus', and discussing the proposal for a system of global democratic governance linked to in-depth reform of the system of international institutions as described in the section that follows it on 'Democratic Worldwide Governance', we are left with at least a couple of important questions: What world model? With what specific policies?

In fact, these questions are partially answered in our analysis of the world political situation where, naturally, we have taken sides. And, in fact, the proposal for institutional reform is far from neutral. Nevertheless, no doubt we need more explicit reflection on the questions that head this section of the paper so as to close it with a modicum of internal coherence.

To this end, we should begin by going back to the analysis of globalization as a new, fundamental context for humanity's 'affairs' on planet Earth. While the focus in the first part was more on economic questions, emphasizing more negative results of this aspect of globalization, making it clear, too, that there are other results that may also turn out to be greatly damaging (those affecting the sustainability of cultural diversity, for example), there are also certain aspects to globalization that go to shape what is at least a different world. I believe it may even be a better world, though I will not expand on this personal perception here and so, therefore, we need to study and conceptualize it as it is, at least, different.

A POSSIBLE SCENARIO	
UN GENERAL ASSEMBLY	• Two-chamber system representing UN states and the world's citizens (see World Parliament) • Unification of general assemblies and conferences into a single institution with a central role in the system: UNGA (*)
UN SECURITY COUNCIL	• Supervision by General Assembly • Representative composition • Abolition of veto • Voting by qualified majority for certain questions
UN ECOSOC IFM WB WTO	• ECOSOC revamped and converted into the Economic, Social and • Environment Security Council with effective control over BWIs, WTO and agencies engaged in these fields
UN AGENCIES AND PROGRAMMES	• Dissolution of general assemblies and conferences of agencies other than UN (*); creation of specific assemblies (**) with the presence of actors from all the relevant sectors
INTERNATIONAL JUSTICE	• Interconnected world legal system embracing both civil and criminal law, with executive mechanisms from local to world level
WORLD PARLIAMENT	• A WP with UN chamber representing the world's population • With UNGA, part of a two-chamber world legislative system (*)
WORLD REFERENDUMS	• Binding world referendums
CIVIL SOCIETY	• Effective participation, along with other actors, in specific assemblies (**)
DEBT	• Cancellation of external debt
TAXATION	• Elimination of tax havens • Interconnected world fiscal system
DEVELOPMENT	• World cohesion funds for development
STATE SOVEREIGNTY	• Transfer of sovereignty to system of global democratic governance See Section 3.2.
UN CHARTER REFORM	• Yes, but first ñand most importantñ reforming the BWI and WTO foundation agreements

Figure 4.5 *A possible scenario*

This is an ever more intervisible and interdependent world where more and more citizens have access to more information, more relations, more experiences, etc., with places, problems and people from other places on the planet from where they habitually live physically. Although we cannot generalize here either, we are seeing more and more significant examples that this is the case. And this leads us to identify clearly with what we might conceptualize as the emergence of a new global or world citizenship, that is to say, a citizenship of people aware that they are citizens of the world!

The global demonstration of 15 February 2003,[6] 'For Peace, Stop the War', was a historic moment that has as yet been little studied, one which marks a turning-point with regard to the reflections in the above paragraph. Never before had a state of world opinion been so clear, so broad, so important as was created at that time on a particular issue: that of the war in Iraq.

And this fact requires and permits us to make a series of considerations regarding the key questions that concern us here:

- It was not an isolated event, but a culmination and one perfectly able to be repeated. It was the result of different, eminently interesting factors, including:
  - the emergence of a clearly-spreading perception on the part of many citizens of the world who feel and identify themselves as such, as world civil society;
  - the emergence of forms of organization that, in fact, were able to find a place in society because, in one way or another, they are the expression of the previous factor. From what have become the 'older' NGOs, though they are continually growing, both quantitatively and qualitatively, to the so-called new social movements that, above all, have collectively identified themselves with the World Social Forum's global and local idea that 'another world is possible';
  - the experience, learning, maturity, etc., that these citizens and movements acquire while demanding and exercising, as and when they can, their right to take part in global decisions that finally also affect their own lives: Seattle, Porto Alegre, Genoa, Johannesburg, etc. (and, more recently, Cancun);
  - the absolutely disproportionate stance taken by the US government over the Iraq question. Unlike, say, the situation in Afghanistan, for example, everyone could clearly see that Iraq was purely and simply about oil. This shows, too, that not even the ferocious control the dominant powers wield over the leading media can fool the people of the world who are, fortunately, capable of using other, alternative, means of communication and

information, independent to a greater or lesser degree but, in any case, clearly identified with both the factor of globalization that concerns us and with its main effect: that of creating a global citizenship, global movements, with their own opinions.

- The worldwide, global nature of the demonstration. Never before had so many of the world's citizens coincided in the same cause and activity in so many different places all over the world or in numbers of people 'taking to the street', or in the different ways they adopted to express one single will.
- The political successes won by the demonstration. Despite what many opinions and, above all, perceptions a posteriori, alleged, the outcome of that demonstration was, in my view, an enormous success and a huge accumulation of 'capital', from which we shall need to extract the appropriate yields and benefits. It is true that the war finally took place and that, therefore, the basic aim was not achieved. But it is also true that never before had many of the world's states and such a key international organization as the UN 'fed' off such a demonstration to proclaim their existence and their opinion, turning the empire's action into an illegal act against international law. It was and is becoming ever more clear in the eyes and judgement of most of the world that this was an illegitimate act! And, although this is not the place to expand on it, let me also reaffirm my conviction that the UN emerged strengthened by that crisis!

From the world under globalization and world citizenship to cosmopolitan democracy; or for what world model?

A lot of water has gone under the bridge since, some years ago, I first wrote my intuitive ideas on the subject, and many new situations and thoughts have emerged. Ulrick Bech and David Held[7] are, for example, two of the best-known authors in the field and with whom I, personally, feel most identified when formulating and ripening my ideas about a new global world, in the age-old tradition of the Stoics, the first Christians, Kant, Russell, Peccei, etc.

We are in a world fast becoming global in a process that is bringing about in what is the most positive reactive element, as discussed in the previous section, the emergence of what is becoming known as world civil society. This, and why not admit it that in different, contradictory forms (NGOs, social movements, etc.), clearly affirms, as part of its collective identity, another world is possible? For the first time, and again, as always, in my opinion, a possible, necessary, progressive alternative can become valid: the construction of a true cosmopolitan or global democracy supported by a political structure that helps to shape this new, emerging world society, to which different nation-states will gradually cede certain types and/or levels of sovereignty. The basic institutions in this future world political movement/structure will, probably, be those resulting from in-depth reform of the system of international institutions, as described in the section on 'Democratic Worldwide Governance' and illustrated by way of a possible scenario in Figure 4.5.

Having come this far we should remember that, at times, we are more afraid of calling a spade a spade than anything. Personally, I have no fear. But we need to tread carefully, needless to say. Why, throughout this paper, do we talk of 'governance' and never of 'government'? Well, because the latter is no doubt associated with the nation-state, where the government is the body with executive power within the state and also denotes the action of governing, what the government does. Governance, on the other hand, denotes a much broader compendium of procedures, means, etc., that make a certain government not necessarily associated with that exercised by a government possible. For this reason, when we speak of international, transnational or world issues, we are only permitted to coin and use the expression 'governance'. Because, if we understand that they are necessary, then the conditions, procedures, means, etc., must be built so that decisions can be taken and even put into practice at this scale too. While world issues were, to a large degree, international questions between nations these dichotomies or disquisitions did not even take place. As transnational and global or world issues take on more and more importance, however, these nuances of language have also become ever more important.

Well, what I would speak of, with the necessary prudence, of course, is of world democratic governance (conditions, procedures, structures, means, etc.) built on a system of international institutions that has undergone the necessary in-depth reform in line, we insist once more, with that described in the section on 'Democratic Worldwide Governance' that is capable of making democratic governance of world affairs possible, that is to say, governance capable of democratically taking and implementing decisions relating to areas of reality that are world or global in scale. This does not need the creation of a world state with its attendant world government. It does, however, require the provision of world or global (we'll find a word that doesn't strike fear into us) political structures and procedures, with an institutional system that guarantees the strictest democratic balance between the different powers and situations that exist, and that is supported and moved, above all, by principles (with human rights at their base, because human rights are becoming ever more widely accepted, even if with certain differences in interpretation) and renewed contracts (social, cultural, environmental, political, etc.) on the world scale that, logically enough, embrace everything at this scale. All this, while also guaranteeing the principle of maximum possible subsidiarity at state, regional, sub-state or supra-local and local level and, inversely, minimum, strictly necessary levels at which sovereignty is ceded in the opposite direction. A more strictly democratic nature should be inherent to this political architecture, enabling us to speak of it as the new cosmopolitan or global democracy.

There are many and there will be more and more. But there is one particular example: global warming for me, yet another manifestation, in many senses, of what we have come to call globalization that shows how absolutely necessary is the above-described political construction. The states cannot continue to exercise complete sovereignty in defining policies in this field. Our planet is in no condition to permit the positions such as those adopted at present and which are completely legal as things stand by the US and Russia, for example. Nonetheless, subsidiarity is indispensable for defining and implementing at local level the great political decisions taken at global level to reduce greenhouse gas emissions.

Clearly, the political construction we are speaking of should run parallel to the global civil society I have spoken of – and I would even dare say ahead of it – improving and finding new forms of organization and action that enable it to play both a participatory role and that of a nest of representative elements consubstantial to the required construction.

With what policies? For the time being, those of a cosmopolitan social democracy!

From the economic standpoint, the globalization of the world no doubt entails a further phase of capitalist expansion, one, however, in its most neoliberal form and with truly negative effects on the social and environmental situation, if the analysis made in the section on 'The Washington Consensus' is anything to go by.

For this reason, in the short and medium term at least, the basic policies that should be formulated and applied in a model such as that described in the previous section, are those that best guarantee that the world as a whole progresses towards higher standards of social well-being, reduced environmental impact and greater equity and justice. Taking the part of the model for European construction based on large-scale use of the cohesion funds, the cosmopolitan democracy described in the previous section can only be built through a world redistributive social-democratic policy that, precisely by making it more cohesive, can change the world and enable it to face the future with truly new confidence and collective efforts.

I believe that, in the final outcome, the key to many of the more neoliberal 'local' fashions lies in the incapacity, of a state for example, to implement a progressive fiscal policy. The result is that large companies, obeying the most easily understandable internal logic, rush to locate elsewhere. In response, a political force in that state, obeying the most easily understandable internal logic, will quickly experience a tendency to adopt neoliberalism, turning into something positive their real incapacity to do anything else rather than something that would be automatically qualified as old-fashioned social-democratic policy. But these postulates become much less implacable if we move onto the planetary, the global level. The elimination of tax havens, followed by the enactment of a simple world fiscal policy beginning, for example, and no doubt popularly, with the more speculative financial transactions, would no doubt enable policies for a world cohesion fund to be implemented, thus beginning to achieve the goals discussed in the previous paragraph.

In other words, the model for cosmopolitan democracy would make little sense in the end if it did not have the real capacity to do 'politics with a capital T'. And, to conclude: in a global world, it will only be possible to do 'politics with a capital T' at ever more global level, and, in fact, this is already occurring! However, with institutionalization and a cosmopolitan model as proposed here, then no player can escape, each player has to coexist, negotiate, agree, etc., with all the others. From this new level of coexistence, which is, in fact that which our very evolution should bring us to, should emerge and bring an end to the exploitation of the weak by the strong and the birth of a more fraternal world. A world in which we are also able to restore a stable dynamic balance with the planet, based, all in all, on human beings valued for what they are rather than for what they have.

5

The 2006 War in Lebanon and the Role of the United Nations

The World Campaign for In-depth Reform of the System of International Institutions has never remained aloof from everyday reality. On the contrary, it has made its stance clear at specific junctures and on specific conflicts directly or indirectly through the UBUNTU Forum, or through its statements aimed at world public opinion. It is in the Forum's nature to seek to go beyond the circumstances of the moment (though those are important too) and clearly state our support for the structural institutional reforms that were being called for, and that in our view best characterized the requirements and possibilities involved in the issue in hand.

In that context, the year 2006 was particularly worrying on account of the entrenchment of violent conflicts (both old and new), the entrenchment of violence as such and the entrenched inability of the political world to find solutions. It was in the face of that scenario that the UBUNTU Forum issued the statement reprinted below.

In response to that statement, Professor Richard Falk (Professor Emeritus of International Law at Princeton University, University of California – Santa Barbara, and closely involved since 2004 with the UBUNTU Secretariat and the World Campaign) sent us his analysis of the serious conflict then raging in Lebanon. This document merits highlighting since it clearly contributes an ever-essential complement to this book: a political analysis of reality.

Afghanistan, Iraq, Palestine, Sudan and elsewhere: STOP THE VIOLATIONS OF DEMOCRATIC INTERNATIONAL LAW! 11 July 2006, Statement issued by the UBUNTU Forum.

Rather than just one specific event that bothers us (there are so many of them!) and rather than a specific complex situation that worries us (again, there are far too many of them!), it is a series of events that we have been concerned about for some time and which we have spoken out against: a whole host of situations, trends, actions (and inactions) that once again demand, with even more energy than before, that we the undersigned participants, members and friends of the UBUNTU Forum collectively speak out and say once again: STOP THE VIOLATIONS OF DEMOCRATIC INTERNATIONAL LAW!

In Afghanistan, Iraq, Palestine, Sudan … deadlock, militarization and the use of all kinds of mechanisms that disregard or do not comply with democratic international law founded on universal human rights **(clandestine prisons, 'illegal' flights, shameful walls, 'selective' killings, collateral damage, disproportionate responses, technical errors, etc., seem to be the flags of the new barbarities of the powerful)** mean that in the conflicts of today the widespread and indiscriminate suffering that civil society is subjected to in these areas seems to be of no importance and to be without limit or end.

The 2005 UN Summit, which was influenced by the events of 11 September 2001 (which we have condemned and will continue to condemn as an act of expression through violence and struggle), dealt, among other issues, with the themes of world peace and security. Even though it was unable to come up with many specific solutions, the summit fortunately did declare:

> *We acknowledge that peace and security, development and human rights are the pillars of the United Nations system and the foundations for collective security and well-being. We recognize that development, peace and security, and human rights are interlinked and mutually reinforcing.*
>
> *The international community, through the United Nations, also has the responsibility to use appropriate diplomatic, humanitarian and other peaceful means to help protect populations from genocide, war crimes, ethnic cleansing and crimes against humanity.*

In this context, and in many others prior to the UN itself, we finally speak out together to firstly DEMAND:

> *An immediate end to the ignominious events, situations and actions such as those described above and in particular that the armed forces should act in these deadlocked conflicts as 'blue helmets' under UN command.*

Real reform once and for all of the UN, giving it the powers, functions and human and financial resources it requires, together with the unwavering and unequivocal commitment from all parties, especially the most powerful states, to redress the sad trends and realities today without delay and with firmness of purpose.

And secondly, we CALL ON the citizens of the world, in particular international civil society organizations and social movements, to continue mobilizing to restore a climate of dialogue in the world and to achieve peace and justice everywhere.

The world order and the role of the United Nations after the 2006 war in Lebanon
Richard Falk

There has been much commentary on the significance of the Lebanon War. There is an unresolved debate about whether there was a victorious side in the war and even what the idea of victory means. There are various suggestions about how to prevent a new war between Israel and Hezbollah, whether by relying mainly on the UN stabilization force or by reviving diplomacy between Israel and its various adversaries. Is it time to talk with Hezbollah and Hamas? What does the inconclusiveness of the war tell us about the benefits and limitations of military superiority in such a conflict? Could Israel have used its military capabilities more effectively, or were deeper structural restraints operative? These are all important issues, deserving of reflection and dialogue, and hopefully encourage a turn away from violence by all sides in their search for peace and security.

Beyond these immediate concerns lies the question of world order and the extent to which some gaps and weaknesses were disclosed by the Lebanon War and its outcome. In a deep sense this question of the shape of world order has been present at least since the collapse of the Soviet Union in the early 1990s. It was given a temporary spin by the first Bush president, George H. W. Bush, who introduced the phrase 'a new world order' to describe the possibility of using the UN Security Council as an effective instrument of collective security in the aftermath of the Cold War. The Security Council was no longer gridlocked by the pervasive antagonism between East and West, as was shown by the mandate to reverse Iraqi aggression against Kuwait in the first Gulf War. It seemed possible to implement the Charter promise to protect victims of aggression and conquest by enlisting the world community as a whole in an undertaking of collective self-defence. There were many criticisms of the manner in which the United Nations Security Council (UNSC) gave unrestricted discretion to an American-led coalition in 1991 to take over the conduct of the war, determine its goals and control the dynamics of post-conflict diplomacy. But the undertaking did effectively restore Kuwaiti sovereignty, and in that sense could properly proclaim 'mission accomplished'. But no sooner were the guns silent in Iraq than the idea of a new world order was quietly abandoned by Washington, put back 'on the shelf' as one senior American diplomat described the new mood. On reflection, the US government seemed reluctant to affirm UN authority to such an extent, or to find itself assigned unwelcome undertakings in the future by a more confident Security Council.

In any event, subsequent developments during the 1990s moved the United States away from a reliance on the UN to address world order challenges. The failure of peacekeeping in Somalia (1993), the non-response to genocide in Rwanda (1994) and the shocking ineptitude of the UN in Bosnia, especially the dismal spectacle of UN peacekeepers standing by as spectators during the massacre of some 8,000 Muslim males at Srebrenica in 1995. These moves away from the UN took place during the presidency of Bill Clinton, a moderate, internationally minded American leader. This new trend reached its climax in 1999 when an alleged imminent threat of ethnic cleansing in Kosovo led to a war under North Atlantic Treaty Organization (NATO) auspices, 'a coalition of the willing' led from Washington, engaging in a controversial instance of 'humanitarian intervention' without the benefit of UN authorization. And then in 2003 the Iraq War went ahead despite the failure of the US and Britain to persuade the Security Council to authorize the use of force. In both these instances, there seemed to be a renewed reliance on traditional alliance diplomacy to pursue both humanitarian and geopolitical objectives. Rather than a new world order, there was a reversion to an older idea of a world order managed by dominant sovereign states to serve their interests and promote their values.

At the same time, outside the security domain, there were other ideas being discussed about the changing nature of world order. Some observers expressed the view that the rise of market forces, combined with the compression of time and space as a result of information technology and the mobility of international capital, was producing a borderless world, leading many to adopt the label of 'globalization'. Others speculated that the Internet was an extraordinary instrument of empowerment that was making the peoples of the world a potential 'second superpower' based on the leverage that could be generated by a networked world civil society acting in unison. And still others emphasized the revolutionary relevance of climate change, bringing about extreme weather in the form of tsunamis, hurricanes, polar melting, droughts and disease, threatening human catastrophe that could be averted only if effective global governance were established as a matter of urgency.

All of these developments have greatly complicated our understanding of the nature of world order in the 21st century, but we have yet to absorb the implications of the 9/11 attacks on the United States, and the American decision to declare a 'global war on terror' in response. The Lebanon War (as well as the Iraq War) reinforces what I would call the unlearned lessons of 9/11. The most important of these is the change in the nature of power and security: even the most traditionally powerful state is now vulnerable to a devastating attack by a determined and skilled non-state actor, and unlike an enemy state, this adversary is itself basically invulnerable to a debilitating counter-attack by military means. Such an actor occupies no territory, offers no targets and has no leadership that can be persuaded to surrender. The failure to heed the lesson of 9/11 resulted in relying on a war strategy to address the adversary instead of adapting the response to the non-state nature of the threat. What was appropriate after 9/11 was not a generalized war, but a set of particularized responses associated with greatly improved international law enforcement, possibly supplemented in exceptional situations by special forces operations undertaken with the consent of either the territorial government or the UN. Such a police approach, to be successful, would need to be combined with concerted efforts to address whatever legitimate grievances had played some part in motivating such extreme violence.

What does the Lebanon War add to this picture? It reinforces in a more vivid fashion this new ratio of power with respect to combat between state power and a non-state adversary. The military machine of the state can inflict virtually unlimited destruction and cause great suffering to civilian society, and yet it cannot consistently destroy the capacity of its non-state adversary to strike back. Israel had repeatedly defeated and deterred Arab states that had challenged its security in a number of wars. Its military might and skill had been successfully used in the past to achieve a series of political victories in a series of wars that expanded its territory, raised its prestige and intimidated its neighbours, while creating a reputation of invincibility. But in this different world order, relying on military muscle against a seemingly weakly armed opponent will not yield a victory, even for Israel. Instead, militarism now exposes the vulnerability of supposed military powerhouses to the increasingly effective tactics of non-state political adversaries. Of course, both sides learn within their respective paradigms. Israel adapts future war plans to overcome failure in Lebanon, while Hezbollah tries to anticipate these adjustments in planning to mount an even more devastating resistance in the course of the next flairup.

In the face of experiences in Iraq and Lebanon, the frustrated states, addicted as they seem to be to military solutions for political problems, are likely to go back to their drawing boards, devising new weapons and tactics, but convinced that in the future it will be possible to restore the relevance of superior military power as measured by wealth and technological capacity. This will be a costly mistake. It overlooks the extent to which war is becoming dysfunctional in the 21st century, wasting incredible amounts of resources that could be put to much better uses in raising living standards and creating a more stable, cooperative world. If military power is not the answer, what is? It has never been more important to find sustainable solutions to the deep, unresolved conflicts of the Middle East. The problems of Israel could be most reliably addressed by a fair political compromise that acknowledges Palestinian rights, restores Syrian territory and produces a full withdrawal from Lebanese territory.

The United States could similarly gain security and confidence by disengaging from wars that have no foundation in law or morality, and joining with other countries to protect the societies of the world from extremist violence, constructing arrangements for improved international cooperation and for global governance. It is instructive to take account of the greatest achievement of Europe since 1945, which is not, as generally believed, the high level of economic integration, but rather the truly remarkable establishment of a culture of peace that has made the outbreak of war within the boundaries of the EU virtually unthinkable.

An appreciation of the Lebanon War from the perspective of world order may encourage this perception that the viability of the war system was based on being able to limit the playing field of international conflict to sovereign states exercising governmental control within recognized international boundaries. Even this role for war has been earlier deeply challenged by the advent of weaponry of mass destruction, especially nuclear weapons, the existence of which continues to threaten humanity in a variety of ways. But with the rise of non-state actors as international players, modalities of war are more and more likely to lead to the persistence of deadly conflict rather than to victory. The United States currently spends more on its military capabilities than the rest of the world combined, and yet it has never in its history felt as vulnerable to attack or as unable to translate battlefield outcomes into desired political results.

All in all, the Lebanon War is likely to be remembered not for the birth pains of 'a new Middle East' (Condoleezza Rice), but as the death throes of a system of world order that accepted war as the inevitable basis of stability and change in relations among sovereign states.

PART 3

THE PROPOSALS – IN GENERAL

6

Proposals for the Reform of the System of International Institutions. Future Scenarios

A document drafted by the Secretariat of the World Campaign and of the UBUNTU Forum with the special collaboration of Aldo Caliari and John Foster, on the occasion of the seminar entitled **Future Scenarios for the Reform of the System of International Institutions.** The event was held in the Polytechnic University of Catalonia and the Pompeu Fabra University (UPF) in Barcelona on 12 and 13 March 2004 in the framework of the World Campaign for In-depth Reform of the System of International Institutions and the World Governance Programme. The book that emerged from that seminar served as a basic precedent for the Conference on Reform of the United Nations and other International Institutions that was held on 23 and 24 September that year in Universal Forum of Cultures Barcelona 2004. Participants in the seminar included: Gemma Adaba, Aldo Caliari, Richard Falk, John Foster, Candido Grzybowski, Eva Hanfstaengl, Sara Longwe, Manuel Manonelles, Fèlix Martí, Federico Mayor, Lluís Miret, Núria Molina, Adil Najam, Jorge Nieto, William Pace, Ferran Requejo, Cyril Ritchie, Roberto Savio, Frank Schroeder, Pere Torres, John Trent, Jose Vidal-Beneyto, Ramón Vivanco and Josep Xercavins.

If any document and/or part of this book had to be singled out as central, this would surely be it. This text was written at the World Campaign's halfway point in time, and probably in conceptual terms too. The manifesto drawn up in 2003 needed a very open propositional follow-up, and that was produced, decisively, at the time and in the way reflected in this next text.

Introduction, framework and summary

This paper presents a collection of proposals to reform international institutions, ranging from piecemeal changes at the system to improve its functioning and enhance participation of all actors at the world scene, to deeper reforms which would path the way towards a truly democratic system of international institutions which is able to deliver policies and resources conducive to a genuine human sustainable development.

The debate on reform is neither recent, nor unique. However, the debate has recently intensified due to the growing mismatch between these institutions and the world where they have to perform. In this ever more globalizing context, world citizens are increasingly affected by decisions taken at the global level, which need to be more transparent, accountable and democratic. Moreover, world problems and challenges – poverty, inequality, violence, injustice, environmental deterioration and cultural homogenization – are to be dealt with by global policies; and the current multilateral system – designed for a fairly different world than ours – is not well equipped to face such an interconnected world.

A number of initiatives have been set up in most recent – and not so recent – years to deal with the challenges currently facing the multilateral system. Whether coming from governments, international organizations or civil society, these initiatives tend to share a concern on the efficiency, legitimacy and democratic credentials of the system. From the Commission on Global Governance[1] to the still ongoing High-Level Panel on Threats, Challenges and Change set up by the UN Secretary-General, there are several initiatives devoted to democratize and enhance the functioning of the international institutions, such as those of the UN Secretary-Generals Boutros Ghali and Kofi Annan, the Panel of Eminent Persons on United Nations-Civil Society Relations established by Kofi Annan, ad hoc groups such as the Independent Working Group on the Future of the UN, proposals by groupings of developing countries, academics and civil society organizations and movements. The International Forum of Montreal, the Club of Madrid, the International Facilitating Group on Financing for Development, the Helsinki Process, the World Political Forum, the International Council of the World Social Forum and the Global Progressive Forum (GPF)[2] are some of those particularly active at the moment.

This collection of proposals is not exhaustive, but tries to gather some of the most representative proposals which have been advocated in most recent times. It is structured around three scenarios – gathering what we have called elementary, substantive and in-depth reforms, which present proposals for reform diverse in scope and depth. Aware that the politics of change are rather complex, we wish to state that there is no time-line assumption behind the succession of scenarios. Sometimes changes which seemed unfeasible can happen earlier than expected. Although the authors and experts who participate in the making of this paper may not subscribe its entirety, in general terms, the proposals for reform included are these which are taken to be desirable to attain and are more or less politically feasible by wide sectors of civil society.

Aimed at putting on the table a sample of proposals which open up debate on a series of questions – what do we mean when we talk about reform? What are to be its guiding principles? And its purposes? What are the reforms put forward by the diverse reform advocates? And what are the diverse steps that could be taken to achieve these goals? This process will – hopefully – engage diverse actors and sectors in a fruitful dialogue to unveil what are the divergences and common points in our respective approaches to the reform of the system of international institutions. Acknowledgement of these eventual commonalities and promotion of complementarities of the diverse processes and initiatives may help moving forward to the common goal of democratizing and enhancing the functioning of the current multilateral system.

Thus, the paper should contribute to sketching out a range of scenarios and proposals to stimulate debate and help find consensus about contents, strategies and the scope of reform, as well as its contribution to designing a new international system for the 21st century.

Summary

This paper contains the following points and scenarios:

- The current system of international institutions: the legacy of the 20th century. This section seeks to facilitate analysis of the current system of international institutions and, highlighting certain serious problems facing the world today, determine the issues reform proposals should cover.
- The main objectives of reform of the international institutions. A general introduction to the scenarios presented, reflecting the reasons and main objectives behind the proposals for reform of the international institutions that follow below.
- Elementary reform scenario: steps towards reform of the system of international institutions. A first scenario for reform of the international institutions that includes proposals best suited to achieving as things stand today the greatest political agreement among government actors, who have the power to put reforms into effect, and other actors forming part of the system. This scenario details certain steps towards immediate improvement in the function of the existing system of institutions.
- Substantive reform scenario: substantial reform of the system of international institutions. A second scenario containing proposals for reform of the international institutions that imply greater changes, and even

slight modification to the founding charters of certain organizations, particularly the Bretton Woods Institutions and the WTO. It entails substantive steps towards achieving great objectives. This scenario would make it possible, in principle, for the international institutions to function considerably more democratically and for the policies necessary to reverse current more negative trends to be implemented to some extent.

- In-depth reform scenario: the system of international institutions after in-depth reform. A final scenario would enable the objectives of democratizing the system and carrying out in-depth reform of the bodies and institutions that form part of it to be achieved, enabling them to confront and resolve conflicts threatening peace and security and implementing policies to promote true, sustainable human development and greater justice in the world. Without forcing complete rupture with the present system, this scenario seeks to sketch out the desired future.

The possibilities for reform are without number and, although this paper does not explicitly develop on them, these possibilities include those that would worsen the current situation as regards the international institutions and the multilateral system. For example, certain proposals for UN reform might, in practice, mean a weakening allegedly seeking greater effectiveness of the organization's resources and mandate, turning the UN into merely a humanitarian agency.

The system of international institutions as it is now: the legacy of the 20th century

The framework at the birth of the present system of international institutions
The origins of today's system of international institutions go back more than 50 years, their original design responding to the desire to prevent another great war like those which took place in the first half of the 20th century. To a large extent, they reflect the situation at that time: as regards peace and security, the victors of World War II obtained a privileged position within the institutional design of the United Nations. And in the economic sphere, memories of the Great Depression convinced the founders of the Bretton Woods Institutions that sometimes the market does not work well and requires government intervention.

The first decades after this system came into being coincided with the process of decolonization, in which the UN played a key role through the Fiduciary Administration Council (Trusteeship Council). The new states' aspirations to be treated as equals served to reinforce the primacy of the idea of the absolute sovereignty of the state within the system of international institutions, a concept largely enshrined in the UN Charter. In line with these ideas, the 'consensus on development' which prevailed at this time was a conscious attempt to limit world economic opening up and integration in order to achieve more independent development, in which the state plays a strategic role. The relations promoted among the states are characterized by functionalism and encouraging supranational cooperation in specific areas (food, health, education, etc.).

Virtues and shortcomings of the original design of the present system of international institutions

Created to safeguard world peace, the establishment of the UN and, soon after, the adoption of the Universal Declaration of Human Rights are crucial events in 20th-century history. They are a great success in human history. The General Assembly is probably one of the most democratic of international institutions and has, over the course of its history, developed international legislation that is fundamental for peaceful coexistence and respect for and promotion of human rights and international cooperation. Nonetheless, the original design of today's international institutions revealed certain shortcomings. The restricted permanent membership of the Security Council, the UN body with binding authority, weakens the chances for the UN – and particularly the UN role in maintaining world peace and security – to achieve a greater legitimacy and capacity of enforcement.

The Bretton Woods Institutions also suffer from the same problem: the unbalanced decision-making system undermines the possibility for a wider legitimacy and democratic credentials and has allowed for a number of policies which lacked consensus and support by all member states and other stakeholders. Despite agreements formally converting the WB and the IMF into specialized UN agencies, and despite the establishment of the Chief Executives Board to coordinate international agencies, programmes and organizations, the BWIs have almost always acted independently, with practically no coordination with the UN. This has resulted in a lack of coherence between policies decided at these institutions and other international policies and standards under UN competence.

Evolution of the system in the second half of the 20th century

Over time, some of the democratic deficit and imbalances of the system were highlighted by the erosion of the original mandates governing certain organizations. The UNGA, which was very active in the 1960s and 1970s, when the Security Council (UNSC) was paralysed due to rivalry between the superpowers, began to play an ever less important role after the late

1980s when, with the end of the Cold War, the UNSC became reactivated. However, while the UN maintains the central role accorded to it by the Charter in peace and security issues, it plays a minor role in economic affairs. Despite having established programmes for development (UNDP), the environment (United Nations Environment Programme – UNEP), etc., the UN has been hamstrung by mandate restrictions and lack of budgetary recourses when it has come to implementation to achieve the goals it has set.

Moreover, when the demands of the developing countries finally achieved a majority in the General Assembly in the 1960s, the Northern countries tended to shift the decision-making locus towards the BWIs, whose decision-making was more favourable to their interests. Parallel to the collapse of the Eastern Bloc, the neoliberal policies enshrined in the Washington Consensus began to gain ground. The BWIs became the institutions supervising global economic governance and ECOSOC, the UN agency designed to play a role in world economic coordination, was clearly sidelined. To the BWIs must also be added the WTO, established in 1994 as a new multilateral organization, but one outside the United Nations system. These institutions have helped in spreading the neoliberal economic policies applied in many parts of the world in recent years.

The crisis of multilateralism in today's world
In the second half of the last decade, the rise of social movements and mass mobilizations on the occasion of intergovernmental summits and gatherings brought to the fore the discontent of the world population vis-à-vis the politics operating at the global level, the de-legitimization of global institutions and distrust with political leadership. At the same time, they evidenced the rise of a sense of common interests and global citizenship among the world's peoples. Worrying recent developments in the world scene, such as the war in Iraq, have shown the divorce between certain decisions in world politics and the opinion of the world citizenry, as well as the inability of the world states to find peaceful, collective and enduring solutions to the world's grave problems. The collapse of the trade negotiations at the Cancun WTO ministerial meeting show, once again, the deep crisis which is currently afflicting the system of multilateral institutions. In this context, the need for reform of the system of international institutions is even more urgent: to deal efficiently with the grave world problems, and to do it in a legitimate and democratic manner.

The current system of international institutions

CURRENT SYSTEM OF INTERNATIONAL INSTITUTIONS (1/2)		
	STRUCTURE AND COMPOSITION	**EVOLUTION**
UNITED NATIONS ORGANISATION, 1945		
General Assembly (Ga)	• Member states: 191 • Voting system: one state, one vote. Two-thirds majority for peace and security questions, election to bodies, entry of new members, budgetary questions... • Recommendatory authority: non-binding resolutions Mandate: international peace and security, international cooperation in resolving international economic, social, cultural and humanitarian problems, promotion of human rights • Functioning processes: high-level dialogue on • Financing for Development implementation	• Great activity in the 1960s and 70s, eclipsed in the 1980s
Security Council (Sc)	• Member states: 15 (5 permanent members with veto: US, Russia, China, France and United Kingdom, 10 elected by the General Assembly for two-year periods) Majority of 9 votes • Binding resolutions • Mandate: International peace and security: military operations, economic and military sanctions, arms inspections, electoral and human rights supervision. Elects ICJ judges jointly with the GA. Establishes UN peacekeeping forces (function later taken on by the GA)	• Paralysed during the Cold War, has increased activities considerably since the 1990s
Economic and Social Council (Ecosoc)	• Member states: 54 (with three-year mandates) • Studies and reports on international economic, social, etc., questions and recommendations; coordination of the activities of specialised organisations, consulting with them and passing on recommendations to them • Functioning commissions: human rights, sustainable development	• ECOSOC does not play the crucial role in international economic affairs conferred on it by the UN mandate. This role is played by the Bretton Woods institutions and the World Trade Organisation
Programmes, Funds And Other Bodies Directly Linked To The Main Organisations (Undp, Unep, Unifem...)	• Provide technical assistance and other forms of practical support in practically all economic and social areas • Independent executive bodies and budgets • Accountable to the GA through ECOSOC • Establish their own lines of action	• Activities limited by UN financial crisis • Pressure to limit expenditure, some run the risk of closure
International Court Of Justice (Icj) Specialised Agencies Or Organisations (Ilo, Unesco, Who, Fao...)	• Some older than the UN • Provide technical assistance and other forms of practical support in practically all economic and social areas • Independent executive bodies and budgets • Assemblies of states independent of the GA • Own executive bodies and budgets • Establish their own lines of action	• Activities limited by UN financial crisis • Pressure to adopt neoliberal policies • Agreements with WB since 1995
Internacional Court of Justice (ICJ)	• Member states: all UN member states • Arbitrates between states. No individual person can appeal to the Court • Jurisdiction: all disputes that the states refer to it and all affairs provided for by the UN Charter or standing treaties and conventions • Magistrates appointed by the GA and the SC • If sentences are not complied with, the parties can appeal to the SC	• In practice, and in accordance with recent jurisprudence, the court has no power of legal review over SC actions

Figure 6.1 *The current system of international institutions*

CURRENT SYSTEM OF INTERNATIONAL INSTITUTIONS (2/2)		
	STRUCTURE AND COMPOSITION	**EVOLUTION**
INTERNATIONAL CRIMINAL COURT, 2002		
ICC	• Member states: 92 • Jurisdiction: brings individuals, not states, to justice, accused of committing the most serious violations of human rights and international humanitarian law, such as genocide, war crimes and crimes against humanity • Complementary to national justice systems	• The Statute of Rome entered into force in July 2002
BRETTON WOODS INSTITUTIONS, 1944		
International Monetary Fund (IMF)	• Member states: 184 • Voting system: basic votes (2.1%) and voting quotas (39.72% of which accounted for by US, 17.16%, Japan, 6.16%, Germany, 6.02%, France, 4.97%, and United Kingdom, 4.97%) • Main objectives: to promote international monetary cooperation, economic grouth, balanced expansion of international trade, stable exchange rates, establishment of a multilateral system of payments, promote resources to correct imbalances in balances of payments, reduce imbalances in member's balances of payments. • Relation with UN: independent specialised organisation which coordinates formally with the UN through the Chief Executives Board of Coordination (CEB); mutual representation, consultations, high-level dialogue with ECOSOC, BWIs and WTO; etc.	• Main policy since the 1980s: loans to countries with balance of payment problems, conditioned on macroeconomic adjustment policies and structural reforms
World Bank (WB)	• Member states: 184 • Voting system: basic votes (2.1%) and voting quotas (39.72% of which accounted for by US, 17.16%, Japan, 6.16%, Germany, 6.02%, France, 4.97%, and United Kingdom, 4.97%) • Main objectives: to fight poverty and improve standards of living in the developing countries • Relation with UN: independent specialised organisation which coordinates formally with the UN through the Chief Executives Board for Coordination (CEB); mutual representation and consultations, high-level dialogue with ECOSOC, BWIs and WTO; etc.	• Main policy since the 1980s: loans to countries, conditioned on macroeconomic adjustment policies and structural reforms, own or partnership projects, promoting IED
WORLD TRADE ORGANISATION, 1995		
WTO	• Member states: 148 • Decision-taking: consensus • Main objectives: deals with rules governing trade between countries; main purpose to ensure that trade (agricultural, goods and services, investment, intellectual property etc.) flows circulate with maximum possible ease, reliability and freedom • Independent of the UN. Informal coordination with other institutions through high-level dialogue with ECOSOC, BWIs and WTO.	• Precedents: GATT, 1947 - instead of the ITO, contemplated by the UN at the Havana Conference, 1948 -UNCTAD, 1964, founded as a result of the South's pressure - Neoliberal raise gave strength to GATT and paved the way for WTO • WTO: The most powerful countries are trying to extend its powers to include the following in its mandate: competition policy, investment, environmental regulations and public procurement

Figure 6.1 *continued*

PARTICIPATION OF OTHER ACTORS IN THE INTERNATIONAL SYSTEM		
CIVIL SOCIETY	• Consultative status in ECOSOC • Affiliation to the DPI • Ad hoc participation at UN summits	Rio/Johannesburg Summits gave birth to the category of "major groups"
BUSINESS ASSOCIATIONS	• Ad hoc participation at UN summits • Global Compact • Consultative status in ECOSOC	
LOCAL AUTHORITIES	• Ad hoc participation at UN summits	
REGIONAL ORGANISATIONS	• Attempt to coordinate the positions of member states by certain regional organisations within the UN	

PRESENT GRAVE PROBLEMS	
GLOBAL DEMOCRACY	• Democratic deficit of international institutions • Delegitimisation of international institutions
PEACE AND SECURITY	• Worsening endemic conflicts • Outbreak of new international and domestic conflicts and fresh threats to international security • UN incapacity for action due to lack of mandate and/or resources
SUSTAINABLE HUMAN DEVELOPMENT	• Poverty, stagnation of development, exclusion and humanitarian crises in general • Growing social inequalities • External debt • ODA: the goal of 0.7% of GDP for development aid - established by the GA - is not met • Speculative financial movements • Unregulated transnational corporation activities • Global and local environmental problems
WORLD JUSTICE	• Impunity in the international sphere

Figure 6.1 *continued*

The main aims behind reforming the system of international institutions

More than 50 years after the creation of the system of international institutions, the world has changed, as have its needs for governance. The globalization process has led to the ever-greater integration of national economies. Thorny new problems have emerged at national level, showing up the present system's deficiencies when it comes to facing the new challenges. To the shortcomings of the original design and subsequent practice highlighted in the previous section then, we must also add the inefficiency of an institutional architecture (which was created in a world of states so much less interconnected) to address the globalization problems.

The international institutions must start a reform process in order to achieve the capacity to meet these new challenges. And it should do so in a legitimate and democratic way that includes all actors, interests and needs so as to adopt policies leading to the solution of the world's problems.

The need for global democratic governance

The globalization process has led to the ever-greater integration of national economies. The rapid growth in international trade, financial flows, direct investment, migratory processes and information and communication flows has drastically increased global interdependence. Although this has created new opportunities for some, most people and most countries in the world have been excluded from the process. The neoliberal policies the rich countries have promoted over the last 20 years have only helped to aggravate some of humanity's endemic problems and have increased inequality in the world. The old problems persist and have even become intensified, while new ones have also emerged: poverty and feminized poverty, inequality, ethnic conflicts and civil wars, displacement, humanitarian crises, global pandemics – HIV/AIDS, environmental problems ...

The neoliberal policies that have dominated over the last several decades have clearly shown the market's grave limitations and that mechanisms are required to correct conflicts and inequality. However, in an ever more interconnected world, many problems cannot be solved at the national level, and the state's capacity for intervention has been greatly eroded. As a result, the need for global governance has increased considerably. Unfortunately, however, the present international system is clearly not capable of solving problems and meeting the challenges of a new framework, vastly different from the circumstances in which it was first set up. Moreover, any increase in the system's responsibilities with regard to global governance merely serves to show up the democratic deficit inherent in it, undermining it in the eyes of the world after years of practices which have made it shackle to the interests of the leading rich and powerful nations – while certain global policies and regimes have rapidly transcended the state and acquired the status of a supra-constitution, we lack an effective 'global constitution' ensuring the primacy of human rights and providing the right balance to global economic, finance and trade regimes. The system of international institutions needs reform, enabling it to address current problems and to contribute to building a fairer and more equitable, diverse, sustainable and peaceful world. The reforms described in this paper form a response to the need to establish international institutions based on a system of values (What ethical framework?), provided with the necessary mechanisms (What institutional reforms? Involving which actors?) to implement new policies to enable us to achieve the great objectives of:

- global democracy with respect for and promotion of an ethical framework based on human rights;
- peace and security based on justice and freedom throughout the world;
- sustainable human development that takes diversity into account;
- global justice to ensure that these objectives are achieved.

Global democracy and human rights

The international institutions should act in accordance with the different interests and needs of the world's citizens, and this necessarily implies a fairer redistribution of power between the countries of the North and South, as well as increasing the possibilities of citizens to be represented and participate in the international institutions. However, democratization does not depend merely on procedural questions, but requires respect for and promotion of the fundamental provisions enshrined in the **'Universal Declaration of Human Rights'**. Reforms, then, should lead to the creation of a new system whose main pillars are respect for and promotion of a universal ethical framework based on human rights.

Peace and security, based on justice and freedom

The international institutions must substantially improve their capacity to prevent conflicts and keep the peace. For this, the organizations responsible for **peace and security** questions should take all positions into account in a balanced way, should be universally accepted as legitimate and should have the capacity to enforce their decisions.

Sustainable human development

The international institutions' capacity for global macroeconomic management should also be increased through financial, economic, trade, social and environmental policies that take into account all interests, and most significantly of those most vulnerable and marginalized in society. To resolve the world's grave problems of poverty and inequality, the priority of human rights (including gender, environmental protection and worker protection) should be recognized in international legislation and jurisprudence. Special priority to the provision of decent work and protection of labour and social rights is essential to economic and social well-being. Economic policy should be brought into coherence with social and environmental priorities and human rights, in an integral way with effective and democratic structures of coordination and accountability.

Global justice

Global justice should be empowered to eradicate international impunity, not only as regards criminal law, but also in the civil, economic, social and

environmental spheres. To make all this possible, the international institutions must be provided with resources and independent financing, enabling
them to implement their programmes without being hostage to the vested
interests of certain actors within the system.

The fundamental reforms scenario: steps on the way to reforming the system of international institutions

The first scenario contains the proposals most likely to achieve at present
the greatest political agreement among governmental players, those with the
power to put such reforms into effect, as well as other actors within the system. They constitute steps towards immediately improving the existing
system of institutions. Most of the proposed reforms do not require amend-
ment of organizations' founding charters. In most cases, they improve the
way the institutions work by reviving existing mechanisms that have fallen
into disuse or were never implemented, restoring the original spirit the
founders brought to certain organizations and which has, in practice, been
lost. Non-state actors would play a merely consultative role in international
organizations, and in many cases the new policies emphasize compliance
with agreements and commitments many states have already ratified.
Generally speaking, most of these proposals enjoy the more or less explicit
support of many actors in the system, including states, and they often reformulate old demands still pending solution.

The substantive reforms scenario: substantive reforms in the system of international institutions

The second scenario includes proposals to reform the international institutions that imply greater changes and even slight modification to the
founding charters of some organizations, particularly the Bretton Woods
Institutions and the WTO. They entail substantive steps towards achieving
the great objectives laid out in the above section on 'The main aims behind
reforming the system of international institutions', and, in some cases,
would pave the way for the new institutions and more ambitious proposals
described in the third and final scenario. This scenario would, in principle,
enable the international institutions to function in a considerably more
democratic way and progress towards implementation of the policies
necessary to reverse the most negative of present trends.

Generally speaking, the UN's role and capacity to control other multilateral organizations is strengthened, while mechanisms are also proposed

The fundamental reforms scenario

FIRST STEPS TOWARDS REFORM OF THE SYSTEM OF INTERNATIONAL INSTITUTIONS	
UN	
GENERAL ASSEMBLY	• Improving working of the General Assembly: - Establishment of a GA general committee and specific working parties • Increase supervision capacity of UN organisations and programmes - Joint GA and SC working party to institutionalise consultations and reports • Create a forum to resolve disputes over jurisdictional limits between international organisations and to establish a hierarchy amongst rules, standards and international legislation
SECURITY COUNCIL	• Guarantee consistent, effective regional representation: maintain or increase number of members? Maintain or increase the number of members with the right to vote? Create regional seats? • Guarantee transparency in decision-making procedures • Discourage the use of the veto in all cases except Chapter VII of the UN Charter
ECONOMIC AND SOCIAL COUNCIL	• Improve mechanisms for coordination with agencies and with BWIs and the WTO: - Establish a regionally representative executive committee • Improve working methods • Improve infrastructure and financing
PROGRAMMES	• Improve coordination between UN agencies and programmes and with, basically, the BWIs and the WTO
AGENCIES	• Improve coordination between UN agencies and programmes and with, basically, the BWIs and the WTO
INTERNATIONAL COURT OF JUSTICE	•Enable greater recourse to the ICJ for constitutionally doubtful SC actions
INTERNATIONAL CRIMINAL COURT	• Work towards universal ratification of the Rome Treaty
IMF	• Review and reduce powers - Restrict policies to original mandate Reform voting system to ensure balanced representation of all members: increase basic votes to original levels • Increase transparency in procedures and decisions • Improve coordination and political coherence with other economic, financial and trade organisations and with human rights declarations - Renegotiate agreements on relations with the UN to clarify responsibilities vis-‡-vis the UN to improve UN capacity to guarantee full respect for international legislation, economic, social, labour and environmental norms and standars, and the full family of human rights
W B	• Review powers in accordance with original mandate • Review practices and procedures • Reform voting system to ensure balanced representation of all members: increase basic votes to original levels • Improve coordination and political coherence with other economic, financial and trade organisations and with human rights declarations - Renegotiate agreements on relations with the UN to clarify responsibilities vis-‡-vis the UN to improve UN capacity to guarantee full respect for international legislation, including non-economic legislation
WTO	• Review practices and procedures to guarantee the democratic participation of all members • Increase transparency in all processes • Improve coordination and political coherence with other economic, financial and trade organisations and with human rights declarations - The UN should develop processes to ensure the legal primacy of human rights, and the coherence of trade and investment agreements with them

Figure 6.2 *The fundamental reforms scenario*

PARTICIPATION OF OTHER ACTORS IN THE INTERNATIONAL SYSTEM	
CIVIL SOCIETY	• Achieve a truly consultative role within the UNGA, the IMF, the WB and the WTO
LOCAL AUTHORITIES	• Achieve a truly consultative role within the UNGA, the IMF, the WB and the WTO
PARLIAMENTARIANS	(See section on Global Democracy)
REGIONAL ORGANISATIONS	• Promote balance between trade integration and regional political integration • Set up GA study groups and regional and subregional organisation working parties to study the measures necessary to strengthen their capacity to foresee and intervene in emergency situations • Improve their capacity for political representation within international institutions
BUSINESS ASSOCIATIONS	• Achieve a truly consultative role within the UNGA, the IMF, the WB and the WTO

NEW POLICIES	
GLOBAL DEMOCRACY	• Creation of an Inter-Parliamentary Assembly (a body for coordinating national parliaments composed by national MPs) • Strengthen and provide expanded resources to the Commission on Human Rights. Define, ratify and implement the optional protocol to the International • Covenant on Economic, Social and Cultural Relations to provide for an individual complaints mechanism
PEACE AND SECURITY	• Improve conflict prevention and peacekeeping mechanisms • Implementation of SC resolution 1325, calling from women's participation and concerns in peace processes and conflict resolution
SUSTAINABLE HUMAN DEVELOPMENT	• Cancel the least-developed nations' foreign debt • Establish framework for impartial arbitration over debt payments. Bankruptcy court • Establish a tax on financial transactions • Devote 0.7% of GDP to development aid • Mechanisms for ongoing monitoring for tansnational corporations • Make Kyoto agreements universal • Universal ratification and full enforcement of Convention on the Elimination of All Forms of Discrimination against Women (CEDAW) and the Optional Protocol • Work effectively towards meeting Millennium Development Goals (MDGs) and • implementing global commitments from UN conferences
WORLD JUSTICE	• Work towards making the ICC universally-recognised • First steps towards creating international courts with specific jurisdictions

Figure 6.2 *continued*

to improve coordination and guarantee that policies governing the system respect and promote human rights. Crucial changes are proposed to further the process of democratizing these institutions, and the establishment of new organizations to promote the development of global democracy is also proposed. Nonetheless, the basic structure of the system of international institutions as it stands at present is maintained. This scenario would provide greater possibility for non-state actors to participate in the system, while the new policies proposed include the creation of new institutions to remedy the shortcomings of the present system of global governance. Some proposals would require new international agreements that, similar to the process by which the International Criminal Court was established, could be launched at first by a smaller group of states in cooperation with other actors in the system, later extending to embrace a larger group and, finally, achieve universal status.

In practice, this scenario also includes and builds on all the reforms put forward in the elementary reform scenario.

The in-depth reforms scenario: the system of international institutions profoundly reformed

The third and final scenario would enable the objectives of democratizing the system and completing in-depth reform of the organizations and institutions that form part of it to be reached, enabling conflicts affecting peace and security to be tackled and resolved and policies developed to promote true, sustainable human development and greater social justice in the world. Without forcing complete rupture with the present system, this scenario seeks to sketch out the desired future. What is proposed is the reorganization of the system's main organizations and institutions to ensure that it achieves the objectives for which it was designed. In a world where not only geographic zones but also problems are becoming ever more interconnected, it is necessary to redefine the functional division that characterized the original design of these institutions to give them greater coordination and a more integral vision of the different problems that face the world. This implies inserting certain amendments to the international institutions' founding charters. Regarding the UN Charter, the changes would affect only procedures and in no case the principles, which continue to be valid and to constitute a basic text in the international architecture. The biggest, most profound changes, those concerning their integration into the UN system, would affect the founding charter of the Bretton Woods Institutions and the World Trade Organization. The proposal for this scenario represents a clear commitment to strengthen the UN and give both it and, in particular, its more democratic bodies a more central role. Effectively bringing multilateral organizations together under the UN umbrella appears to be the best way of guaranteeing that their policies promote all interests and needs, and not those of a minority with greater capacity to influence the system. In turn, the scenario would also ensure greater respect for and promotion of human rights in all policies enacted and actions

The substantive reforms scenario

SUBSTANTIVE REFORM OF THE SYSTEM OF INTERNATIONAL INSTITUTIONS	
UN	

GENERAL ASSEMBLY	• Continue improving the function of the General Assembly (annual work calendar)
	• Increase supervision capacity of UN organisations and programmes
	  - Capacity to query the ICJ over constitutionally doubtful SC actions
	  - Increased role in decisions over intervention and establishment of rapid reaction forces in conflict prevention and peacekeeping
	• Effective control of UN agencies and all multilateral institutions

SECURITY COUNCIL	• Restrict right to veto to certain specific questions (UN Charter Chapter VII) and requirement of two simultaneous vetoes in order to exercise said right • Establishment of permanent, transparent procedural rules • Subjection to ICJ review of resolutions
ECONOMIC AND SOCIAL COUNCIL	• Effective control and real coordination of UN agencies and programmes and all multilateral institutions with mandates in relevant areas • Increase the Executive Committee's prerogatives and capacities
PROGRAMMES	• Adequate infrastructure and financing
AGENCIES	• Effective responsibility before the UNGA through ECOSOC • Adequate infrastructure and financing
INTERNATIONAL COURT OF JUSTICE	• Creation of a chamber with capacity to pass down opinions on the constitutionality of action by UN bodies, including the SC
INTERNATIONAL CRIMINAL COURT	• Universal status
IMF	• Review governing bodies' decision-taking and selection mechanisms to balance weight of all members (equal weight of debtor and creditor countries) • Increase transparency • Responsible to UNGA through ECOSOC
WB	• Review governing bodies' decision-taking and selection mechanisms to balance weight of all members (equal weight of debtor and creditor countries) • Increase transparency • Responsible to UNGA through ECOSOC

WTO	• Review decision-taking mechanisms and democratise negotiating practices
	  - Provide financing to ensure permanent presence and participation in Geneva of delegations from countries with less resources
	• Responsible to UNGA through ECOSOC
	  - Establishment of an agreement linking WTO to UN, obliging WTO to present regular reports to ECOSOC

Figure 6.3 *The substantive reforms scenario*

undertaken by the system of international institutions. This scenario presents an integral view of the system of international institutions, including all the actors in the system, providing political and budgetary capacity to develop suitable policies to resolve the great problems facing the world and to promote sustainable human development.

PARTICIPATION OF OTHER ACTORS IN THE INTERNATIONAL SYSTEM	
CIVIL SOCIETY	• Possibility of requesting ICJ for opinions on a consultative basis
LOCAL AUTHORITIES	(See previous scenario)
SECOND-TIER AUTHORITIES	• Achieve real consultative status within UNGA, the IMF, the WB and the WTO
PARLIAMENTARIANS	(See section on Global Democracy)
REGIONAL ORGANISATIONS	• Formalise capacity to be represented on international institutions
BUSINESS ASSOCIATIONS	(See previous scenario)

NEW POLICIES AND INSTITUTIONS	
GLOBAL DEMOCRACY	• An independent Assembly of Representatives (World Parliament), with consultative functions within the UN system • World referendums with consultative status
PEACE AND SECURITY	(See previous scenario)
SUSTAINABLE HUMAN DEVELOPMENT	• Gradual cancellation of developing countries' debt • Develop and ratify an international agreement on tax cooperation, and establish an International Tax Organization under the United Nations • Establish and universalise different global taxes • Abolition of tax havens • Devote 2.8% of GDP for development aid • Mandatory codes of conduct for transnational corporations • Establish new, more demanding goals for Kyoto agreements • Advance towards meeting MDGs. Establish new, more demanding goals building on MDGs as well as commitments of from UN conferences
WORLD JUSTICE	• Council of World Justice • Establishment of a new international court of human rights • Establishment of a new international court for economic and financial crimes • Establishment of a new international court for environmental crimes

Figure 6.3 *continued*

The politics of change and final comments

The recent crises suffered by the system of international institutions – the war on Iraq, the collapse of the negotiations at the WTO Cancun Ministerial, … – have contributed to increase the risks and threats at the world scene but, on the other hand, as with every crisis, they have provided new opportunities for change. Indeed, civil society in recent years has stood up and raised its voice against an increasing mismatch between political decisions taken and the opinion of world citizens. The actors nowadays concerned with the need to regain legitimacy, democratize and enhance the system of international institutions are increasing and, most important, raising voices not only from the world civil society but also from governmental and intergovernmental sectors. This is a key opportunity for

The in-depth reforms scenario

SYSTEM OF INSTITUTIONS AFTER IN-DEPTH REFORM	
Global democracy: representation and participation	
GENERAL ASSEMBLY	• Two-chamber system representing the states and the world's citizens (see Assembly of Representatives - World Parliament- below) • Unification of general assemblies and conferences into a single institution with a central role in the system: UNGA • Binding authority: capacity to adopt binding resolutions
ASSEMBLY OF REPRESENTATIVES (WORLD PARLIAMENT)	• Direct representation of the world population by universal suffrage • Participation in the international legislative process • Capacity to make recommendations to other organisations in the system • Capacity to exercise parliamentary control over other organisations in the system
WORLD REFERENDUMS	• Binding world referendums
Peace and security	
PEACE AND SECURITY COUNCIL	• Supervision by the UNGA • Representative composition by regions • Review/abolition of the permanent member status • Abolition of the veto • Straight majority voting, with 2/3 majority voting for very important issues (to ensure regional balance and prevent less powerful states and regions from being marginalised)
Economic, social and environmental institutions	
ECONOMIC, SOCIAL AND ENVIRONMENTAL SECURITY COUNCIL	• Economic, Social and Environmental Security Council with effective control over BWIs (IMF, WB), the WTO and relevant agencies and programmes that, suitably reformed, would become specialised technical agencies fully integrated into the system • All organisations, agencies and programmes accountable to the GA and the World Parliament through the Council
UN PROGRAMMES	• Dissolution of general assemblies and conferences of states other than the UNGA • Creation of specific assemblies similar to the system adopted by the ILO, with the presence of actors from all the relevant sectors in each case
UN AGENCIES	
BW INSTITUTIONS	
WTO	
World justice	
• Interconnected world legal system embracing both civil and criminal law, with executive mechanisms from local to world level	
INTERNATIONAL COURT OF JUSTICE	• Capacity to pass sentence on the constitutionality of decisions adopted by organisations forming part of the system
INTERNATIONAL CRIMINAL COURT	• Full integration into the UN system
SPECIFIC COURTS	• Establishment and entry into service of specific international courts within the UN system

Figure 6.4 *The in-depth reforms scenario*

improving cooperation and dialogue among these actors to further our common goals. These alliances are not new, they have taken place in recent years and some of them have ended up in relevant successes. This is the so-called 'New Diplomacy', which is not constrained to traditional state-centric action but includes other actors who have come to be very relevant in the international scene. This has been the case of the Treaty of Rome and the ICC, the Treaty to Ban Landmines .... Acknowledging the

PARTICIPATION OF OTHER ACTORS IN THE INTERNATIONAL SYSTEM	
CIVIL SOCIETY	• Effective participation, along with the other actors, in the specific assemblies
LOCAL AUTHORITIES	• Effective participation, along with the other actors, in the specific assemblies
SECOND-TIER AUTHORITIES	• Effective participation, along with the other actors, in the specific assemblies
PARLIAMENTARIANS	(See proposals in the section on Global democracy for this scenario)
REGIONAL ORGANISATIONS	• Participation in different organisations through mechanisms for regional representation
BUSINESS ASSOCIATIONS	• Effective participation, along with the other actors, in the specific assemblies

NEW POLICIES AND INSTITUTIONS	
GLOBAL DEMOCRACY	(See proposals in the section on Global democracy on previous page)
PEACE AND SECURITY	• Effective resolution of endemic conflicts at the root of much world tension • Real and effective development of mechanisms for conflict prevention with the participation of regional organisations • Autonomous peace force
SUSTAINABLE HUMAN DEVELOPMENT	FINANCIAL, ECONOMIC AND SOCIAL POLICIES • Cancellation of external debt and adoption of mechanisms to prevent new unsustainable debt from being generated • Elimination of tax havens • Regulation of transnational corporations activities • World tax system and elimination of fiscal competition (one of its functions would be to co-finance the system of international institutions and world cohesion funds for development) • Enhanced capacity for protection of workers rights. World cohesion funds for development • Economic and social policies to promote sustainable human development • Full achievement of Millennium Goals and partial compliance with new, more demanding objectives and goals set to resolve the world's problems ENVIRONMENTAL POLICIES • Effective reversal of more unsustainable production and consumption trends • Transfer of sovereignty to system of international institutions over world environmental issues
WORLD JUSTICE	(See previous scenario) • World Legal Police

Figure 6.4 *continued*

need for wide alliances to advance the reform agenda, the UBUNTU Forum and the World Campaign are trying to create synergies with several civil society processes and organizations, but also governmental and inter-governmental actors.

Proposals for the Reform of the System of International Institutions to Make Another World Possible – The London Declaration

This declaration brings together a set of proposals worked on during 2003 and 2004, and closely bound up with the World Campaign for In-depth Reform of the System of International Institutions, since they were gradually given shape through the presentation and public-consultation stages of the Campaign within world civil society and through contact with other processes pursuing similar aims, such as the Montreal International Forum, the International Facilitating Group on Financing for Development, the Global Progressive Forum, the World Governance project, etc. This declaration was not intended to be a closed proposal: rather it was to serve as a starting point for debating and disseminating proposals relating to the reform of the system of international institutions. It was presented for the first time on **1 April 2004 in the London School of Economics (LSE)**, with the support of 47 persons and organizations, headed by Federico Mayor, Boutros Boutros Ghali and Javier Pérez de Cuellar.

Background

The globalization process increases both the interdependent nature of the problems facing the world and the gap between rich and poor. Markets are more and more global, but the influence of the political institutions necessary to ensure that these operate in a democratic, equitable and efficient way diminishes day by day. Global economic institutions increasingly apply policies that favour the market and the large corporations to the detriment of policies promoting sustainable human development approved at the 1990s and the Millennium UN summits.

The weakening and marginalization of the system of international institutions over peace and security issues has led to unilateral use of force in recent conflicts. Rather than promoting conflict resolution through processes and rules established by the UN, the interests of the main superpower are imposed through military superiority, sowing the seeds of further violence throughout the world.

The present system of international institutions, established over 50 years ago in what was an important step forward in the history of humanity, suffers from considerable shortcomings, leaving it ill-equipped to resolve the grave problems that face the world today. **For this reason, it is necessary to reform the international institutions so that they can, once more, help to build a fairer, more equitable, diverse, sustainable, free and peaceful world, and ensure that new policies are implemented to pursue the great objectives of global democracy and the promotion of human rights, peace and security throughout the world, sustainable human development and cultural diversity, as well as the consolidation of a global rule of law.**

Global democracy and human rights

Democratization is a key priority in the reform process of international institutions. The international institutions should act in accordance with the different interests and needs and aspirations of all the world's citizens, and this requires a more equitable redistribution of power between the North and South countries, as well as providing increased possibilities for citizens, civil society, different levels of government, etc., to effectively be represented and participate in international institutions and forums. Transparency, public accountability, the decentralization of power and the principle of subsidiarity should be basic characteristics of this democratization process. But democratization not only concerns procedural questions; it also requires respect for and defence of the fundamental rights of citizens as enshrined in the '**Universal Declaration of Human Rights**' and its development.

It is necessary for the world's citizens to be directly represented in the international institutions,[1] and not only the states members of the United Nations General Assembly. The UN General Assembly should evolve, gradually unifying other general assemblies and conferences, to play a central role in the system with authority to adopt binding resolutions and to exercise effective control over the other bodies, agencies and programmes forming part of the system.

All actors on the world scene should be empowered to effectively participate in the international institutions,[2] and different forms of representation should be provided for each.

Peace and security

The international institutions must substantially improve their capacity to prevent conflicts and keep the peace. To this end, it is essential to work towards a collective system for human security that can achieve gradual demilitarization and use of legal and arbitration processes, etc., to resolve conflicts. Bodies engaged in peace and security issues should take into account the views of all in a balanced way, and should be empowered to enforce their decisions.

To this end, the present Security Council should be reformed and placed under effective UN General Assembly control, with a composition representative of all the world's regions. The right to use the veto must be restricted to certain issues while steps are taken towards its eventual abolition, and votes over the most important issues should be according to a system of qualified majorities.

Such reform should make it possible to effectively resolve all conflicts, to develop effective conflict prevention mechanisms – with the participation of regional organizations – and to establish an effective world peacekeeping force. All this should be accompanied by a global disarmament process – focusing, particularly, on non-conventional weapons, while not forgetting all other types – restoring a climate of confidence among all the world's countries.

Sustainable human development and cultural diversity

The international institutions' capacity for global macroeconomic management should also be enhanced through **financial, economic, trade, social and environmental policies** that take the interests of all into account, particularly those of the weakest. In order to resolve the world's grave problems of poverty and inequality, all these policies should be implemented in an integral and coordinated way, and should be subordinate to the primacy of human rights. It is essential to establish a hierarchy in international legislation to promote coherence between economic policies and social rights and environmental issues.

All this requires the implementation of mechanisms to coordinate global financial, economic, social and environmental policies.

A proposal currently enjoying broad support from different sectors is that of reforming ECOSOC (the Economic and Social Council) to transform it into an Economic, Social and Environmental Security Council with effective authority over UN agencies, funds and programmes, the Bretton Woods Institutions and the World Trade Organization. The International Monetary Fund and the World Bank should return to their original mandates (IMF: world monetary and macroeconomic balance; WB: reconstruction and development), establish democratic decision-making processes and become effectively integrated within the UN system. The World Trade Organization should be refounded within the UN and, in cooperation with UNCTAD, draft world trade policies consistent with human rights and world social and environmental standards. At the same time, the UN should, furthermore, take urgent steps to establish a framework to regulate world financial flows.

Such reform should make it possible to finally resolve the problem of foreign debt, eradicate tax havens, establish world tax cooperation mechanisms and global taxes and promote increases in Official Development Aid provisions. All this should enable the operation of the international institutions to be cofinanced, and world cohesion funds for development to be established. Only in this way can we ensure that the Millennium Development Goals are met, and promote true sustainable human development to conserve the planet's environmental and cultural heritage and diversity.

The worldwide legal framework

All these reforms and policies should ineluctably be accompanied by **international strengthening of democratic rule** and measures to prevent impunity at the international level in criminal, civil, economic, social and environmental law. To this end, we should **advance towards ensuring global rule of law**, ensuring compliance with current international treaties, strengthening existing international legal institutions and establishing those necessary in other areas, and providing all these tools with the appropriate and necessary executive mechanisms.

The system of international institutions must also urgently begin taking measures to establish a framework guaranteeing plurality of information in the world.

Finally, we should stress that only if gender equality impregnates all these proposals can we advance towards another possible world.

London, 1 April 2004

8

Reforming the UN and other International Institutions

Boutros Boutros Ghali, former Secretary-General
of the United Nations

> As mentioned in the previous chapter, the presentation of what later came to be called the London Declaration was staged in the London School of Economics on 1 April 2004. The event was chaired and moderated by the highly regarded LSE professor Dr. David Held, with Federico Mayor, Mary Robinson and Josep Xercavins also taking part. Boutros Boutros Ghali was also to have been there, though he was unable to attend in the end for pressing personal reasons. However, he did film a video address for the event, the text of which we naturally reprint here.
>
> This is thus a direct transcription, now published for the first time, of the speech given on film by Boutros Boutros Ghali, that video having been shown at the LSE on 1 April 2004 as part of the debate 'The Reform of the United Nations and Other International Institutions' – specifically, within the public presentation of the London Declaration.

Ladies and gentlemen, I am very sorry not to be among you to participate in this very important forum. I will talk about the reform of the United Nations and other international institutions. I believe that this reform is a must. It is a must for three political reasons and four legal reasons.

The three political reasons are: the end of the Cold War and the necessity to manage the post Cold War; the globalization of the world; and the technical revolution in different fields (communications, telecommunications, armaments, etc.).

Now, let us see the legal reasons. The first one is that nation states are no longer the unique source of sovereignty. The second one is that state sovereignty exercised over a geographical territory is today under question. The third one is that states are no longer alone in the international scene. Other actors (non-state actors) emerge, for example: transnational corporations and non-governmental organizations. Finally, supranational legal rules have appeared. These include: humanitarian law, protection of environment and protection of human rights. Therefore, for all those reasons, we need a drastic change in the United Nations system and in the different international agencies related to the United Nations.

I will talk about the reform of three items: the democratization of the UN system; the reform of the Security Council and of the peacekeeping operations, which are related to the work of the Security Council; and the economic and social cooperation.

Democratization

Let us begin with democratization. Before I left the United Nations I published an agenda, called *An Agenda for Democratization*. It was 16 December 1996 when it was presented at the General Assembly. In this Agenda, I mentioned the reasons why we must democratize the international community and international relations. And this democratization begins democratizing the United Nations system.

In my opinion, the basic reform of the UN system is the participation of the non-state actors in international institutions and international forums. Non-governmental organizations, regional organizations, multi-national corporations, municipality of big countries, universities, political parties: all of them represent the international civil society.

I would like to mention the three main non-state actors: the non-governmental organizations, the regional organizations and the transnational corporations.

Non-governmental organizations – and today there are more than 20,000 – can bring to the international community the democratic dimension which we are advocating. NGOs are proving extremely powerful in fighting isolationism, in fighting indifference in both governments and citizens.

However, how they will participate in the United Nations system is a technical matter. They can be represented according to their specialization: NGO dealing with human rights, NGO dealing with environment. They can be represented according to the region: African NGO, Latin American NGO, European NGO. This is a technical matter, but what is important is that they must participate in the work of the United Nations.

Furthermore, it is important to highlight that in the last international conferences (Rio de Janeiro in 1992, the Conference on Human Rights in Vienna in 1993, the Conference of Social Development in Copenhagen in 1995, the Conference of Women and Development in Beijing in 1995, etc.) there were two conferences: the governmental one and the non-governmental one. So the non-governmental organizations are already participating in the elaboration of the rules of tomorrow.

Regional organizations are another non-state actor. In the 'Charter of the United Nations', Articles 52, 53, 54, the presence of regional organizations is foreseen: the Arab League, the Organization of African Unity, the European Union, the Commonwealth, etc. And I, as Secretary-General, had two annual meetings with representatives of those regional organizations. My successor continued this tradition and once a year had a meeting with representatives of different regional organizations existing. The cooperation with regional organizations is very important because they represent a kind of decentralization. They can cooperate with the United Nations in the field of the peacekeeping operations. In fact, they have done it in Africa with the Organization of African Unity, in Yugoslavia with NATO, and in Kosovo with many regional organizations.

Transnational corporations are also another non-state actor. Those transnational corporations are more powerful than the majority of the member states of the United Nations. They are playing an extremely important role in economic development, not only through foreign investments, but also through the transfer of technology and skills. They can play a very important role and it is important to obtain that participation in the United Nations system.

The participation of non-state actors to obtain the democratization of the United Nations system is not an innovation. The International Labour Organization (ILO) brings together at its general conference, delegates from governments, employers and workers from each member state, all of whom are entitled to vote individually on all matters. The ILO was created even before the League of Nations. It is the oldest international organization and it is based on the participation of non-state actors, all representatives of the civil society.

Reform of the Security Council

Now let us talk about the second reform. The second essential reform is – we have been discussing this in the last 20 years – the reform of the Security Council. The present Security Council should be reformed and its composition should represent the different regions of the world. The composition of the Security Council was done after World War II; it met in 1945. We are in 2004. The equilibrium of forces has changed. We must admit that the Security Council does not represent the international community and needs a change. It needs a change in its composition. It needs a basic change to represent the international community, the family of nations.

I also believe that the right to use the veto must be restricted to certain issues. We know we need the 'big players' and we will not have the big players in the game without the right to veto, but the problem is that nowadays the use of the right to veto is exaggerated. This was discussed in 1955 (ten years after the creation of the United Nations) and it is crucial to restrict the use of veto to certain issues and to not allow it in all the fields related with the work of the United Nations.

The peacekeeping operations must be reformed too. These must be based on the creation of permanent brigades, as a step towards the estab-lishment of permanent UN military forces. On 31 January 1992, just one month after I took the job of Secretary-General, the Security Council had its first annual meeting and I was asked to present a paper on the reform of the new role of the Security Council. In *An Agenda for Peace*, I mentioned the importance of having a permanent presence of military forces at the dis-posal of the United Nations. We need a rapid deployment of forces, because the first weeks after the ceasefire represent the most dangerous period and we need to have a rapid deployment of blue helmets to maintain the peace.

As I mentioned before, I believe it is important to have a closer cooper-ation with the non-governmental organizations. This could be done by giving a mandate to a regional organization like NATO or the Commonwealth, or to give a mandate to an arrangement; an ad hoc arrangement. For instance, we have multi-national forces on the Sinai between Egypt and Israel, and this is not a UN operation and it is a purely multinational force composed of a certain number of countries who have accepted to put troops at the disposal of the two former, the two countries that have signed a peace treaty, Egypt and Israel.

Reform of social and economic cooperation

Let us talk about the third reform, the reform of social and economic coop-eration. The UN role in economic and social development is made more complicated by the split between the North and the South. Developing countries continue to press for the extension of the UN economic and social programmes, while rich countries have little interest in more economic and social activities within the framework of the UN. They prefer to back the IMF, the World Bank, the World Trade Organization, or even bilateral assistance, assistance through the Commonwealth or through the European Union.

We have to overcome a basic contradiction. On one hand, according to some scholars, UNCTAD should put forward an arrangement where trade, development and environment issues are formulated and interpreted by a wider body of global organization. According to them, UNCTAD should become the world parliament of economic globalization. On the other hand, others say 'forget about UNCTAD; what about the social and economic council?'; it is important to transform this social and economic council which is a weak organization, into an economic and social security with effective authority over all the UN agencies, funds, programmes, and on the IMF, the World Bank and the different other economic organizations.'

These are in a certain way the three basic reforms we need if we want a new United Nations. A new United Nations which help us to cope with the problem of globalization, the problem of the post Cold War and the problem of the technical revolution. The above analysis suggests that obstacles to the large scale United Nations reform reside above all in the split between the North and the South, between rich countries and poor countries, and, in a second split, between the superpower, the United States, and the international community. The United States considers that the UN should serve as a mere extension of the foreign policy of the most powerful nations. On the contrary, the developing countries and a group of European countries stress the need to democratize the United Nations.

According to the pessimists, there is little evidence that the United States will accept any reform which may decrease their power within the United Nations system. Ever since the events of 11 September there is much more a tendency to reinforce unilateralism at the expense of multilateralism. They do not believe that the role of the United Nations is even more important now than it was in 1945 at the end of World War II.

But I belong to the optimists, those who believe that reform leaders and activists should keep up the mobilization in order to meet the final objective of building an international democracy, and who believe it is possible to create the political will necessary to achieve a real reform of the UN, to achieve global democratic governments within the UN system. They dream, and I dream, about the possibility that a coalition of developing countries, along with progressive nations of the developed world, might arise to counter the unilateralism of the United States. Further, they believe that the American diplomacy and the American democracy, who gave birth to President Wilson, the father of the League of Nations, and President Roosevelt, the father of the United Nations, will be able to provide a leader with a transcending vision, with imagination, generosity and the will to create a new United Nations organization, able to respond to the needs of humanity, to force a renewed dialogue between North and South and to promote the democratization of globalization before globalization destroys democracy.

PART 4

THE PROPOSALS –
ARRANGED BY THEMES

9

Concerning Two International Conferences, Two Different Yet Complementary Momentums for Progress Along the Analytical and Propositive Path Towards the In-depth Reform of our International Institutions

This substantive part of the text is essentially the result of the two international conferences organized in the framework of the World Campaign:

- the 'Conference on Reform of the United Nations and other International Institutions', held in Barcelona on 23 and 24 September 2004 in the context of the Universal Forum of Cultures – Barcelona 2004

- the 'International Conference on the Reform of International Institutions – Dialogues between different levels of governance and civil-society actors', held at the ILO headquarters in Geneva on 20 and 21 November 2006.

Owing to the role of these conferences in the World Campaign process itself and to their conception, development and results, we can now present this fundamental part of the book not in the guise of 'proceedings of the congress', but rather as guiding threads that point to clear trends in the analytical and propositional work of the World Campaign.

Democratization of the international institutions is a high priority within the reform process. The international institutions should act in accordance with the different interests and needs of the citizens of the world, and this necessarily involves a fairer redistribution of power between the countries of the

North and South, as well as offering more possibilities for citizens to be represented and to participate in the international institutions. The nation-state is not the only actor in the world arena and it is clearly no longer possible to persist with the idea of the state as being an entity that is able to act with absolute sovereignty within its own territory and that has the exclusive privilege of participating in the international institutions. Global civil society, transnational corporations and the different levels of government now have greater influence in the political sphere and must be taken into account in the design of international forums.

In an increasingly interconnected world, it is necessary to redefine the division of functions that characterized the original design of these institutions, ensuring that they are better coordinated and that they share a more integrated vision of the different problems of the planet. This involves introducing certain changes into the foundational charters of the international institutions. In the case of the UN Charter, it means changes that would only affect procedures and none of the original principles, which are still valid and still constitute a basic text of international architecture. Greater and more far-reaching changes – concerning their integration into the UN – would affect the Bretton Woods Institutions and the World Trade Organization.

The UN must be reinforced to become the central institution in the international system, in particular its more democratic organizations. Effective integration of the multilateral organizations under the UN umbrella seems to be the best way of guaranteeing that their policies foster the interests and needs of everyone and not just those of a minority that has more influence within the system. Again, greater respect for and promotion of human rights must be guaranteed in the policies that are introduced and actions that are undertaken by the system of international institutions.

Despite the agreements that officially designate the World Bank and the International Monetary Fund as specialized agencies of the UN, and the setting up of the Chief Executives Board to coordinate UN agencies, programmes, funds and international organizations, the BWI have almost always acted unilaterally with hardly any coordination with the UN. The result has been a lack of coherence between policies decided in these institutions, and with other international policies and regulations that fall within UN jurisdiction. The BWI have become the supervising institutions of world economic governance, while ECOSOC, a UN organ that was conceived of with a view to its playing a role in world economic coordination, has clearly been sidelined. Apart from the BWI, the WTO, which was created in 1994 outside the scope of the United Nations, should also be taken into account as a new multilateral global organization.

A renewed institutional architecture must incorporate an integrated vision of the system of international institutions so as to include all the actors in the system, who could then contribute their political and financial skills in order to work together on policies that would make it possible to resolve the great problems the world is facing and to foster sustainable human development.

With the aim of making progress in producing general and specific proposals in those respects, the UBUNTU Forum organized, in the context of its World Campaign for In-depth Reform of the System of International Institutions, the 'Conference on Reform of the United Nations and other International Institutions' (Barcelona 2004) and the 'International Conference for the Reform of International Institutions' (Geneva 2006).

Conference on Reform of the United Nations and other International Institutions (Barcelona, September 2004)

During the Universal Forum of Cultures – Barcelona 2004, a dialogue took place from 22 to 26 September on 'Contributing to the Global Agenda'. The aim of this meeting was to bring together institutions and individuals with different backgrounds and opinions on the problems and challenges that are currently on the global agenda. On 23–24 September, during the dialogue the UBUNTU Forum – in cooperation with other international initiatives working to democratize and improve the system of international institutions – was organizing a 'Conference on Reform of the United Nations and Other International Institutions'.

Growing awareness of how important it is to have effective, democratic international institutions to contribute to resolving the world's serious problems has led to the emergence of various initiatives aimed at achieving reform of the international system. The UBUNTU Forum sought to organize this conference jointly with some of these initiatives in order to increase dialogue and cooperation to make this event more plural and diverse. The organizations involved included Forum 2000, Montreal International Forum, Club de Madrid, International Facilitating Group on Financing for Development, Helsinki Process, World Political Forum, Global Progressive Forum and the World Governance Programme (Miguel Servet, College of Higher European Studies, Paris).

Proposals to reform the United Nations and other international institutions, such as the Bretton Woods Institutions or the World Trade Organization, are many and varied. The conference sought to provide a forum **for debating existing proposals** for the reform of the system of international institutions, presenting and discussing new alternatives, facilitating interaction between the different governmental and non-governmental actors with interests in this issue, identifying common ground and divergences in their positions and even **exploring the possibility of working towards shared goals within the current global context.**

International Conference for the Reform of International Institutions (Geneva, November 2006)

Two years later, in 2006, at the meeting of the Coordinating Committee of the UBUNTU Forum and Organizing Committee of the World Campaign in February 2006, it was decided to launch the second phase (2006–2009) of the World Campaign for In-depth Reform of the System of International Institutions.

Among the renewed objectives of the campaign was calling the second international conference, in the form of dialogues between different levels of governance and civil society actors, to serve as the framework for one of the campaign's objectives: 'contributing to the construction of an international social and political movement that is capable of being the stimulus for the process or processes of reform.'

The International Conference for the Reform of International Institutions took place at ILO Headquarters, in Geneva on 20–21 November 2006. We envisaged these dialogues as the beginning of the road towards shaping, articulating, defining ... a global social and political alliance of many actors, which would be able to promote advances towards the goal of real reform of the multilateral international institutions. A necessary scenario, to change existing policies on the world scale, begins to confront the huge challenges that humanity now faces and advance towards truly global democratic governance.

Multiple actors had the opportunity to put forward their views of the main weak points in the current system of international institutions as regards global democratic governance and, consequently, their visions of the corresponding reforms to the system that were most crucial for us to undertake, and the level of their urgency and/or necessity. The conference thus contributed to the analysis of the points of consensus, of understanding and of common focus in that reform.

How can we construct an international social and political movement that is capable of initiating a process or processes of reform of the system of global governance? How might this process be initiated? What should the characteristics of this

process be? These were some of the questions that the conference tried to answer.

Likewise, these dialogues offered a suitable space for analysing one of the possible items on the agenda of the second stage of the World Campaign for the In-depth Reform of the System of International Institutions: creating a '**World Committee for the Reform of the System of International Institutions**' that would become a singular, multi-actor and proactive element necessary to attain the desired reforms. In the short-term, we took advantage of the dialogues held to define and provide the tools for a simple model to continue them.

Naturally, an international conference of this nature also contributed towards advancing other goals of the world campaign: (a) to involve in the process the greatest possible number of actors then present on the world stage (to which the multi-actor conception of the proposed international conference contributed); and (b) continue to work, along with other actors, on proposals from civil society concerning the conceptual and methodological base proposals of the reform.

Next, you will find the issues generating the greatest interest, the different participants' positions and possible future action, which have been collected through the work carried out by the team of rapporteurs and, naturally, the texts that some speakers sent or presented at the two above-mentioned conferences.

Proposals for a New Architecture for the System of International Institutions for Democratic Worldwide Governance

The Millennium Declaration and the final document of the United Nations World Summit in 2005 state: 'We are determined to establish a just and lasting peace all over the world in accordance with the purposes and principles of the Charter. [...] We recommit ourselves to actively protecting and promoting all human rights, the rule of law and democracy [...].'

Poverty, gender equality, environmental problems, dignified work, peace, human security, and the governance of globalization: these are the chief issues and challenges facing humanity now. The policies that the international institutions can and should apply are essential in tackling these problems, and the fact that the UN's declarations and action plans for dealing with them have not been implemented clearly shows how the system of international institutions has been weakened, and has launched the debate on the need for reforms and for the establishment of a new worldwide institutional architecture.

We then raise the question: What really operative reforms and measures to attain a democratic worldwide governance must we introduce into the system of international institutions, and how?

The reform proposals framed below were drawn up by the Secretariat of the World Campaign and the UBUNTU Forum, and served as the starting point and the underpinning structure of the debates in those international conferences of 2004 and 2006 mentioned and presented previously herein. The speakers structured their talks around some of these proposals (which were sometimes just questions, sometimes hypotheses, and generally proposals as such), and those talks are set down, arranged by theme, in this chapter and the following ones (11, 12 and 13).

Readers should note that the terminology employed in these, such as improvements in the functioning, substantive reforms and in-depth reforms, comes from the central chapter – chapter 6.

Some proposals on world institutional architecture: UN, UN agencies; BWI, WTO

Improving the functioning of institutional architecture
* Improving coordination between UN agencies and programmes, and essentially with the BWI and WTO, through ECOSOC.

Substantive reforms
* Effective control and real coordination by ECOSOC of UN agencies and programmes and of all the multilateral institutions with mandates in the relevant fields.
* Answering to the UNGA through ECOSOC.

In-depth reforms
* Economic, Social and Environmental Security Council with effective control over the BWI (IMF and WB), the WTO and relevant agencies, funds and programmes that, once they are appropriately reformed, would become specialized technical agencies that are fully integrated into the system.
* All organizations, agencies, funds and programmes to be accountable to the UNGA and the World Parliament through the Council; Dissolution of all general assemblies and conferences of states; Creation of specific assemblies similar to those in the system adopted by the ILO, with the presence of actors from all the relevant sectors in each case.

To attain global democratic governance, the System of International Institutions must resolve fundamental problems concerning participatory democracy as they affect new international political players such as local governments, new regional realities, organized civil society, etc.

Some proposals on global democratic governance and multi-level governance (global, regional, national, sub-national and local) and participation of other actors (civil society, corporations, local authorities, etc.)

Relations between regional organizations and global institutions
* Fostering a balance between commercial integration and regional political integration.

- Creating UNGA study groups and work groups of regional and sub-regional organizations with the aim of defining measures to reinforce their own capacity to foresee emergency situations and to intervene therein.
- Improved capacity for political representation of these regional organizations in the international institutions.
- Formalizing the capacity for representation of these regional and sub-regional organizations within the international institutions.

Participation of non-state actors in the system of international relations
- Civil society, local authorities and other interested groups should continue advancing towards a truly consultative and participative role in the UNGA, the IMF, the WB and the WTO.
- They should be empowered to seek consultative opinions from the ICJ.

Participation of non-state actors in the system of international relations: in-depth reforms
- In a scenario in which all general assemblies and conferences of states are dissolved and specific assemblies like those adopted by the ILO are created, the effective participation of the different actors in the specific assemblies should be guaranteed.

Relevant recent reports dealing with these issues
- Report on the Panel of Eminent Persons on United Nations–Civil Society Relations: 'We the Peoples: Civil Society, the United Nations and Global Governance'; http://daccessdds.un.org/doc/UNDOC/GEN/N04/376/41/PDF/N0437641.pdf?OpenElement
- The World Commission on the Social Dimension of Globalization: 'A Fair Globalization: Creating Opportunities for all'. ILO, February 2004.

The United Nations Millennium Campaign

Salil Shetty, Director of the UN's Campaign for the Millennium Development Goals

There can be no two options on whether the current global governance arrangements require a radical rethink. Traditional notions of national sovereignty have been overtaken by changes in technology, defence, the financial sector and indeed new doctrines and attitudes. Cross-national transmission and movement of money, disease vectors, electronic media, environmental crisis and most importantly ideas and people offers an entirely new global framework. From this perspective, many would argue that the current global governance structure is obsolete, inequitable and on the whole not equal to the task.

The manifestations of this have been described by many, including the Secretary-General of the UN, Kofi Annan, as a series of inter-linked crises.

The first is the crisis of security. Of course, Iraq is the most talked about case of a failure of the current global governance structure to prevent a violation of the UN Charter. But this is not the only one. We have an on-going struggle on violation of resolutions of the Security Council in relation to Palestine, not to talk of several other places. As we speak, millions of people of Darfur and the Great Lakes region in Africa are losing their lives because of this very crisis and our utter inability to deal with it. But too much is made of security at an aggregate or macro level. The greatest insecurities continue to be faced by women and excluded groups and individuals at the individual level, where there is a daily threat to their very existence. The on-going violence and violation of women's rights epitomizes this problem. Expanding the Security Council to reflect the new distribution of power in the world will only start to begin addressing the imbalances. The world does face a crisis of security at so many levels.

The second is the crisis of intolerance. Again, the most visible display of this is in relation to Islam with very deep and long-term implications. Let me give you an example of this from my own country, India, that surfaced in the media just a couple of weeks ago when there was some new census data that was released. The headlines were not that the population growth rate was unacceptably high in all religious groups. Instead, the headline was that the Muslim population was growing at a more rapid pace. To any rational person, this fact would simply indicate that the Muslim population in India suffers from a high concentration of poverty, women's illiteracy and, more broadly, social exclusion. Instead, many media houses, themselves controlled by Hindu fundamentalist thinking, preferred to use this to generate more hate towards the already beleaguered minority groups. We can see the same prejudice and intolerance towards indigenous people, racial minorities and women in so many countries and societies in the world. So the world indeed faces a crisis of respect of tolerance and diversity.

The third is the crisis of representative democracy. Again, much has been said about this at a local and national level. On the one hand, more countries today are adopting democratic systems of governance based on elections. On the other hand, although there are not many models at scale of a better alternative, it is increasingly evident that citizens across the world have not seen enough benefits from representative democracies. This has led to a growing disillusionment and apathy with governments as an institution and with electoral politics as a means of representation. With the illegal invasion of Iraq, this crisis of confidence in governments to represent public opinion has been worsened as governments in several countries allowed this to happen against the wishes of the majority of their population, even in the leading proponents of the invasion in Europe, North America and Asia. Independent civil society, a free press and the rule of law are essential elements in creating a much more participatory form of democracy and counter-balancing the over-dependence on electoral democracy.

And finally the crisis of poverty and inequality. There is no greater crisis in my view than that of extreme poverty and its related manifestations. Unfortunately, we have all become insensitive to the scale of the problem. As we speak, one out of six people in the world, which is almost a billion people, go hungry every day. It is estimated that 30,000 people, many of them children, die every day because of poverty. I am told that the way to get this in the media is to express it in terms of number of planes crashing simultaneously – 100 plane crashes apparently is the headline grabber. Half a million mothers, no less, died last year alone for no justifiable reason – from child birth, from malnutrition. Does this have to be expressed in terms of deaths from a famine or floods to draw attention? The so-called international community has an appalling record of acting too late. We prefer to deal with the consequences than act when we see the early warnings. The case of the current locust attacks in West Africa is a very graphic case in point, not to repeat the Darfur case. Almost three million people died from HIV/AIDS last year; 120 million children are denied the right of a primary education and are out of school, let alone the much larger numbers who go to completely ineffective schools, notionally enrolled. One billion people have no access to sanitation. Most of these are women and girls. Should I say more? The paradox, of course, is that at the same time the world has never seen so much prosperity before. The 1,000 richest people in the world are said to have a personal wealth greater than the 600 million people living in the so-called 'least developed countries'.

Shamed by the sheer magnitude of this violation of basic human rights and troubled by the potential backlash on global security of such deprivation for the majority of the world's population, in the largest gathering of Heads of State in the history of humankind in September 2000, world leaders committed themselves to the Millennium Declaration. In this sobering document, they rededicated themselves to the Universal Declaration of Human Rights, and to the right to development and to free their fellow citizens from the indignity and suffering that goes with abject poverty. And at the turn of the century and the millennium, they recapitulated the outcomes of the different UN Summits of the 1990s and gave themselves 15 years, up to 2015, to meet a set of very minimal but concrete goals and targets, later christened the eight Millennium Development Goals.

In doing this, they knew that the world has enough financial resources to address all these problems. Best estimates are that an additional $100 billion could help achieve all the Goals in all the countries of the world within the next decade. The world spent $900 billion on arms alone last year. Not to speak of the money that is lost due to tied aid, agricultural subsidies and corruption.

In the past we could say that we did not have the technology or resources to address these issues of meeting even the basic needs of all human beings. That is simply not the case any more. We know what needs to be done.

The key to the Millennium Compact is that rich countries have to meet their obligations to helping poverty eradication as spelled out rather shoddily in Goal 8 of the MDGs. This means meeting their commitments to the 0.7 per cent of Gross Natural Income (GNI) to ODA, big improvements in the quality of aid including untying and simplifying procedures and putting an end to conditionalities, and much deeper and quicker reduction of debt – Africa continues to pay out in debt every year more than it receives. Debt sustainability has to be now redefined in terms of the achievement of the MDGs. And we need a much more level playing field in the trade arena. This includes time-bound elimination of agricultural subsidies that make the poor poorer, policy space for developing countries, reviewing all intellectual property agreements that simply benefit TNCs and hinder food security and the health needs of the poor; indeed, concluding the Doha Round in favour of poor countries is essential for the achievement of the MDGs.

Much as rich country commitment to their side of the bargain is critical, there is no doubt that poor countries can do a great deal more to achieve these basic human rights on their own steam. Having the right policies and plans in place, raising and allocating domestic and external resources for fulfilling the needs of the majority of the population on an inclusive basis, being accountable to our own citizens and stopping corruption don't need too much external help.

The MDGs are far from perfect. They are indeed minimum goals. Countries are being encouraged to go much further at the national level – and many have improved on them, particularly in terms of the poverty/hunger goals and on gender. They cannot be seen as techno-fixes, there is no solution outside a full political economy analysis. And they are only meaningful when they build on national planning and decision-making arrangements. The global and national aggregates are meaningless and misleading. They only make sense when we take these goals down to every community and individual. But even these minimal and flawed goals mean a lot to the people who are far from realizing them. They offer the best hope in the current scenario as they have the commitment of the world leaders at the highest level, in the South and the North. We cannot allow the best to be the enemy of the good.

We need to focus on implementation, enough rhetoric, we need action. But the only way in which governments will actually act is when there is pressure from citizens to hold them to account for their promises.

That is really what we at the Millennium Campaign are focusing on. To support citizens' action to hold their own governments and international institutions to account for achieving the Millennium Goals, as translated into the national and local context. And indeed these Campaigns, which are now starting to gain momentum in about 30 countries of the North and South, each look different, as they should. So the Campaign in the Philippines is focused on tracking government budgets towards the Millennium Goals, while the Campaign in El Salvador is focused on local authorities delivering services that really reach the people in terms of education, water and health. The Ghana Campaign wants to change the Poverty Reduction Strategy to make it focused on the rights of poor people. The Italian Campaign is intent on getting the Government to commit itself to the 0.7 per cent target. The Irish Campaign is called Keep Our Word. The Indian Campaign is tentatively called Vaada na Todo (Don't break your promise). What binds them together is that they see the MDGs within a human rights and justice framework as described in the Millennium Declaration, not as a superficial set of targets but looking at the underlying and structural causes of poverty.

The Spanish Sin Excusas 2015 Campaign is off to an excellent start. The national Civil Society Organization (CSO) led part of the Campaign is being directed from the Spanish NGOs for Development Liaison Service (CONGDE), the national development NGO platform. Petitions are already going to President Zapatero to implement the 0.7 per cent commitment, regional authorities are starting to engage with public awareness campaigns on the Millennium Goals, Regional Working Groups are already up and running in the Basque country, Andalusia and Catalonia. 10 December might see the launch of the Catalan Campaign joining an international Skip a Million Meals effort. From now until December 2004, other regions are starting to get involved to launch a much broader mobilization from January 2005.

The interesting thing is that the MDGs are becoming a unifying force, bringing CSOs working on different sectors and thematic priorities together. It is bringing the service-delivery programme/operational NGOs together with the advocacy and human rights-oriented ones. And more importantly it is bringing new constituencies beyond the development NGOs into the process. Youth, parliamentarians and local authorities are all joining forces for a combined fight against poverty.

The good news is that already things are beginning to change. For a start many of the poorest countries in the world are already showing that these goals can be achieved if there is political commitment, even in most adverse circumstances, as faced by Sub-Saharan Africa. Malawi, Eritrea and the Gambia are some examples on primary education and Bangladesh, Ghana and Mozambique are all picking up on the health front, not to speak of Thailand, Uganda and Senegal on education.

Many rich countries are starting to face up to their responsibilities. Half the EU countries now have a clear deadline to get to 0.7 per cent on aid, including some large economies like Spain and the UK. Overall aid levels have gone up in 2003 after a very long gap. There is some glimmer of hope on the trade negotiations through the July announcements on agricultural subsidies. Cancun was a wake-up call and the subsequent victories by Brazil on their complaints on unfair trade practices in the WTO are also positive signs. And discussions on debt have been reopened in the last G8 and will continue into the next one. But none of this is anywhere close to what we need to achieve the goals.

Civil society at the national and global levels is getting stronger through initiatives such as the World Social Forum and now the Barcelona Forum. And many excluded groups are beginning to exercise their rights. We have avowedly progressive and pro-poor governments and parties in power now in many strategically important countries in the world and elections on the cards in several others.

The world needs to bring development back on the agenda, away from the obsession on security and the so-called war on terror. The Heads of State meeting in September 2005 to review progress against the Millennium Declaration is very important. This is preceded by the G8 in the UK which will focus on Africa and the MDGs. At the end of the year, there is likely to be the Ministerial meeting of the WTO in Hong Kong. Recognizing this, a very important Coalition of all major NGOs, trade unions, churches, etc. has come together initially in the UK and now globally. Under the name of the Global Call to Action Against Poverty, this Coalition is planning a series of mass mobilizations on bringing world attention to these issues. Major media houses like the BBC and MTV are joining forces with us. At the political level, President Lula, supported by a large number of Heads of State, has taken the initiative to push hard to create the enabling conditions for the achievement of the Millennium Development Goals. This includes new and innovative financing mechanisms and serious reform to many of the key international institutions, particularly the IFIs and WTO.

Many proposals have come from this Conference on reforming the international institutions to help us move forward – many of these are crucial in the fight against poverty and the struggle for justice and human rights. We are the first generation that can actually end poverty and we are running out of excuses.

We hope you will join forces with the Campaigns in your own country and at the global level.

Reforming the United Nations and other international institutions: observations from the South

Asha-Rose Migiro, Minister for Community Development, Gender and Children of the United Republic of Tanzania

Coming from the South, I find the reform both relevant and timely, as it appeals for a stronger, responsive, transparent, accountable and democratic United Nations and other international institutions for the betterment of all people in the world, regardless of their geographical location, level of their social-economic development and whether they are rich or poor. After all, we all live on the same planet.

The current political, economic, technological and institutional changes taking place all over the world are, to say the least, having significant impacts on systems and institutions of governance, both at national and international levels. In particular, the end of the Cold War signified the beginning of a new era in international relations, in which the political and economic ideologies of the major market economies gained a new ascendancy. Liberalization, deregulation, privatization and monetary considerations as policy prescriptions have come to be considered universal panacea to the various development problems and challenges, particularly those confronting the underdeveloped South.

Admittedly, this new drive has created significant development opportunities in the global economy. As a result and under very difficult conditions, many countries, especially those in the South, have taken significant steps to deregulate, liberalize and integrate further into the world economy. However, the high hopes for meaningful change and development out of these post-Cold War changes are yet to be realized. To the contrary, development challenges among the countries of the South are becoming more complex and overwhelming, and opportunities for growth are becoming increasingly elusive. On the other hand, even those developing countries, which had established a history of fast growth and sound economic fundamentals, are also experiencing severe economic setbacks.

This has been partly caused by socio-economic instabilities associated with financial liberalization and inappropriate policy prescriptions that are offered in dealing with the post-Cold War globalization challenges.

For the South, it is of major concern that the reforms, which have led to a greater integration of developing countries into the world economy, have not narrowed the economic gap between rich and poor countries. What is more worrying is the fact that many countries of the South are currently facing worsening internal economic disparities, which in turn are now generating complex social and political tensions.

At the level of North-South relations, this new trend has had far-reaching implications particularly for developing countries. Almost exclusive emphasis on the role of unfettered markets has displaced key principles that under-pinned earlier multilateral discussions and negotiations on economic issues. The role and responsibilities of the international community, the need for non-commercial international transfers and the necessity to give developing countries special and differential treatment no longer orient or inform inter-national policies and action in the face of severe development challenges of the South. Instead, the international agenda is dominated by overwhelming concern on developed countries to gain greater freedom for their foreign investments, capital flows, Third World resources and markets.

Consequently, the countries of the South are increasingly becoming unable to advance an agenda of their own, in promoting their key interests. Against this background, it is imperative that the countries of the South evolve and put in place appropriate policies and strategies that would sig-nificantly enhance their capability to face the enormous challenges and exploit the vast opportunities that are located in the new world of globaliza-tion. Equally important, they must also review and strengthen their role in multilateral systems and institutions of governance, and work out approaches and actions that will enhance their effectiveness on the interna-tional scene. Their unity and cohesion remain, therefore, the source of their strength. As such, a new agenda of the South needs to identify major issues around which all can rally. It is in this context that the work of the Helsinki Process on Globalization and Democracy becomes extremely significant, particularly as the process seeks to address and look for possible solutions to the dilemma of global governance.

An agenda of the South: Priority issues towards reform of international institutions

Allow me now, at this juncture, to identify principal and priority issues that must make up any new agenda for developing countries, outlining in broad terms what their objectives might be in respect of each of these issues. These, old and new, are as follows:

Governance and the global economy

In a world of growing linkages, the governance issue of the global economy and of representative mechanisms for dealing with multilateral political governance assumes a special importance. At present the G7 and G8 groupings, and the institutions over which they exercise almost executive influence, have virtual monopoly in determining policies affecting the entire globe. The South needs to give serious consideration to the development of institutional mechanisms at the highest level, representative of the interests of all countries or groups of countries, to deal with the task of global economic surveillance management and governance.

Monetary and financial environment for development

Developed countries have begun to distance themselves from the earlier edifice of development cooperation in the area of money and finance. Instead, the current emphasis is on market forces and private financial flows. Any agenda of the developing countries ought, however, to emphasize the following:

Official financial flows
- Official development assistance, both bilateral and multilateral, must remain an important means of meeting developing countries' needs for external financing.
- The contribution of the multilateral financial institutions towards meeting the capital needs of developing countries must be enhanced.
- Creation of international liquidity to replace the dollar and other national currencies as internationally accepted reserves, and proposals for these to be channelled to developing countries, are policy propositions that deserve renewed attention.
- New revenue raising instruments, urged as a means of resolving a number of environmental problems and a means to curb short-term speculative capital movements, could also help to enhance official capital transfers to developing countries.

External debt and other issues related to the need for finance
- Means to achieve a speedy resolution of the continuing debt burden which hinders growth and development in many developing countries must be sought and effectively promoted, including efforts to improve the Heavily Indebted Poor Countries (HIPC) initiative and its implementation.

- Regional funds to contain financial crises to facilitate resumption of economic growth could provide financial assistance associated with locally and regionally generated development policies and programmes.

Private capital flows

Drawing lessons from the financial crisis that affected South East Asia as a result of financial liberalization and the prescriptions insisted and enforced by multilateral financial institutions to the South, a South Agenda must give serious attention to the following:

- Measures and mechanisms to control and moderate short-term and speculative international capital flows to reduce vulnerability and instability.
- Calling upon the IMF to revisit its articles of agreement in order to accommodate and empower developing countries to play a bigger role in making decisions that affect the well-being of their economies.

Reform of the multilateral financial institutions

In the context of the overwhelming influence of the Bretton Woods Institutions on developing countries' policies either through structural adjustment or through prescriptions for crisis management, a range of issues relating to the conduct of the institutions needs to be placed on an Agenda of the South. In particular, serious consideration needs to be given to establishing new policies and mechanisms in these institutions to achieve improvements in:

- the objectivity of their analysis;
- criteria for lending;
- the relevance and impact of conditions;
- transparency and accountability of these institutions;
- voting procedures to end the marginalization of developing countries in the policy and decision-making processes.

International trade and trade-related issues

World Trade Organization matters

In addition to trade, the WTO agenda now covers a wide range of trade-related matters and agreements that circumscribe wide areas of domestic development policy in developing countries. The experience of the Uruguay Round and its aftermath demonstrate the need for developing countries to ensure a mutually reinforcing relationship between trade liberalization and development goals. These matters must be a continuing agenda for the reform of the United Nations and other international institutions as perspectives from the South. Developing countries will need to develop proposals relating to the implementation of agreements already reached, as well as to the new issues that have subsequently emerged, or to any new negotiating round proposed for the future. In doing so the South must:

- Give consideration to the pace, direction and content of liberalization, taking into account levels of development and the need to build up national capabilities.
- Make concerted efforts to prevent technical, environmental, social, health and other grounds being used to introduce what in effect are measures with a protectionist intent.
- Formulate and present a united policy front in WTO negotiations and with respect to implementation of the Uruguay Round Agreements.
- Develop a common position on whether there should be a new round of WTO negotiations or whether a sector approach is acceptable. In any event, the South must take the initiative and place proposals of its own on the WTO negotiating agenda.
- Suggest improvements in WTO procedures and mechanisms on the basis of which agreements are negotiated and implemented, so that these do not prejudice developing countries' interests. There are other key issues, which must form part of the South Agenda relating to reforms on trade and trade-related matters. These include:
  - food security;
  - rapid and full implementation of the Marrakech Ministerial Decisions concerning least developed and net food-importing countries;
  - special and differential treatment for developing countries;
  - competition policy.

A multilateral investment agreement

The advanced industrial countries' quest to establish a multilateral regime to liberalize foreign investment and to establish standard rules of treatment has far-reaching implications for developing countries, and therefore ought to be reconsidered in any new South Agenda. In considering whether it is in their interests to participate in possible negotiations, developing countries need to define a set of principles for a policy framework, which correspond to developing countries' interests in this matter.

The importance of commodity trade in the exports of developing countries as a whole has declined. Nevertheless, the weakness of commodity prices and their terms of trade in recent times have severely affected many developing countries, particularly the poorest of the poor. The commodity issue must therefore remain an important element in any new Agenda of the South in reforming the United Nations and other international institutions. In particular, the rationale underlying the dismantling of the framework of international commodity agreements must be contested, while giving consideration to schemes of supply management among the producing countries themselves.

Regional and other trading arrangements

The growth of preferential trading arrangements, including mega-blocs, which embrace both developed and developing countries, raises a number of important issues for developing countries. Two of these issues are the discriminatory treatment of developing countries that do not belong to these groups, and the erosion of generalized preferences. Such issues aimed at evolving a new international trading system must be part of an agenda to reform the existing framework.

Reform of the United Nations

Changes in the global political scene have equally brought into focus the role and reform of the United Nations system, in particular in relation to the management of the global economy. The South Agenda must include the bolstering of the United Nations role in placing the development problem in a global perspective, strengthening its contribution to the development field and resisting any retrogression in this area.

In recent years, considerable international attention has been given to social and related aspects of development in contrast to that devoted to 'hard core' international economic issues affecting development. But the former cannot be a substitute for addressing the key economic issues. As part of this agenda, the South must try to rectify this situation and continue to encourage initiatives in the United Nations that are intended to bring about a mutually reinforcing relationship between these two dimensions.

Let me conclude by reiterating that partnerships are crucial to global problem solving. Surely, one could argue that partnerships are the only way to earnestly tackle global problems. In order to work effectively, partnerships have to be based on equality and be goal-oriented. I believe that the best way to reach more effective multilateralism is to develop innovative and genuine partnerships between all stakeholders. It is in this context that the views from the South need to be given more attention. We need to devise better instruments for the governance of globalization and the functioning of the multilateral system. Better governance of globalization must enlarge the space for national policies to stimulate enterprise development, employment creation, poverty reduction and gender equality. It must reinforce social protection and enhance skills and capabilities. It must support action to overcome infirmity, inequality and exclusion.

'A better world is possible, let us play our part.'

What future for the United Nations?

Samir Amin, Forum du Tiers Monde

It is good form today to say that the UN has gone bankrupt and that it is henceforth the duty of the G7/8 and even of NATO to ensure the 'security' of the international order, and even its 'democratization'! On the contrary, in this document I will demonstrate how the UN is the victim of a plot whose aim is no less than to assassinate it. To demonstrate this, we must take a look at both the UN – in the past as well as its present state of crisis – and the strategic political options taken by the ruling powers in their real perspective, based on the analysis of the challenges of the 21st century.

Market/State conflict and coincidence in their first expressions

- The space defining the sphere of reproduction of a society is always multidimensional: it is that of its political management, its economic life and the expression of its cultural identity. The consistency of a society therefore depends on the degree of coincidence of these various spaces – political, economic and cultural. This coincidence operates at times in a relatively large geographical sphere or, on the contrary, is disperse, being effective only on the level of micro companies in villages, for instance.

    The coincidence in question does not exclude the possibility of contradictions and conflicts between the internal logic particular to the different authorities of the social reality considered (political, economic and cultural). Quite on the contrary, it is the unfurling of these contradictions that reveals the dynamic of history and social transformations.

    In any case, the coincidence in question is always relative, in the sense that the societies defined on its basis only rarely unfurl in an absolute or nearly absolute autarchy, but are usually in line with 'society systems'. The spheres of Christianity, Islam, Hinduism or Confucianism, for example, define cultural dimensions (religious and philosophic) common to all societies. By the same token, one can observe the spheres of commercial exchange that associate many societies to one another, which become more or less interdependent due to this exchange. In modern capitalism, this sphere is constituted by the entire planet, lending the economic authority of social reproduction its quality of 'world economy'. Yet in previous periods, there were also vast spaces of exchange, such as those designated by the 'silk routes', for instance.

The nebula constituted by interdependent human societies reveals, in some of its constituent areas, strong agglomerations lending the societies located in these areas an evident consistence that identifies them. One could then, for the societies in question, speak about a coincidence of 'market' (a disputably simplistic term for designating the economic aspect)/State (sphere of political power management)/society (recognizing itself in a cultural identity) aspects.

- Capitalism was first successful in a particular region of the Old World – the small, north-western corner of Europe. It had precedents elsewhere, but it was there that it took its 'definitive' historical form, spreading (or attempting to spread) elsewhere.

Now, the region in question was characterized by a high degree of dispersion of both its conditions of economic reproduction (largely limited to those of the subsistence of the fief) and those of its political management (equally largely limited to the powers of the local lord). The vaster spaces of which the base feudal units were a part continued to have a weak density: the shared 'Christianity' was not accompanied by real political power, exercised by neither its head (the Pope), nor the Emperor (of the Holy Roman Empire) nor Kings; commercial exchange remained limited in its effects (and in any case, the 'long distance' type of exchange – the 'Silk Routes' – predominated in comparison with local commercial exchange). Precisely for this reason, I have qualified this ('feudal') form of society of 'tributary' families in the periods in question as a 'peripheral' form, as opposed to centralized forms characterized by an economy/power (operating in considerably larger areas) coincidence. The precocious coagulation of new capitalist forms in these peripheral areas of the tributary world seems to me not to be purely by chance.[1]

- At first, during the period of its initial coagulation, the intensification of commercial exchange unfurled in what I call the chaos of the origins of capitalism. The coincidence between spaces of political management and economic reproduction was broken. Juxtaposed to the ancient feudal powers and the limited powers of guilds were the commercial networks that transcended them. The map of Europe of this transitional period from the Middle Ages to modern times took the form of a puzzle of principalities, lordships and free towns, all of them increasingly dependent on the network of merchants that escaped their power. This model contrasts with that of centralized tributary worlds characterized by the submission of the commercial economy to political powers,[2] a major handicap to the emergence of fully developed capitalist forms.

The chaos was overcome and the 'market/State' coincidence (economic and political) was reconstructed through the emergence of the modern Nation-State. The United Provinces, above all England and France, invented the Absolute Monarchy of the Ancien Régime which paved the way for the spread that would reach its zenith in the 19th century, producing the 'model' par excellence of the organization of the modern world.

This model has entered a phase of final disintegration that excludes all possibilities of reversal, as we will see later. A return to chaos under conditions that comprise a new challenge: that of going beyond capitalism, which has become obsolete.

- The establishment of the UN occurred precisely during the long phase characterized by 'market/State' coincidence (management of the economy/management of politics). It was its late culmination. The philosophy of this world system was based, in effect, on two principles: the absolute sovereignty of States (considered by nature as 'Nation-States') and polycentrism. They were to constitute the foundation of the United Nations Charter. We will later write up the balance sheet (with positive results – it is far from being negative as is too often and too quickly asserted today) for this world system, though without ignoring the limits and increasing contradictions that have led to its contemporary crisis.

The Treaty of Westphalia (1648) inaugurated the establishment of this system based on the dual recognition of the sovereignty of States and polycentrism. The system was then only specific to the space of Old World Catholicism, whose unity was broken by the explosion of the Reformation. It was generalized throughout Europe by the Treaty of Vienna (1815) and was first made partially universal by the creation of the League of Nations (1920). I say partially universal because the League of Nations did not question the colonial statutes that excluded Asia and Africa. The League of Nations remained an organization representing a world system reduced to its centres (Europe and Japan), amputated from the United States (which distanced itself after having been the main promoter) and flanked by the peripheral area of 'independent' Latin America. The UN was conceived from the beginning in an authentically universal perspective, which would rapidly become a reality with the regained independence, firstly, of the countries of Asia and the Arabic world, and then of Africa.

Hence it is not surprising that the apogee of the United Nations was precisely during this relatively brief period that, from the early 1960s to 1975–1980, coincided with the so-called 'decades of development', which I will discuss later.

The doubts and the crisis that followed were not those of the UN, but of the world system in which the organization was inscribed. Because, as one will see later, discord between the different authorities of world management (especially between its economic dimensions – the 'market', in simplistic terms – and its political dimensions) has reappeared, following upon two or three centuries of coincidence, though limited to the central regions of the system. Yet discordance is no longer of a nature analogous to that characterizing the chaos of the beginning. The new chaos is that of a system henceforth obsolete.[3] It cannot be overcome by the reestablishment of previous forms of coincidence. It requires the revision of all the data of the challenge on its local ('national') level, but also on that of the world system (and any possible regional sub-systems).

Just as the solution to these problems on the local ('national') scale cannot be found through a 'return' to practices institutionalized by the capitalism of the previous stage and, likewise, the UN crisis (one of the major dimensions of the crisis of the globalized management system which we are discussing here) cannot be overcome by maintaining the functions that brought the organization success and glory in the period after World War II.

Balance sheet of the actions of the United Nations (1945–1980)

• World War II ended with a double victory, that of democracy over fascism and that of the peoples of Asia and Africa over colonialism. The creation of the UN must thus be understood in the context of this atmosphere.

This double victory commanded the economic, social and political forms of the management of systems both on their national levels and on the international organization level. It established the three fundamental 'historical social commitments' of the time: the Welfare State in the West, a work/capital commitment that allowed the working classes who were victorious over fascism access to a degree of dignity unknown in the previous stages of capitalism, really existing socialism and that which I call the national populisms in the countries of Asia and Africa that had gained independence.[4]

At the same time, it opened the way for a negotiated political management of international relations, likewise promoting the role of the United Nations. It is good form today to say that the bipolarity of the Cold War and the powers of veto (of the five, but especially the two superpowers) have 'paralysed' the UN. Far from this and on the contrary, the bipolarity reinforced by the veto gave the countries on the periphery of the system (Asia, Africa and Latin America) a margin to manoeuvre that they lost later. For a time the imperialist centres were forced to 'adjust' to the demands for respect of the sovereignty of the peoples in question and accept (or collaborate with) their projects for national and social development.

The significance of this positive change can be grasped once one has understood that globalized capitalist expansion has always been, throughout all stages of its spreading and from the start (the centuries of mercantilism, 1500–1800), imperialist by nature. That is, its immanent – and dominating – internal logic has generated a polarization of power and wealth on the planetary scale without parallel to anything throughout the preceding millennia of history. This permanent dominant tendency of really existing capitalism (which the discourse of 'liberalism' deliberately ignores in order to substitute it with a veritable mythology that the acrobats of simplistic economy attempt to present as reality) was, if not called into question in a radical manner, at least tempered during the period I have labelled as 'Bandung' (1955–1975). The rise – and glory days – of the United Nations coincide with this period, and this is not by chance.

• It is not difficult to draw up the (positive) balance sheet of the period: the highest economic 'growth' rates of all modern times, enormous social progress, both in the centres of the system and countries of really existing socialism and in the great majority of those on the liberated periphery, as well as a blossoming of modern national identities and new pride. No more difficult than it is to identify the limits and contradictions, to which we will later return.

The United Nations accompanied these upheavals and facilitated their realization. The double principle of national sovereignty and polycentrism constituted an effective means. On the political level, the UN banned the brutal interventions that had been commonly practised by the former imperialisms and which have once again become common practices since NATO invested itself with the responsibility of imposing its order on the Planet. On the level of economic management, the UN imposed the principle of negotiation, the Nation-States remaining free – on their territories – to organize their systems of production and distribution of wealth as they deemed appropriate. Certainly, the 'pessimists' will state that the negotiations in question (among others, for instance, through the UNCTAD) have rarely resulted in anything more than declarations with no real effect. Nonetheless, the States continued to be sovereign – on the internal level – and therefore they had real power of negotiation, of which they made the use that their ruling classes wished.

- Yet it is quite as easy to identify the limitations of this system. In the first place, observe that the system makes no reference to democracy apart from purely verbal reference. Today peoples have become more demanding in this aspect – though to differing degrees – than they had been in the period of the Welfare State, really existing socialism or national populisms. I certainly consider this evolution positive, even if the democratic demands in question remain the object of manipulations that are at times facile by the imperialist powers. In the spirit of the period, absolute sovereignty was that of the States, considered as exclusive representatives of their people. At the time, the denial of democracy was often justified by the ruling classes on behalf of the requirements of 'building the nation'.

  With the reversal of the economic situation, the slowed economic growth has put an end to the repercussions from which large segments of the population (especially the middle class, but also the working class, to the extent to which the social rise of young generations actually functioned) benefited. Suddenly, the 'national' discourse lost the legitimacy that allowed it to ignore democratic rights and even fundamental human rights.

  In the second place, observe that the concepts of economic and social development themselves were based on the postulates of the paradigm of the time, founded on the market/State coincidence, or more generally speaking, management of the economy/exercise of political power. The concept of economic development was in keeping with a capitalist expansionist logic characterized by 'recouping', which in turn presupposed the 'neutrality of technologies' and the reproduction of hierarchical modes of organization produced by the historic processes of capitalism. The fact that this model has always involved at least an active regulating role of the State, at times substituting the absent capitalist (or 'compradorisé' capitalist, i.e. dependent on foreign capital) class, which here and there – and to differing degrees – has taken on social dimensions, does not lend it the quality of socialist that it has often too hastily been ascribed (which is why I prefer to qualify it as a populist national model).

  Furthermore, this form of development was in line with the capitalist globalization of the time. Yet this alignment was founded on the negotiation of its conditions. The 'decades of development' that were the glory of the United Nations actively supported the deployment of these strategies at the time.

  It goes without saying that, precisely for this reason – because they were within an ultimately capitalist perspective, both in the logic of internal social relations of the nations concerned and in the logic of globalized expansion – the development projects of the time must have quickly reached their limits. The accumulation of contradictions that their implementation involved necessarily had to lead to the erosion of their efficiency and thus pave the way for the imperialist offensive and the reversal of the economic situation.

- Through its political actions of protection and respect for national sovereignties and support for polycentrism, the United Nations positively contributed to allowing the implementation of these experiments. And the political regimes that assumed the responsibility, though not democratic (or at best, democratic to a very low degree), were not in general as 'horrible' as is often asserted today. Modernizers, open to laicization, promoting the social rise of women (within limits ...), these autocracies were often close to forms of 'enlightened despotism'. The most horrible regimes that existed at the time were for the most part put into place or supported by the imperialist adversary, which did not hesitate to do this whenever it could: Mobutu in Zaire, Suharto in Indonesia and the dictatorships of South America are all testimony to this. The subsequent events of history – including the support of the Taliban in Afghanistan (here, an obscurantist dictatorship succeeded enlightened despotism, too hastily qualified as 'communist') – testifies to the decline that followed the erosion of national populisms.
- Criticism today directed at the United Nations actions in that period does not generally take into account the overall reality of the time. This type of criticism thus remains superficial, placing an emphasis, for instance, on the 'mediocrity' of the 'UN bureaucracy'. A tranquil comparison between the UN apparatus and that of other national or transnational institutional systems (such as the European Union apparatus, for instance) would invite more qualified conclusions.[5]

In retrospect, it is more seriously legitimate to place an emphasis on the illusions generated by the success of development at the time. But that which is certainly not legitimate is the use of this 'failure' as an instrument by the neo-liberals. Because what they imposed thereafter was an even more devastating illusion: that the deployment of deregulated capitalism would assure a 'better' development. An illusion associated with a dogmatic rhetoric refuted by the entire history of really existing capitalism (development, even in the limited sense of catching up in the system, whenever it occurred, always occurred via strategies accepting the conflict with the dominating logic of expansion of the dominating globalized capital) and cruelly refuted by the events of the past two decades, characterized by stagnation (development was sent through the trap door, substituted by the discourse of inefficient charity

– the 'struggle against poverty') and by the most scandalous aggravation of social injustices.

It is not at all surprising that under these conditions, democratization and peace were, like development, sent through the trap door, despite the resounding rhetoric of the representatives of the ruling powers. The debate that should emerge in response to liberal chaos concerns is the necessary democratization in its relation with social progress. It is replaced by a series of empty discourses designed to dispose of the real problems: the discourse of 'good governance' (accompanied by insipid developments concerning the 'struggle against corruption'!), substituted for the analysis of the reality of powers, the promotion of communitarisms under the fallacious pretext of respect for the right to difference, the so-called 'postmodernist' bric-a-brac, the discourse on the supposed civilization conflicts (which substitutes the real debate concerning the conflict of political cultures, which we will discuss later). It is easy to recognize the trademark indicating the source of this discourse: the US department of propaganda. We know how these discourses are relayed by the World Bank (the ministry of propaganda of the G7, as I call the institution) and imposed upon the United Nations (which admittedly does not put up much of a fight). Insofar as the promised peace, it takes the form of permanent warfare (supposedly against 'terrorism'!), repeated aggressions by Washington and its allies ('preventive' wars), and civil wars produced by the disintegration of States and societies subject to the treatment of liberalism!

• The United Nations has been invested with an unprecedented task of supreme importance: ensuring peace, condemning recourse to warfare (and preventing it insofar as possible).

The spirit of the United Nations Charter implies a polycentric view of globalization. This is understood as the forms of globalization that are based on the principle of negotiation, the only guarantee of authentic respect for diversity in all of its dimensions: cultural and linguistic, certainly, but also those that are the historical product of the inequalities of economic development. Polycentrism respects all States, all nations, be they 'large' or 'small', accepts that each of them, in a way, constitutes a centre in and of itself, and that therefore the interdependence involved in globalization must be able to handle the legitimate demands of the 'self-centred' viewpoints of all of its partners. Globalization is thus 'negotiated' and, if not perfectly egalitarian, at least conceived to reduce inequalities and not to favour their growth. Reconciling de facto differences on the one hand, and the universal demands for peace, democracy and development in solidarity on the other; this is the challenge.

Moreover, in the perspective of affirmation of polycentrism, the Charter of Nations has gone quite far, to the point of condemning the very principle of war, which is only accepted in case of legitimate defence, the aggressor being condemned without hesitation. The only legitimate military interventions are those ordered by the UN and conducted under its operational and political command. And these should in any case be measured and provisional.

The balance sheet of the implementation of these principles by the UN until the Gulf War (1991) shows rather positive results. The United Nations lent legitimacy to the wars of liberation against (British, Dutch, French, Belgian, Portuguese) colonialisms and thereby provided positive support to polycentric construction. In comparison with what occurred thereafter, there were few 'civil wars' during that period; and if, as has always been the case in history, certain powers have sought to take advantage of this and throw fuel on the fire, the United Nations system did not favour their manoeuvres (as reflected in the case of the War of Biafra). Certainly, the United Nations have perhaps been at times manipulated (this was the case in the War of Korea), or neutralized (in the US war against Vietnam or the Soviet invasion of Afghanistan). In the Palestinian issue, it is true that the United Nations legitimized the creation of Israel in a highly disputable manner (authorizing the Zionists not to apply the plan for sharing), but they later attempted to put a brake on the expansionist ambitions of Tel Aviv: the tripartite aggression of 1956 was condemned, and by Resolution 242, it condemned the occupation of Palestinian territory since 1967 as well.

The responsibilities I held at the time in the 1960s and 1970s led me to frequently attend the General Assemblies of the United Nations, held every year in New York in September. It was a major event every time, followed by the highest political figures the world over. That is to say, even if the positions expressed by the different participants did not always allow for a positive compromise to be found, these positions had to be taken into account by everyone.

The UN did not therefore die a natural death; it was assassinated in 1990–1991 by a decision of the United States, supported by its allies of the triad, putting an end to its responsibilities in managing and guaranteeing peace. The UN was assassinated by Washington's decision to implement its project – that is, to extend the Monroe Doctrine throughout the entire Planet.

This project, which I would qualify without hesitation as insane and criminal for its implications, was not born in President Bush Junior's mind. It is a project that the ruling classes of the United States have nourished since 1945.

The project has always assigned a decisive role to its military dimension. It was conceived after Potsdam, based on the nuclear monopoly. Very quickly, the United States implemented a global military strategy, divided the Planet into regions and assigned the responsibility of controlling each of them to a 'US Military Command'. I refer you to my writings on this issue.[6] Even before the USSR collapsed, and on the priority position occupied by the Middle East in this global strategic vision, the objective was not only to 'surround the USSR' (and China), but also to have the means to make Washington the master, as a last resort, of all regions of the Planet. In other words, to extend throughout the entire Planet the Monroe Doctrine, which effectively gives the United States the exclusive 'right' to manage the ensemble of the New World according to what they define as their 'national interests'.

The project implies that the 'sovereignty of national interests of the United States' be placed above all other principles structuring political behaviour considered as 'legitimate' means; it develops a systematic mistrust with regard to all supranational law. Certainly, the imperialisms of the past behaved no differently and those who seek to attenuate the responsibilities – and the criminal behavior – of the United States establishment at present, and to find 'excuses' for them, take up this same argument – that of indisputable historical antecedents.

Yet this is precisely what one would have wanted to see change in history and which has been in progress since 1945. It was because the conflict of imperialisms and the disregard of international law by fascist powers had produced the horrors of World War II that the UN was founded on a new principle proclaiming the illegitimate nature of war. The United States, you could say, not only made this principle its own, but was by far the precocious initiator. At the end of World War I, Wilson advocated restructuring international policy precisely on the basis of principles other than those that, according to the Treaty of Westphalia (1648), gave the sovereignty of the monarchical States and then of the more or less democratic Nations its absolute character, called into question by the disaster to which it has led modern civilization. Little does it matter that the vicissitudes of domestic US policy postponed the implementation of these principles. F. D. Roosevelt, and even his successor, H. Truman, certainly played a decisive role in the new concept of multilateralism and the condemnation of the war accompanying it, which is the basis of the Charter of the United Nations.

This excellent initiative – backed by the peoples of the entire world at the time – which effectively represented a qualitative leap forward and opened a path for the progress of civilization, nevertheless never enjoyed the conviction of the ruling classes of the United States. The Washington authorities always felt ill at ease with the UN entente and today brutally proclaim what they had previously found themselves constrained to conceal: that they do not accept the very concept of an international law superior to what they consider to be the demands of defence of their 'national interests'. I do not believe it is acceptable to find excuses for this return to the vision that the Nazis had developed in their time, demanding the destruction of the League of Nations. The plea in favour of law made with talent and elegance by Villepin at the Security Council is not, in this sense, a 'nostalgic look back at the past', rather on the contrary, a reminder of what the future should be. It was the United States that, on that occasion, defended a past that had been proclaimed definitively outdated.

The United States is not solely responsible for this downfall. Europe has generally participated, throwing fuel on the fire in Yugoslavia (through its hasty recognition of the independence of Croatia and Slovenia), then by a reallegiance with the positions taken by the United States concerning 'terrorism' and the waging of war in Afghanistan. It remains to be known whether, after the War in Iraq, Europe will embark upon a revision of its positions. In any case, the return to the principle of polycentrism and the restoration of the role of the United Nations will not be on the agenda as long as Europe accepts the substitution of the UN by NATO (!) as a means of managing globalization.

The new challenge of the 'market/society' conflict

Contemporary chaos is not analogous to the chaos that prevailed during the formation of capitalism. By the same token, the responses to the contemporary challenge cannot be similar to those that were given by the construction in the past of the 'market/State' coincidence.

In its time, this construction had certainly constituted a real social advance that accompanied the deployment of the superior capitalist mode. Today, capitalism has exhausted its historic role as a progressive force and can offer nothing but its barbarous downfall. The challenge compels us to think of a situation 'beyond capitalism' and based on focusing analysis on the conflict between the economy (the 'market', that is, capitalism) and society. This conflict concerns all the dimensions of reality, both national and global. One cannot, therefore, make proposals regarding the role that one would like to have assigned to the United Nations without having first clarified the nature of the challenge confronting humanity.

In order to do so, we will necessarily have to make a digression and examine the two sets of issues concerning: (i) the nature of liberal chaos and the illusions developed in this regard; and (ii) what I call the conflict of political cultures in the face of this chaos.

This digression is indispensable, and without it, the proposals concerning the UN which I will develop in the final section of this paper would make no sense.

Chaos and 'liberal' illusions

Having already expressed my opinion on these matters in some detail, I will be brief:

- We are confronted today with a single project for the future, implemented through the systematic use of violence (including military violence) by the dominating powers, themselves at the service of the dominating segments of globalized capital.

This project – which is the only possible project of 'really existing capitalism' that has reached its current state of natural development according to its immanent internal logic – has nothing to do with the project that the 'liberal' discourse describes in terms of the market rule (both 'competitive and transparent'), of democracy promoted by the substitution of the 'civil society' for the State ('bureaucratic' or even 'autocratic'), guarantor of peace (on the sole condition that a stop be put to practices of savage 'terrorism' ...). This discourse is empty.

This project is that of the dominating segments of globalized capital (the 'transnationals' of the imperialist triad). I have qualified the future that it envisages for the majority of humanity as 'apartheid on a global scale'.[7] Permanent warfare against the peoples of Asia, Africa and Latin America is therefore considered an inevitable necessity of its gradual success. In this perspective, obviously, the United Nations can no longer have a role to play: either they accept becoming one of the docile instruments of those who conduct permanent warfare against the 'South', or they must disappear.

The only questions to be asked here are who will direct the camp of barbarianism and to the benefit of whom?

The answer to this question is already evident from the events: the Unites States put itself in that position by its unilateral decision. I have moreover proposed an analysis of the situation that governed this option, placing the emphasis simultaneously on the elements of power that are its source (the enormous destructive military capacity of the United States) and on its military vulnerability (limited military combat capacity) and economic vulnerability (a deficit that, should it fail to be 'spontaneously' funded by the entire world, will have to be tapped in the form of an authentic tribute). For all of these reasons, this choice is not only that of the American extreme right wing behind Bush Jr., it is also that of the democrat opposition. The latter would be far better disposed to reformulate the methods of implementation and to make some concessions (to what extent?) in order to associate their allies in the triad (which continue to be subordinated).

The alternative in this context is not of great interest to the peoples of the rest of the world. The 'sharing' – of responsibilities and benefits – does not eliminate the barbarous nature of the future it would bring, which remains well and truly apartheid on a worldwide scale.

The project of really existing imperialism does not pave the way to social progress nor to the progress of democracy, nor to the peoples who are the victims (70 per cent of humanity) nor even to the workers of the triad nations, as the implementation of liberal policies over the course of the past 20 years has amply illustrated. It remains that its success – not very likely – would allow 'concessions to be made to consumers' of the triad, if this were necessary. By way of example, let us imagine the petrol shortage. The military control and pillage of productive regions (the Middle East, in the first place) would allow the consumption of this unavoidable source of energy to be reserved exclusively for the countries in the triad, annihilating the possibilities of development for China in particular, and for the South in general.

Despite all of this, does the project stand any chance of pursuing its deployment under the banner of 'authentic economic liberalism'? In the present state of things, one cannot ignore that a significant part of public opinion, particularly in Europe, believes in the possibility of such an alternative. Even more numerous are the ruling milieus of the South, which accept to do battle on its terrain, simply considered 'realistic'. The accession of China to the WTO and the positions taken by developing countries in Cancun (September 2003), which I have analysed elsewhere, testify to this.[8] History will take it upon itself to dissipate these illusions, but will it be quite soon or too late?

In the face of the reality of the project of capitalism – really existing imperialism, there is but one true alternative: it involves thinking 'beyond capitalism'. And it is then in this long-term perspective that it will be necessary to conceive the stages of the transformation sought, both of national plans and those of the organization of a negotiated globalization. The United Nations recover an important role, in this perspective.

The conflict between the political cultures of the past/present and those of the future/present

The Washington propaganda machine has placed on the agenda a supposed conflict between 'civilizations' (in fact, religions) that has supposedly become inevitable and therefore governs the future. Through the systematic means implemented – promotion of communitarisms under the pretext of respect for differences, an offensive against laicism ('old-fashioned'), praise of religious obscurantisms (placed by postmodernism on an equal level with all other 'ideologies'), systematic promotion of nauseous ethnocracies (in former Yugoslavia and elsewhere), even cynical manipulations (support by the CIA of terrorist groups mobilized against adversaries in Afghanistan, Chechnya and Algeria, among other places), deceitful warfare declared against supposed 'terrorism' (when such terrorism does not serve Washington's interests) – the United States has managed to put a real face on the conflict. This is an integral part of the barbarous downfall of capitalism and in no way does it constitute an obstacle to the deployment of its project.

The downfall annihilates the fundamental values of universalism and thereby illustrates the senility of the capitalist mode. Because the latter, in previous stages of its development, had been universalist, though this universalism had remained truncated due to the imperialist dimension innate to capitalist globalization. In counterpoint to this political culture of capitalism, whose past is always present (this culture always occupies dominating positions in contemporary societies), the political culture of the alternative (socialism) is likewise universalist and potentially capable of far surpassing the truncated universalism of capitalism. This culture of the future is not only that of a 'theoretical' creative utopia; it is already present in the real conscience of peoples today.

The real ideological/cultural conflict of the 21st century is therefore not the 'shock of civilizations' à la Huntington, but the conflict that opposes the political culture of capitalism, drifting in the direction of barbarity, to that of socialism.

The political culture of capitalism had defined rights and developed a concept of law and democracy that is inherent to it. In order to define its contours, it is useful to subject to analysis the manner of thinking prevailing in United States society, because this culture is present there in a form that is least 'contaminated' by that of its victims and adversaries. At first the only 'rights' recognized were those of individuals (even the acknowledgement of the personality of 'corporations' did not come until much later), in fact 'white' males (and excluding women, who are slaves that can be compared to colonized peoples). Hence, the 'contract' between individuals prevails over law, reducing the legislative role of the State to a marginal one. A banal 'contract' in the United States can contain 200 pages, where elsewhere, in Europe, for instance, where law prevails, two pages would suffice.

These fundamental concepts accompany a political culture based on a rigorous separation of the economic domain of life (managed by private property and the owners' free will, ignoring the social dimensions that are associated with it and, by the same token, devaluing the term 'equality') and that of political life. The latter, cramped, is thus reduced only to the practice of 'representative democracy', that is, the formula of the 'multi-party system and elections'. It excludes all more advanced forms of democracy, participative by definition.

The concept of 'civil society' in its American definition crowns the edifice. Civil society is thus reduced to a nebulae of 'apolitical', non-government organizations, believed to be – above all if they are based on religious 'communitarian', para-religious, ethnic or neighbourly principles, which they most often are – alongside the private business sector, 'closer to the public' (itself conceived as constituted by consumers more than by citizens) and thus more efficient in managing social goods (education and health in particular). The fact that these procedures increase inequalities does not bother it, as the aspiration to equality is not considered an important ethical value.

Since the French Revolution, the political cultures of France and continental Europe, though they fall perfectly within a capitalist structure, are significantly different.

Here, from the beginning, the values of liberty and equality were placed on an equal footing, which implies social management of their conflict. The State is thus called upon to regulate the deployment of capitalism according to its objectives. This different approach allows for the possibility – if social struggles assert themselves – of embarking upon a participative democracy that, by its very nature, accentuates the conflict through the logic of accumulation of capital, as the 'majority' of citizens can thus oppose the minority of 'owners', only recognized as real active citizens by the excluding logic of capitalism. The approach opens the door to the recognition of positive social rights, ignored by principle in the American model. Because, as you know, these rights entail the active intervention of the legislative and executive branches of the State, as opposed to simply the political and civic liberties that only require the State to abstain from hindering their use. The concept of public administrations assuming the management of collective services (education, health) with a view to ensure the maximum equality takes up a major position in social management. The fact that this formula is in fact more efficient than that implemented in the United States is demonstrated by a comparison of health expenditure (7 per cent of the GDP in Europe versus 14 per cent in the United States) and the associated results (much better in Europe). Under these conditions, a different concept of civil society is possible here; one that lends full importance to popular organizations in defence of social rights (such as trade unions and politicized citizen organizations).

The political culture described here paves the way for going beyond the limits of the logic that capitalist expansion imposes. The socialist future already exists as a potential power in the still-capitalist present.

The conflict between the culture of past/present and that of present/future was begun by the offensive made by Washington to impose on the entire Planet its vision, nonetheless limited and retrograde. An objective that is all the more arrogant, given that the English Common Law comprising its legal infrastructure is a primitive form of law, largely outmoded elsewhere, in Europe and numerous countries of the South. This does not mean that the objective has not been declared: the law of the United States should be accepted as a substitute for international law. Moscow's ambition of imposing a reduced vision of socialism in imitation of the Soviet model is largely outmoded here.

In order to measure the reversals registered in this contemporary battle, it suffices to examine the terms of today's dominating language in politics and the media. Terms that have disappeared: State, policy, power, classes and class struggle, social change, alternatives and revolutions, ideologies. They have been replaced by the insipid terms of governance, communities, social partners, poverty, consensus and changeover.

The attempts of member countries of the OECD to impose a 'universal' business law code that would prevail not only over specific national laws in this domain but also over all other local laws, whether social or political (the so-called AMI project), is part of this offensive. It resembles an attempt to impose the option of 'sharing', reserved for the partners of the imperialist triad. Therefore, it does not constitute a real obstacle to the aggressive deployment of the project by Washington.

The rallying of all of the triad partners behind this retrograde view of law and democracy is not at all mysterious. It can be explained by the desire common to all segments of the dominating imperialist capital of opening new spaces for the increase of profits. Calculated in the short term, true, but with a lack of social resistance capable of making it adjust to its demands, capital never reasons otherwise.

In view of this regression of democracy, the United Nations no longer has specific functions to fulfil. The UN thus loses its essential role, which is, on the one hand, to support democratization by integrating social rights to the set of rights of individuals and peoples, and, on the other hand, to promote an authentic international law system that would be a product of negotiation and commitment to the stages indispensable for the progress of humanity.

The conflict between the 'market' (brutal national and globalized capital) and society (in its local and globalized dimensions) finds its full expression here.

The 'market' (capitalism)/society conflict

The capitalist system in which we live has entered a stage of profound, real transformations whose impact cannot be ignored in the long term and whose foundation is formed by the scientific and technological revolution. In the analysis that I have proposed of these transformations, I emphasized the qualitative novelty of this revolution in comparison to preceding ones, and have reached the conclusion that the implementation of the creative potential of this revolution demands going beyond the social relations innate to capitalism (that is, the domination of capital and its privative appropriation) and the construction of a 'cognitive economy', to use the terms put forth by Carlo Vercelone.[9] My analysis, like that of Vercelone, calls attention to the obsolete nature of this aspect of capitalism.[10]

Yet capitalism is still in effect. It is thus employed to 'direct' this revolution, to subject it to the demands of its reproduction. Conventional economic analyses of the 'economy of growth' (as opposed to the cognitive economy) fall within this strategic framework, which 'postmodernist' discourses attempt to legitimate.

This new contradiction – between the potentially liberating impact of the development of productive capacities and the maintenance through all means of the relations of capitalist social domination – lends the conflict between the logic of capitalist expansion and the affirmation of social interests an unprecedented scope. The strategies employed by the dominant capital reveal themselves, under these conditions, to have a gigantic destructive (barbarous) scope, both in their local effects (in 'national' plans) and in their globalized dimensions.

The system of dominating powers is thus employed in order to flee discussion, substituting it with false debates. The emphasis is then placed on phenomena of the economic situation produced by the capitalist management of the crisis ('financing' constitutes a good example), which are presented as 'irreversible' structural transformations. But above all, the intention is to limit the debate within the biased alternatives of either 'market' or 'State'; the option in favour of the 'State' is rejected (and along with it, the nation), which is qualified simultaneously as 'old-fashioned' (globalization abolishes nations!) and powerless (the failure of socialism has demonstrated the ineffectiveness of the State), leaving nothing except for the option of full submission to the so-called market demands; in fact, those of the dominating oligopolistic capital of the imperialist triad.

This is an ideological discourse devoid of scientific value. Capitalism has never been reducible, and never will be, to a single 'economic' dimension. It does not exist without a political organization of power – the State. In its global dimension, really existing capitalism has always been synonymous with 'markets plus canons'. The globalization that it attempts to manage to its exclusive benefit would thus in principle demand the organization of a legitimate globalized political power. Yet the conditions that would allow the construction of such a State (benefiting all the more so from a democratic legitimacy!) do not exist. It is precisely because nations exist. This means that there is, beyond the interests of the capital segments dominating the imperialist oligopolies, what can be called 'national interests', whose precise content is defined by historical social commitments of each nation, capable of ensuring the stability of their social and political reproduction (whether within or outside of more or less democratic practices). Especially since, as products of the history of capitalist deployment, unequal by nature, these nations are far from enjoying comparable economic and political power.

The real alternative choice is thus: accepting that socialization on all levels, from national to global, be operated by the sole virtues of the 'market'; or on the contrary, building (on the long term and by stages) the necessary forms of socialization through democracy (in the richest and fullest sense of the term). Because peoples aspire simultaneously to social progress, the democratization of the management of their lives and respect for their national identities. And capitalism is less and less capable of allowing the effective fulfilment of these aspirations, on both the national and global levels.

The capitalist management of this crisis thus quite clearly requires the intervention of a political force capable of imposing its barbarous demands. For want of an impossible global State, the US State will take charge of this responsibility, as it intends and feels that it can. Europe itself, as it does not constitute 'one nation – one State', but only a series of associated nations and States, does not have the means with which to contest the US leadership of the imperialist triad. 'Sharing' would go no further than substituting NATO (under the direction of Washington) for the United States army; and this does not change things greatly for the rest of the world. In putting this management into practice, the United States (or, if necessary, the triad accepting its leadership) are called to act outside of all reference to law, international, among other types, and conduct themselves as 'ruffian States'.

The 'globalized liberalism' by which the management of the crisis is designated has no future. Either the societies of the entire Planet accept their submission to the so-called market demands (the future would then bring a world certainly different to that which we have known to date, something worse, infinitely more barbarous, and in this perspective, the UN would no longer make sense); or – and this seems to me not only desirable, but also more probable – they will eventually impose, through a long transition, the construction of local social systems and a global system progressively integrating the submission of the 'market' (and more amply, of the economy, beyond the market – this particular form of managing it) to the demands of socialization through democracy. The UN would have an important role to play in this perspective.

When I say that these are the only two alternatives, I understand that the idea of a 'third option', defined in terms of a market management on local and global scales that would be 'liberal' (possibly even tinged with social correctives), is perfectly illusory. The dominating capital cannot allow this.

The illusion that it is not only possible and is viable, but that it would even give chances to individuals and peoples who knew how to play the game intelligently, is nevertheless still very strong. The opinion in Europe, bogged down in the quicksand of its project, seems to believe in this. The Chinese ruling class also believes in it. The former and the latter at times even wage combat – though yet hesitant – along these lines. Giovanni Arrighi[11] and André Gunder Frank,[12] in their recent writings, imagine that China will be able to rise, in this framework, to the summit of world hierarchy. I do not believe this. Through the implementation of the 'five monopolies' by which the imperialist triad profits (and the form of law of the globalized value that expresses its efficiency), really existing capitalism prohibits this type of 'recouping'. In agreement with Lin Chun,[13] I suggest that China cannot 'develop' (in the sense of emerging from its peripheral state within globalized capitalism) unless it distances itself from the strategies it is implementing at present.

Putting the alternative, 'socialization through democratization', into practice entails meeting urgent demands in order to derail the project underway and especially that of the military control of the Planet by the United States and/or NATO. Then it would entail undertaking the reconstruction of a 'Southern Front', which cannot be a remake of Bandung in the 1955–1975 period, the reconstruction of the European project, stuck at its foundation, such that it would allow the progress of socialization through democracy, and the invention in China of an authentic 'market socialism' constituting the first stage of a long transition to socialism itself. This project implies, on national levels, that the social struggles of the victims of the system, through their politicized and constructed convergence, manage to reconstruct the unity of the workers' front, without omitting the farmers (half of humanity). On these issues, I refer to developments that I have proposed elsewhere.[14]

It is within this framework and in this perspective that one should identify the functions that the UN should fulfil in order to manage the proposed alternative 'globalization' in coherence with the requisites of socialization through democracy. One could then concretely envisage proposals of stages allowing the desired path to be embarked upon.

Proposals for the rebirth of the UN

The proposals that follow are grouped into four ensembles corresponding to the functions for which it would be desirable that the UN assumed important responsibilities.

Proposals concerning the political functions of the UN

*   Restoring the UN the major responsibility corresponding to it: ensuring the security of peoples (and States), guaranteeing peace, prohibiting aggression under any pretext whatsoever (such as that invoked in the case of the war in Iraq – which incidentally proved to be a lie). This principle should be emphatically proclaimed once again.

    In this spirit, it is necessary to condemn without ambiguity the declarations of the United States government, NATO and the G7, by which the powers concerned adjudicated themselves 'responsibilities' that are not theirs.

    This condemnation should be complemented by the drafting of political plans to resolve issues relative to the future of countries that are the victims of illegitimate interventions by imperialist powers (former Yugoslavia, Afghanistan and Iraq). These plans should explicitly establish the withdrawal of foreign military forces. It would by no means be acceptable that the UN be reintroduced 'by the gang' to legitimize the conditions created by the condemned interventions. The UN should be invited only to 'facilitate' the withdrawal of the invaders.
*   Restoring this major function to the UN could obviously imply certain reforms of its institutional architecture.

    But one must be wary here. Certain 'criticism' has been made and hasty proposals deduced from there, that are not in keeping with the perspective of reinforcing the role of the UN but rather in line with its domestication by the imperialist triad.

    Other criticism, apparently 'democratic and realistic', could be considered just as bad. I am particularly referring here to the attacks directed against the right to veto: one can easily imagine that if France had not been one of the beneficiaries, the Unites States would have managed to 'legitimize' its aggression. Possible reforms of the Security Council (its enlargement to include India and Brazil, ensuring a stronger representation of the diverse regions of the world) should be the object of in-depth examination before being put forth. Lending more importance to the General Assembly and improved articulation of resolutions (having or not the force of law according to the hypotheses, to be defined) on the measures required of the Security Council could constitute the axis of this reflection.

• Reinstating this central function of the UN does not imply the return to asserting the 'absolute' sovereignty of States, considered the only representatives of their peoples. In the following section, I will discuss proposals aimed at substituting the sovereignty of peoples with that of the States only, in the perspective of democratization of societies.

• Restoring the UN's functions should allow effective progress in the path of a solution for the major crises characteristic of our era and largely produced (or facilitated) by the strategies of 'generalization of chaos' put into practice by certain powers, first and foremost the United States.

In this spirit, the following should be imposed:

• The establishment of a UN interposition force between Israel (with its 'borders' as per the green line previous to 1967) and Palestine. Israel would not be able to withstand severe economic sanctions such as have been imposed on others.

• The establishment of UN peacekeeping forces in the regions of former occupied Yugoslavia (Bosnia and Kosovo), as well as in African countries that are the victims of so-called 'civil' wars.

   These operations could possibly be conceived in close collaboration with the regional organizations concerned (the European Union, Europe in the wider sense, the African Union).

• The UN should actively participate in drafting a 'plan for general disarmament'. This plan would not be able to be reduced to the implementation of the 'Non-Proliferation Treaty', which, in its current form, reinforces the monopoly of the production of weapons of mass destruction to the benefit of those who have proven to be their most frequent users! Disarmament should begin by that of the Powers and be controlled by the UN, which would substitute the 'bipolar' control formerly practised by the two superpowers but now non-existent.

   General disarmament should establish the evacuation of all military bases established beyond national borders, and therefore especially those through which the US intends to pursue the implementation of its 'military control of the Planet'.

- The UN should actively participate in the definition of the framework of possible 'humanitarian interventions' and their operational modes.

The need for such interventions is not disputable, given that, unfortunately, in the current state of development of societies, occasions of plunging into savagery (ethnocide, 'ethnic' or 'religious' cleansing, apartheids) are possible. But these interventions cannot be left to the Imperialist Powers, thereby facilitating manipulation, the use of double standards, etc.

- By the same token, the UN should be invested with the main collective responsibility in defining what constitutes 'terrorist' actions. The organization should likewise determine the conditions of measures designed to eradicate these practices and should oversee the modes of putting these measures into practice. It would not be possible to entrust the waging of a 'war against terrorism' to Powers, and in particular to the United States.

Proposals concerning the rights of peoples and the creation of international law

- The principle guiding these proposals are based on the observation made above that the concept of sovereignty of States should be redefined.

That the general public opinion today considers that all human beings are responsible for what occurs, not only within the borders of the States of which they are citizens, but all over the world, constitutes – in my opinion – an indication of progress of universal awareness. This progress brings back the issue of the old concept (from the Treaty of Westphalia to the Charter of the United Nations) of the absolute and exclusive sovereignty of States.

The contradiction between said sovereignty and the rights of peoples is real. Yet this contradiction cannot be eliminated by the abolition of one of its terms: that of the right of peoples (by maintaining the old concept of sovereignty) or that of sovereignty (which would in fact be to the benefit of interventions and manipulations by imperialist powers).

This contradiction can only be overcome by the real progress of democratization of all societies. This consists of a process which, it must be admitted, must simply be allowed to follow its pace, that of the progress of the affirmation of the need for democracy. The international organization must intervene here to sustain this progress, accelerate its translation into real change in the exercise of powers. The UN is the place par excellence where this debate should be unflaggingly pursued.

• There are already charters of rights which are beginning to show signs of progress in the expansion of their definitions. To the first charters, limited to political and civic rights understood in a restricted sense, were added the Charters of Collective and Social Rights. These efforts must be unflaggingly pursued, the Charters being far from sufficient in the present state. The right of peoples to development, for example, which was the object of in-depth reflection in 'private' circles (the Lelio Basso International Foundation for the Rights and Liberation of Peoples, for instance) or groupings partially under state control (the Non-Aligned Movement, for instance), should be declared an integral part of the universal rights of individuals and peoples. The right of all farmers on the Planet (half of the human population) to have access to land and to human and viable conditions for its use, which is an integral part of the right to development, has not, to date, even begun to show signs of being recognized.

It is likewise within this universal framework – as represented by the United Nations – that the efforts should be pursued to establish rights whose recognition is only in its infancy, or at least far from being attained to date. The rights asserting in principle and establishing in practice the equality of men and women belong to this family of rights. Those concerning 'collective' rights through which 'identities' are expressed – cultural, linguistic and religious identities, among others – should likewise be the object of in-depth debate allowing their definition and that of their fields of application. In no case should the recognition of these rights to diversity allow the demand for the 'communitarian organization' of societies (by the same token denying the 'right to resemblance' and the rights of the individual outside of the community). In other words, the rights in question would be unable to question the principle of laicism.

Many 'realists' lend but little importance to charters of rights that are only valid to the degree to which there are measures taken to ensure their effective execution. These people probably underestimate the importance of law, which can become an effective weapon used to enforce these charters. Action can be sustained through the creation of a system of universal tribunals, which we will discuss below:

• The UN should exercise particular responsibility in the creation of an international business law code.

The increase of all sorts of relations in a globalized economy makes the creation of an international business law code more necessary than ever. Nevertheless, this particular law domain would not be allowed to prevail over the fundamental rights of individuals and peoples nor over their national formulations. The option provided in this sphere by the AMI project is therefore unacceptable.

Moreover, the drafting of this law would not be entrusted to a single partner represented by the set of interests of the dominating capital (the 'Club of Transnationals'), as is the case with WTO projects. Especially considering that the partner in question invests itself as legislator, judge and party, as it is the sole master of its business tribunal project. Rarely have the elementary principles of law and justice been trampled with such impertinence! In its absence, allowing, as is in fact the case, the courts of the United States (whose impartiality is more than doubtful) and the (especially primitive) law codes of that country to dominate the practice with regard to regulating business is no less unacceptable.

International business law should be drawn up through transparent debate involving all interested parties, that is, not only the business world, but also the workers concerned (of the businesses in question as well as of entire nations, who are suffering the consequences of the legislation put into effect) and States. There are no premises other than those of the UN (and the ILO, which is one of its expressions) for conducting this debate.

• The UN cannot be invested from one day to another as a 'World State' nor a 'world government', or even as a supranational authority vested with powers too ample in varied spheres.

Acknowledging this does not rule out that a path be embarked upon that could lead to this in the longer term.

The proposals put forth in this perspective should be the object of our undivided attention, true, but also of our greatest vigilance. Today, there are many proposals being put forth that aim to associate the 'civil society' (defined in the Washington manner as described above) with the life of the organization and some of these proposals attempt to give the representation of the 'business world' a major position in this association! In contrast, the workers' world – the majority of human beings as opposed to the minority of millionaires – is always ignored by the advocates of this 'reform' of the UN. The latter have gone as far as intending to reduce the powers, already insignificant, of the ILO. Unfortunately, the administration of this organization truly seems to be an accomplice of this project for social regression.

Proposals concerning the institution of a 'World Parliament', composed of representatives of national parliaments (which do not always exist and are only seldom truly representative of the people), are not necessarily trivial or unrealistic. An evolution moving in this direction could be undertaken, even if it is clear that the democracy that it supposedly supports could not advance on a universal scale more quickly than it could on the scale of the nations concerned.

Proposals concerning the economic management of globalization

- So-called 'deregulated' globalization, as it is at present, is in fact one form of globalization among many, which is regulated exclusively and wholly by the dominating globalized capital (the 'transnationals') and their political debtors (the G7). This form, which is neither 'inevitable' nor 'the only alternative' nor even acceptable, should be substituted by institutionalized forms of regulation on a world-wide scale, supporting and possibly complementing the regional and national forms of regula- tion that peoples will eventually impose here and there, even granting that there may be contradictions and conflicts between these different levels of the economic management of the modern world.

The task is thus complicated and the progress that could be made in the short term, even if the UN were mobilized in this field, would long remain modest. But it should allow the beginning of evolution favourable to peo- ples and their workers and should therefore not be disdained.

- Considering their enormously devastating effects, international debts could constitute a solid starting point for opening a debate on the func- tions of the UN in managing the world economy.

The prevailing discourse attributes the sole responsibility for debt to the borrowing countries, whose behaviour can supposedly not be justified (cor- ruption, facility or irrationality of the political decision-makers, extremist nationalism, etc.). The reality is quite another thing. A significant percent- age of loans were in fact the result of systematic policies implemented by the lenders, seeking to place an excess of capital that – due to the profound economic crisis of the past 20 years – could not be used in productive investment, neither in wealthy countries nor in those deemed able to receive their capital. Artificial alternative uses were thus fabricated to prevent the devaluation of excess capital. The explosion of 'speculative' capital move- ments made on a very short term resulted from these policies, such as their placement in the 'debt' of the developing countries and the former Eastern Block countries. The World Bank in particular, but also many large private banks in the United States, Europe and Japan, as well as transnationals, share a major responsibility which is never mentioned. 'Corruption' is added to these policies, with the double complicity of the lenders (the World Bank, private banks, transnationals) and the authorities of the States concerned in the South and East. A systematic audit of these 'debts' is called for as a priority. It would demonstrate that a large part of the debts in question are legally illegitimate.

The weight of paying this debt is absolutely unsustainable, not only for the most impoverished countries of the South, but even for those that are not. We should recall here that when, in the aftermath of World War I, Germany was condemned to pay reparations amounting to 7 per cent of its exports, liberal economists of the time concluded that this charge was unsustainable and that the productive machine of that country would be unable to 'adjust' to it. Today, economists of the same liberal school do not hesitate to propose the 'adjustment' of the economies of the developing countries to the demands of paying debts that are five or at times ten times heavier. Therefore, in reality, collecting the debt is today a form of pillaging the wealth and work of the peoples of the South (and the East). A particularly lucrative form as it has managed to make the poorest countries of the Planet exporters of capital to the North. Also a particularly brutal form that frees dominating capital from worries and from the vicissitudes of managing the businesses and workforces that they implement. The debts are payable, that is all. It is the duty of the States concerned (and not of the capital of the 'lenders') to extract it from its people's labour. The dominating capital is freed of all responsibility and concern.

A 'classification' of debts is called for. These can be ranged under one of the three following categories:

Indecent and immoral debts

A good example of these is the loans taken out by the apartheid government of South Africa in its time, loans taken out to purchase weapons in order to put down the revolt of its African peoples.

Dubious debts

These consist of loans taken out largely at the suggestion of the financial powers of the North (including the World Bank) and made possible by processes of corruption whose creditors are the actors involved as well as the debtors. The majority of these loans were not invested in the projects that justified their issuance (and this fact was known to the lenders, who were accomplices). In this case, the debts are purely and simply illegal in the eyes of a justice minimally worthy of the name. In some cases, the loans were indeed invested, but in absurd projects imposed by the lenders (and especially by the World Bank). Here also, it was the Bank's process that was worth carrying out. But this institution is not financially 'responsible', having placed itself above the laws and the discourse of liberalism on 'risks'!

Acceptable debts

In cases where loans were effectively used to the ends for which they were intended, the acknowledgement of the debt is indisputable.

Not only should indecent and dubious debts be unilaterally repudiated (after an audit), but the payments made in their name should also be reimbursed by the 'creditors', after their capitalization at the same interest rates as the debtors had to pay. It would then see that it is the North, in fact, that is deeply indebted to its victims in the South.

The debt management proposed for the 'Heavily Indebted Poor Countries' (HIPCs) reveals a completely different logic. The entirety of the debt is considered perfectly 'legitimate', with no examination or audit whatsoever. The proposal is based on the sole – and unacceptable – principle of 'charity'. The intention is to 'alleviate' the charges for these 'very poor peoples', but at the same time, impose upon them draconian supplementary conditions that definitively place them in a category approaching that of 'colonies administered directly by foreigners'.

But beyond the proposed audit and the adoption of measures that would allow the accounts to be balanced and in order to prevent analogous situations from being reproduced in the future, it remains necessary to draw up an international debt law code, to date in its infancy, and of authentic courts to dictate the law in this sphere (which would allow going well beyond what one can expect of arbitration commissions).

- Reinstating the full responsibility of the United Nations in the organization of the world economic system involves the redefinition of the functions of the major institutions that comprise it (the UNCTAD and ILO, among others) or that are external to it (the WTO, IMF and the World Bank).

The principal priority objectives that could be assigned in this sphere could be as follows:

- The resuscitation of the UNCTAD and the identification of its new (or renewed) functions, such as: (i) drawing up a global framework for a 'foreign investment code' allowing the regulation of relocation and the protection of the workers of all the partners concerned; (ii) the negotiation of conditions of access to the markets for the different national and regional partners. These proposals call into question the total marginalization that the UNCTAD has suffered, all of its powers having been transferred to the WTO. This organization should be thoroughly rethought if we wish to have it escape from the orbit in which it is imprisoned, strictly defined by the Club of Transnationals.

- The resuscitation of the ILO, not in the sense proposed by the current administration of this organization, but precisely in the opposite sense, that of reinforcing the representation and rights of workers.
- The renegotiation of the world monetary system, of the institutionalization of regional arrangements guaranteeing the stability of exchange rates, a new IMF (which would have hardly anything to do with the organization by the same name existing today) with the responsibility of managing the interconnection between the regional systems concerned. In the current state of affairs, the IMF, which is not responsible for relations between the dominating currencies (the dollar, euro, yen, pound sterling, Swiss franc), operates as a colonial, collective (for the Triad) monetary authority in charge of managing the finances of dependent countries by subjecting them, on the one hand and through 'structural adjustments', to the demands of the pillaging of their resources to the benefit of floating capital, and on the other hand, to the tributary drain represented by the repayment of debts.
- The construction of a world capital market worthy of this name and designed to orient monetary movement towards productive investment (in both the North and the South) and, as a necessary complement, equipped to discourage so-called 'speculative' financial flows (the Tobin Tax could be considered in this context). This market would call into question the functions of the World Bank (the Ministry of Propaganda of the G7) and of the WTO (the agent executing the will of transnationals).
- In the sphere of the economic management, the UN can certainly do no more than it could in the political management of the world. But it could likewise undertake the construction of a globalized economic government (and policy). And where there is a government, there are finances.

The sphere of managing the natural resources of the world without a doubt constitutes the best entranceway leading to this path.

Access to natural resources is always relevant insofar as the principle of national sovereignty. But this principle has been and often continues to be disdained by events, not only in colonial situations (where national sovereignty disappears), but also through the exercise of power relations that are generally analysed in terms of 'geopolitics', or even 'geostrategy'. This de facto unequal access is the source of immense waste by the societies of the 'North' of the planet's resources, and by the impossibility of foreseeing the extension of the forms of consumption concerned to the totality of peoples, who are thus condemned by the imposed form of globalization to the state of victims of 'apartheid on the global scale'. Ecologic movements, which are the source of the awareness of the dramatic scope of the problem, have not really managed to make the world system of powers (represented by the Conferences of Rio and Kyoto, which led to the Conference of Johannesburg in August 2002) accept appropriate and efficient forms of democratic global management of access to these resources. The militarization of globalization should likewise be associated to the objectives of the control of the natural resources of the world by hegemonic power.

The exploitation of the resources in question arises in principle from that of 'existing capitalism'. The latter is based on the short-term view of financial profitability and the decision-makers in this domain – the transnationals – know no other perspective. We are fully in a domain where the supposed rationality of management according to the market is in fact irrationality from the viewpoint of the interests of peoples considered in the long term. The discourse on 'sustainable development' proceeds from an awareness of this contradiction between the market and the interests of humanity, but often does not arrive at concrete and practical consequences.

The alternative of a rational ('sustainable') and democratic (in local plans and in those of the global system) management of natural resources could be discussed on the basis of proposals that have always been hinted at, such as that of a world taxation of income associated with excess and exploitation of these resources and the redistribution of the product of said taxation to the benefit of the peoples concerned, designed to favour the development of disadvantaged countries and regions and to discourage waste.

This could be the manner of creating the embryo of globalized taxation.

The issue embraces a great number of resources – minerals, oil, water and climate. I suggest initiating debate in two domains, concerning oil and water, respectively.

- Management by the UN of water, a common asset of all peoples:
  There is no life without water, which is just as necessary as air. Among the multiple uses of water, we will focus here only on those concerning agriculture – which consumes the largest amount.

The supply of water is distributed by nature among the different rural societies of the planet in an extremely unequal manner. There are regions of the world that receive water for free from the 'heavens'. In the meantime, in other places – in arid or semi-arid regions – water must be collected from wells or rivers, and distributed via irrigation throughout the entire farmland area. There, water has a production cost that is far from insignificant. Should one respond to this situation of dearth by putting a price on this resource in these cases?

By accepting to strictly follow the reasoning of conventional economy and of commercial alienation that constitutes its pedestal, by accepting to play the game of competitiveness within the framework of unbridled globalization, one cannot but either accept a systematically lower remuneration of the work of some, or simply stop producing. Liberal globalization condemns agriculture in vast regions of the planet to extinction.

But peoples, nations and States exist. They occupy spaces on the surface of the planet that are theirs and that do not enjoy identical natural conditions. A realist political economy should take this into account. The conventional economy, feigning ignorance of these dimensions of reality, substitutes them with the theory of an imaginary globalized world, defined at once by the merchandising of all aspects of social life and all conditions relating to human activity, and by its extension to the planetary level. This theory allows it to legitimize the unilateral ambitions of capital without being concerned about social reality. If the liberals, who defend this fundamentalism of capital, were coherent with their own logic, they would arrive at the conclusion that the optimal use of natural resources (in this case, water) requires a massive redistribution of peoples of the world due to the unequal distribution of this resource on the surface of the Planet. In this case, water would become the public property of all of humanity.

In the meantime, water is one of the public goods particular to a given peoples or country. If, for these peoples, this good is relatively rare, access to it must be rationalized. The cost of access to its use should be distributed among all inhabitants in one way or another, that is, through the regulation of the market by means of an acceptable system of subsidies and taxation. The formula for this system would be the result of a series of compromises defined by internal social conditions and those governing the way in which the country is integrated in the world economy. Compromises between the farmers and the consumers of foodstuffs; compromises between the demands of a development defined in terms of a project of society and the possible need for exportation that the implementation of this project could require at a given stage of its deployment (in this spirit, one could 'naturally' conceive of subsidizing non-competitive exports). This formula cannot be defined in absolute terms once and for all; it remains relative and historically dated.

The response to these problems lies in the sphere of what should be called 'the right of peoples and humanity'. This right is, with regard to water, nearly inexistent since each country is, in principle, free to use the underground and surface waters within its borders as it sees fit. Agreements governing water management, should they exist, are but the product of private international treaties. The need to advance in this domain towards a real right of peoples and of humanity has already become urgent. The international business law that the interests of capital have imposed, and which currently constitutes the exclusive concern of international institutions created to this effect (the WTO in particular), is not a possible substitute for the absence of a right of peoples to manage this public property of humanity. On the contrary, it is quite the opposite.

Proposals concerning the institutionalization of an international justice system

- There are already a series of international courts of justice, some of which were established even before the creation of the UN; others are the recent product of the denunciation of war crimes and of crimes against humanity.

The archipelago comprised by these international institutions of justice nonetheless remains of quite limited effectiveness, both because of the restrictive definition of their competencies and due to the refusal by certain powers (the United States in the first place) to acknowledge their legitimacy.

A preliminary task is called for: make a thorough inventory of the institutions, propose critical analyses of the shortcomings of the institutions concerned, and identify the areas of legal void which should be gradually filled.

Furthermore, there are so-called 'opinion tribunals', which have no legal status, yet fulfil functions of great utility in alerting public opinion (the Bertrand Russell International War Crimes Tribunal constitutes a good example). The missions accomplished by these institutions deserve to be pursued, their actions supported and their echo amplified. Nevertheless, this should not constitute an obstacle to conducting campaigns in order to create recognized international tribunals in charge of sentencing law. Obviously, at the same time, by pursuing the action of encoding the rights that the tribunals concerned will be entrusted with enforcing.

As an indispensable complement to the proposals put forth in the preceding paragraphs concerning the responsibilities of the UN, a series of international courts of justice should be conceived and proposed in order to aid implementation. The proposals whose objective is to reinforce the juridical dimensions of action taken by the United Nations concern three sets of courts of justice whose establishment would seem desirable.

- The first group of juridical institutions to be considered concerns the political aspects of managing globalization.

If the actions and interventions of States beyond their boundaries, whatever their pretexts, are to be subject to the judgement of the United Nations, it is advisable that a relevant court of law of this organization have a word to legitimize or condemn these interventions. The International Court of Justice in The Hague can hardly do this under the present conditions of definitions of its competencies. The revision of the competencies of this Court in order to expand its powers is called for. One could imagine that the victim State, like the General Assembly of the UN, could have recourse to the Court, even in the hypothetical case of opposition by the State who was the author of the intervention being questioned.

Otherwise, the imperialist powers (the United States first and foremost) will never be able to be judged for their violations of international law, even if these violations are undisputable.

Some progress has nevertheless been made after actions and interventions by States, thanks to the definition of war crimes and crimes against humanity; some ad hoc international criminal tribunals have been established in this spirit (for the crimes committed in Yugoslavia and in Rwanda) and an agreement was made allowing the establishment of a general criminal court. This progress remains insufficient, as the refusal of certain powers to undersign the agreement renders their accusation in this tribunal impossible. The crimes committed by the United States are hence beyond the reach of any ruling other than one of 'opinion'. This is absolutely unacceptable and considerably reduces the legitimacy of rulings made against other possible criminal States. It is high time that the Ruffian State par excellence – the United States – be forced to confront the judges. All cases should be able to be submitted to the Court (simply at the request of the victim State, among others) and the criminals judged in absentia, if necessary.

- A second group of juridical institutions deserves to be established in order to consolidate the rights of individuals and peoples recognized by the United Nations.

One could take inspiration from the European Court of Justice, to which, within the domains of its competence, the victims – whether individuals or collectives – can submit their cases directly – without necessarily gaining the previous authorization from the State from which they come. Yet one could – and even should – expand the domains of competence of international justice (to include, among other things, social rights), and to this effect, Chambers other than the Court of Human and Peoples' Rights of the UN could be established.

- A third group of juridical institutions to be established concerns business law.

One could imagine diverse Chambers in the Court of Trade Law of the UN, with specified competencies, one of which would be called criminal chamber and would judge criminal economic acts. The case of Bhopal illustrates the scandalous impunity that transnationals are currently enjoying.

It is likewise in this context that a Chamber of the Court could be established to handle cases of litigation concerning foreign debt.

Action plan for implementation of proposals

The proposals put forth here are certainly ambitious and the execution of only part of them will require time. But the future starts now and there is no reason for postponing the launching of an action plan to ensure progress.

I do not believe it useful to appeal to governments to negotiate as of today the 'UN reform'. They will do it themselves if they deem it necessary. But the power relations that prevail today are such that there is little chance that these reforms – if they were pursued – would go in the right direction. On the contrary, there is every reason to fear that they would be in line with the dominant imperialist strategies of the time, which aim to marginalize and domesticate the international organization even more. One can expect to have to rather make a campaign against the reforms proposed in this spirit rather than supporting them!

I thus believe that another approach must be taken, by first addressing public opinion. In this spirit, I propose the establishment of ad hoc International Commissions (on each topic of the project concerned). These commissions could then supply analyses and proposals to the vast nebula of movements recognizable in the Social, National, Regional and Global Forums. The World Forum of Alternatives, through the channel of its centres for critical reflection constituted by its network of correspondents and members, could help to coordinate the enterprise.

Once the commissions' works were sufficiently advanced, they could – and should – become the object of vast campaigns of global scope based on objectives defined precisely by each of them. One would thus contribute to correcting the imbalances that characterize the power relations prevailing in the contemporary world.

Democracy, the United Nations and Civil Society

Birgitta Dahl, former Speaker/President of the Swedish Parliament; Member of the Panel of Eminent Persons on United Nations–Civil Society Relations

When the Secretary-General of the United Nations, Kofi Annan, opened the first Security Council debate on terrorism after September 11 he did so by reminding the meeting of the fact that all the items that were on the agenda of the United Nations before September 11 are still there and have to be addressed, also, if we want to fight terrorism. He was referring of course to the fight against poverty, diseases and famine, underdevelopment and debts, oppression and homelessness, for sustainable development and social welfare of all human beings, as expressed in the Millennium Development Goals adopted by the General Assembly in 2000. Of course he was, and is, right in calling for common action against the evils that are tormenting millions of our fellow-mortals today.

The history of mankind is a history of violence and wars, oppression and unspeakable distress. But mankind has always, all through these sufferings, sustained the dream of peace and freedom, democracy and human rights, economic development and a healthy environment, social welfare and culture. Indefatigably and persistently mankind has struggled to find ways to realize this dream. And we have experienced, in our time, how people with these ideals have been victorious after a long struggle in the former colonies in Africa, Asia and Latin America, in Spain, Portugal and Greece, in Germany, in the former Soviet Union, in South Africa, East Timor and Cape Verde.

Democracy is based on respect between individuals, popular move-ments, interest groups and political parties. In a democracy we use the respectful dialogue and the trustworthy compromise as the method to solve conflicts and reach decisions. In a democracy there is a distinct – and dif-ferent – role for individual citizens, Non-Governmental Organizations and political parties. Each of us has a role to play and duties to perform. Democracy does not solely imply freedoms and rights, but also responsibil-ities to contribute to the common work and goals. NGOs, popular movements which are there to mobilize citizens for particular causes, put an issue on the public agenda, rouse opinion and call for action. Political parties are there to sustain the representative democratic system at all levels – local, regional, national and international. Their role is to find priorities and compromises, reach decisions, based on a holistic and ideological perspective. In most democracies this also calls for cooperation, coalitions, compromises based on a respectful dialogue. In a good democracy this fosters a thinking and performance that is the mere opposite to the funda-mentalism and irreconcilableness that is today plaguing so many peoples.

A working democracy is based on three very important principles – working methods:

- Democracy and human rights, universal suffrage, equality between sexes and ethnic, cultural and religious groups.

- Education, adult education, culture.

The individual citizen should be in a lifelong process of learning and development. Culture should be present throughout society. NGOs and political parties, organized as popular movements, should be the core and initiators of this kind of adult education and cultural work.

- Peace and international cooperation.

The pioneers and popular movements, who struggled for independence, democracy and universal suffrage, have always been peace activists, internationalists. Based on their experiences of the atrocities of war and violence, they had a vision of a world in peace: 'Never more a war'. Democracy was conceived as the guarantee for peace. A country ruled by its people would not make use of violence against its own citizens or neighbours. A democratically elected government would not start wars, but seek cooperation with other countries and peaceful solutions to conflicts.

Today most of us live in a multicultural society, composed of citizens with different backgrounds and experiences, different cultures and religions. We all live in a globalized world, where cooperation is more needed than ever, but the risk of extinction of cultural heritage is evident. We need to establish a good balance between national-cultural identity and international cooperation.

I was once – 40 years ago – quite amazed by a statement by Kwame Nkrumah, the first president of independent Ghana, saying: 'To be a good internationalist you have to start by being a good patriot.' To me and my likeminded radical friends, working for internationalism, it first seemed to be 'old fashioned' to speak about 'patriotism'. I was wrong. He was right. A person, a people, who is confident and proud of her identity, is also confident, secure, open for cooperation with others. There is no real conflict between national, cultural identity and international cooperation. But if globalization, international cooperation leads to the weakening and levelling of cultural heritages, there is a risk for popular resistance against international cooperation that can be misused, exploited by charlatans and evil populists fostering xenophobia and racism. I believe that it is important in today's multiplex reality to have a clear identity and to preserve cultural traditions. It is in the active and dedicated meeting between cultures that new and rich development can arise.

In this connection I would also like to quote Amílcar Cabral, leader of the liberation movement African Party for the Independence of Guinea and Cape Verde, PAIGC:

The ideological weakness, not to say the total lack of ideology within the national liberation movements depends ultimately on their lack of knowledge of the historical reality they claim to change and represents one of the biggest, if not the biggest, deficiency in our struggle against imperialism.

Our lack of experience made us believe, that we could fight in the cities with strikes and other actions. But we were wrong and the reality showed us that this was not possible.

Therefore, the struggles of PAIGC and the society in the liberated areas were organized on the basis of the cultural and social heritage of the farmers in the rural areas. But it was not unconditional. Amílcar Cabral again:

Another aspect that we consider very important is the religion of our people. We avoid all kinds of hostility against that and against the bonds that our people still have with nature, because of the economic underdevelopment. But we do firmly oppose everything which is contrary to human rights.

On these grounds, Cabral and PAIGC worked for the equal rights of women and for the respectful understanding between religions and ethnic groups.

He was of course right. Revolution, change, can never be imported. The development of each nation must be based on its cultural and social heritage. But cultural traditions can never be used to excuse and legitimize violations of basic human rights. They must always be respected and come first.

The introductory words of the Charter of the United Nations express the eternal dream – vision of mankind:

We, the peoples of the United Nations, determined to save succeeding generations from the scourge of war, which twice in our lifetime has brought untold sorrow to mankind, and to reaffirm faith in fundamental human rights, in the dignity and value of the human person, in the equal rights of men and women and of nations large and small, and to establish conditions under which justice and respect for the obligations arising from treaties and other sources of international law can be maintained, and to promote social progress and better standards of life in larger freedom, and for these ends to practice tolerance and live together in peace with one another as good neighbours, and to unite our strength to maintain international peace and security, and by the acceptance of principles and the institution of methods to insure that armed forces shall not be used, save in the common interest, and to employ the international machinery for the promotion of economic and social advancement of all peoples have resolved to combine our efforts to accomplish these aims.

These ideas have not lost their significance – they must be protected and strengthened more than ever in the world and harsh reality of today. They represent the good alternative that does as a matter of fact exist. As expressed recently by an 80-year-old survivor of the Holocaust: 'The best way to fight the evil is to hold up the good!'

It is an irrefutable fact that the world should have been, should be, much more horrible than it is today without the United Nations. But there is no doubt the United Nations needs to be strengthened and reformed.

The United Nations can never be stronger than its members want it and allow it to be – and this support needs to be reinforced.

The United Nations needs to reform its work and organization. The world has changed since the United Nations was founded by the victorious powers of World War II. Today the United Nations has four times as many members (around 200 as compared with around 50) as it had at the outset. The majority of the new members are countries that 60 years ago were not free and independent. A majority of them are also developing countries or countries in transition, still much poorer than the rich north-western minority.

Today we see new strong actors on the international arena, parallel to national states: regional organizations, economic forces – multinational companies and financial empires, popular and social movements, academia – and the scientific society. New technologies enable instant coordination of action on a global level. The United Nations and international cooperation suffers from a democratic deficit, which creates distrust. There is an obvious risk that international cooperation is conceived as a threat to democracy and cultural identity – quite contrary to the close connection between peace, international cooperation and democracy, that was the initial vision.

Today we do have a great number of international agreements and commitments – final documents from global conferences. They are concluded in The Millennium Development Goals in the 'Millennium Declaration' of the General Assembly of 2000. Thus we do have a very good common agenda for peace, poverty eradication and sustainable development. For this to be attained, we require a strong support among citizens, popular movements and democratically elected representatives in the member states.

Civil Society, popular movements and NGOs have had an explicit role in the work of the United Nations from the beginning, clearly worded in the Charter of the United Nations. Their role has increased considerably during the last 15 years, particularly in connection with the major global summits and international negotiations. Today there are about 2,000 Civil Society Organizations accredited to the United Nations and around 500 new ones, which call for accreditation every year. So we have seen a really strong development.

On the other hand, this has also caused tensions and problems, not only for financing and the ability to host so many. For instance, at the last summits we had around 30,000 NGO-persons present each time. It is also a fact that some governments do not like this development and the growing influence of Civil Society. From the South there are many who feel that the North, the rich north, is tormenting Civil Society in a way that is provocative to them. There was a feeling that these problems have to be addressed in a systematic way so as to allow for a higher participation for Civil Society.

The Secretary-General Kofi Annan wants to strengthen the role of Civil Society and the popular support for the United Nations. In his report to the General Assembly in September 2002, entitled 'Strengthening of the United Nations: an agenda for further change' (A/57/387 and corr.1), he stated that he would establish a panel of eminent persons to review the relations between the United Nations and Civil Society. The General Assembly, in its Resolution 57/300 of 20 December 2002, concurred with his intention and decided to consider the recommendations through the respective intergovernmental process. Accordingly, in February 2003, the Secretary-General appointed the 'Panel of Eminent Persons on United Nations-Civil Society Relations' and asked Fernando Enrique Cardoso, former President of Brazil, to chair it. The Panel included 12 members – I was one of them.

The terms of reference are short. They say: 'The High-level Panel will undertake an assessment of relations between the UN and Civil Society with the objective of formulating recommendations to the Secretary-General for enhancing' ... I stress this ... 'enhancing interaction between the organization and Civil Society, including parliamentarians and the private sector ... The Panel will consult broadly and submit its recommendations to the Secretary-General within twelve months.' We have done so and we submitted our report in time.

We had our first meeting in June 2003 in New York, where we agreed on the basis of our work. We used the following six months for extensive dialogues with Civil Society and other actors all over the world. They were invited to participate in different forms and we also travelled and met them all over the world. In December 2003 we met in Geneva to agree on the principles in the report. The last days of March 2004 we met in New York agreeing on the report. In June we submitted our Report, 'We the Peoples: Civil Society, the UN and Global Governance'.

Many of our proposals are of a kind which the Secretary-General can implement according to the mandate he has and his office. Others need to be part of intergovernmental negotiations and agreements. The intention is that the Secretary-General will present his proposals to the General Assembly this autumn. Hopefully, there will be a quick implementation.

We have, after thorough analysis, agreed to use a fairly limited understanding of 'Civil Society'. When we say Civil Society, we mainly mean CSOs, NGOs. We also address other constituencies that are needed in the kind of international networks that we want to see in the future. So, we address the role of local councils, national parliaments, the scientific community, the private sector and some others. But with Civil Society we mean the organizations, popular movements, and not the wider perspective.

At our first meeting we were told by the Secretary-General to be both bold and pragmatic. We have understood this to be as bold as possible without creating resistance that could block the process. We want a change to take place and we want to start that change with our proposals.

Our recommendations are based upon the principle that Civil Society, popular movements, NGOs and elected representatives must have a significant role, a real and substantive influence on the work of the United Nations and in international cooperation. Our proposals can be realized in the framework of parliamentary democracy and the rules of international law, defining governments as the negotiating and contracting partners.

We have agreed on some paradigm shifts that we would like to see, as the basis of our proposals. The first one is that the United Nations should emphasize its role of convening, of leading, of facilitating partnerships, multi-stakeholder partnerships, global policy networks, coalitions of like-minded governments and other actors. We believe that the United Nations should act not only on the notion that all governments, and only governments, should be present at all deliberations. We propose that the United Nations should actively initiate global policy networks with the participation, different on different issues, of governments, of national parliaments, of Civil Society, of NGOs, of academia, of the private sector. The idea is that likeminded partners come together, join their forces, to try to change the world. We believe this is very important.

This method has been used in a number of cases. The first one was in 1979 when the World Health Organization (WHO) and the United Nations Children's Fund (UNICEF) brought together the stakeholders to address the problem of marketing of breast milk-substitute. It has been used on questions like debt, landmines, the tackling of major diseases like

HIV/AIDS, malaria and others. As Minister of Environment 15 years ago, I used this method extensively in the preparations for Rio 92 and for the ban on the use of chlorofluorocarbons. It was by forming informal networks of those countries, ministers, parliaments, CSOs (particularly on the environment) and the academic world that we were able to achieve much more than it would otherwise has been possible. So I have personally a very good experience of this way of working.

The second shift we want to see is the focus on the national level in implementing global agreements, commitments, in supporting sustainable development, and in analysing how this could best be done. In many countries the UN family plays a crucial role for the eradication of poverty and diseases, for sustainable and economic development. Likeminded responsible groups, organizations and institutions should go into alliance on the national and local level to find good solutions to problems. By this one could say that we act both according to the classical approach 'Think globally, act locally' and, at the same time, according to the revised principle 'Think locally, act globally'. This means that ideas can come from both sides and converge. The way that we are able to improve our commitments should be improved. This calls, of course, for resource allocation and for the strengthening of Civil Society in countries where Civil Society is weak and needs to be better organized. We propose both a fund to assist this process and also what we call Resident Coordinators in 30 to 40 countries, mainly developing countries and countries in transition, where Civil Society needs to be strengthened to be able to participate on an equal level, and also to be actors implementing international commitments and the support coming from abroad.

The third shift we would like to see is that the United Nations and its members address the problems of democratic deficit in international cooperation. Traditionally and by constitutions and international law it is the government that represents the country in all international deliberations. This is part of the government's executive power. The very weak parliamentary control, that is the reality in most countries today, gives rightly rise to the feeling of democratic deficit. But there are no constitutional restrictions or rules in international law against strong parliamentary control also in this area. Such a parliamentary control could give democratic legitimacy to international cooperation. It could create popular support to international commitments.

We propose that national parliaments should take on the role to be an active controller, to execute parliamentary control of the government, also when it comes to international affairs and UN-issues. National parliaments should receive all important UN documents at the same time as governments. All standing committees in national parliaments should follow very carefully what is happening in their respective area, also on the global, international scene. Open public debates should be held in parliaments on major issues. We need the parliaments to implement international commitments. International commitments must be followed by action – decisions, legislation in national parliaments. We need the parliament as the national arena making international cooperation and solidarity part of our daily political work.

We also propose that national standing committees should send representatives to Global Public Policy Committees to be held in the United Nations on certain issues that need to be addressed carefully, jointly and globally. The parliamentary representation in national delegations to the General Assembly and global summits should be strengthened. We propose that the Secretary-General should organize public debates and hearings on major issues to which should be invited parliamentarians, local constituencies, Civil Society, the academic world, etc. We conclude that there should not be an absolute stop to global conferences, but that there still may be some on major issues.

We propose that the Security Council's work be reformed, particularly in the way that the 'Arria Formula' is used systematically, inviting Civil Society to a dialogue with the Security Council. Every delegation of the Security Council, that visits an area in conflict or with problems, should always meet with representatives of Civil Society. We propose that the Security Council should arrange seminars and public hearings on questions of importance from time to time.

We are addressing a number of other issues as well. We propose a totally new system of accreditation of CSOs to the United Nations to be handled by a unit under the General Assembly. With the approval of Member States, the Secretary-General should appoint an Under-Secretary-General in charge of a new Office of Constituency Engagement and Partnerships (OCEP) comprising:

- A Civil Society Unit to absorb the Non-Governmental Liaison Service.
- A Partnership Development Unit to absorb the United Nations Fund for International Partnerships.
- An Elected Representatives Liaison Unit.
- The Global Compact Office.
- The Secretariat of the Permanent Forum on Indigenous Issues.

The Panel suggests the establishment of a special Fund to enhance Southern Civil Society capacity to engage in UN deliberative processes, operations and partnerships.

The Panel urges the Secretary-General to use his capacity as chairman of the United Nations system coordination mechanism to encourage all agencies, including the Bretton Woods Institutions, to enhance their engagement with Civil Society and other actors, and to cooperate with one another across the system to promote this aim, with periodic progress reviews.

The Panel invites the Member States to encourage, through the forums of the United Nations, an enabling policy environment for Civil Society throughout the world and expanded dialogue and partnership opportunities in development processes. The Secretariat leadership, resident coordinators and governance specialists should use their dialogues with governments to similar effect.

The basic idea in our Report is that the United Nations should exercise global leadership in a world where the multilateral system and international cooperation is changing. It is not any longer omni-governmental – only governments meeting with each other, agreeing on the lowest common denominator. We need a multilateral society, which is characterized by coalitions of the willing seeking cooperation around the highest common principle. Coalitions of the promoters of the good alternative that want to join their forces to create a better world – to get things changed quicker than they could otherwise have been achieved.

In such a way we could, in our time, realize the classical vision of the close connection between peace and democracy.

How and what truly effective measures should we introduce in the UNGA, the ECOSOC and other multilateral organizations to comply with the commitments taken at UN conferences and summits, including the MDGs?

Renata Bloem, CIVICUS representative and President of the Conference of NGOs in Consultative Relationship with the United Nations (CONGO)

How and what truly effective measures should we introduce in the UNGA, the ECOSOC and other multilateral organizations to comply with the commitments taken at UN conferences and summits, including the MDGs?

*   The High-level meeting of the General Assembly (September 2005), convened to endorse the most ambitious reform proposal of the UN since its creation, has not lived up to the expectations of NGOs, as expressed in the first ever Hearings of the General Assembly with CSOs in June 2005.

Most notably, NGOs had underlined the need of a strengthened ECOSOC that would become a high-level development forum. It was argued that for the UN reform to be effective there must be a reinvention of the WB and the WTO and a coordination mechanism with enforceable power over all intergovernmental organizations.

- This mechanism has certainly not been created and this may be the reason of our gathering here today. However, the Outcome Document adopted by 175 heads of state and government contains a strong commitment in favour of the strengthening and empowering of ECOSOC, since it recognizes:

> *The need for a more effective ECOSOC as a principal body for coor-*
> *dination, policy review, policy dialogue and recommendations on*
> *issues of economic and social development, as well as for the imple-*
> *mentation of the international development goals agreed at the major*
> *UN summits and conferences, including the MDG.*[15]

In order to do so, ECOSOC should 'hold a biennial high-level Development Cooperation Forum (DCF) to review trends in international development cooperation, promote greater coherence among the development activities of different development partners and strengthen the links between the normative and operational work of the UN'. Even though only biannual, the creation of this Development Cooperation Forum mirrors the expectations of NGOs.

ECOSOC is also expected to 'hold annual ministerial-level substantive reviews to assess progress of the MDGs, drawing on its functional and regional commissions and other international institutions'.

ECOSOC is also mandated to 'play a major role in the overall coordination of funds, programmes and agencies, ensuring coordination among them and avoiding duplication of mandates and activities'.

Finally, the outcome document acknowledges that 'in order to fully perform the above functions, the organization of work, the agenda and the current methods of work of ECOSOC should be adapted'.

What has happened to date?

The draft resolution of the General Assembly on Strengthening the Economic and Social Council has decided that:

- The biennial high-level Development Cooperation Forum would be held within the framework of the ECOSOC High-level Segment (HLS) to review progress in international cooperation, identify gaps and obstacles, exchange lessons learned. This Forum will be open to civil society and other stakeholders.

- Concerning the annual ministerial level reviews, these should also be part of the HLS with a cross-sectoral approach.

What does CONGO do?

The Conference of NGOs in Consultative Relationship with the UN (CONGO) strives to fill the deficit in global governance by creating spaces where NGOs can give targeted input into UN decision-making bodies.

Therefore CONGO has organized for years now NGO forums prior to the ECOSOC HLS in order to produce recommendations that would hopefully impact into the Ministerial Declaration. The theme of the forums was drawn from the one of the HLS and it has been, for example, rural development in 2003 and employment and decent work in 2006. In 2006 we have also managed to discuss interactively the recommendations with dignitaries and high-level UN officials, even though not in an institutionalized way yet.

For the next few years, we intend to organize major development forums prior to ECOSOC sessions, focusing each time on the issue of the session and on MDGs (MDG+, including decent work and gender equality). The idea is to cover all MDGs by 2015 and to see how civil society can have an impact into their realization. The launch of the first DCF will be held during the 2007 HLS of ECOSOC, in Geneva.

Our aim is to involve always closer civil society in the decision-shaping of UN organs. Even though the final decision-making power lies exclusively with the States, we believe that NGOs can help governments take the most appropriate decisions to reduce poverty and reach the MDGs. ECOSOC being the UN institutional partner for NGOs, we most naturally concentrate on this principal UN organ, particularly if it lives up to the 2005 Summit expectations and really manages to become *the* overall international development forum.

Reform of International Institutions: Dialogues between different levels of governance and civil society actors

William R. Pace and Lene Schumacher,
World Federalist Movement (WFM)

As many of you know, WFM has the great honour to serve as the Secretariat and convener of the NGO Coalition for the International

Criminal Court, which is one of the most successful civil society and human security campaigns ever.

Also, having mentioned the CICC, I want to point out that it is seen as one of the greatest examples of the so-called 'new diplomacy' model of reforming existing and creating new international laws and institutions. During this process global civil society coalitions from the South and North have worked in informal partnership with like-minded governments from different regions and government groupings, and when possible leaders of international organizations, to establish strong new global governance goals. The convention establishing ICC and the one banning landmines are the most well known examples of the effectiveness of this new diplomacy – a strategy that we apply to our goals for deep reform of international organizations.

The WFM is a 60-year-old international NGO. We advocate for the creation of democratic global structures accountable to and representative of not only states, but also the citizens of the world. Inspired by the democratic and human rights values of federalist political philosophy, WFM believes that international democracy requires legal and institutional structures to underpin a responsive, accountable system of democratic global governance.

The questions before us are thus central to WFM's mandate which is also why I thought of starting by giving a short outline of the developments within the World and Regional Federalist Movements before outlining some of our proposals for reform of the UN, specifically focusing on Security Council reform and the importance of independent funding of multilateralism.

WFM was established not far from here in Montreaux in 1947 as a coalition of peace movements, largely as a reaction to the two catastrophic world wars, and also because our founders and many peace leaders believed that there were fundamental flaws in the newly adopted UN Charter. While the UN and its Charter showed a tremendous commitment to cooperation by the international community, it was clear already in 1946 and 1947 that the deficiencies of the new Charter and structure of the UN would not allow it to achieve even its first preambular goal – 'to save future generations from the scourge of war'.

In particular, several major flaws determined its inability to maintain international peace and security:

- It did not establish international enforceable law to end anarchy and imperialism of political and economic powers.
- It did not prevent major powers from re-occupying territories, and trying to re-establish their empires.

- The Security Council was fundamentally flawed in its conception. The victors of World War II were given permanent membership status and the veto powers. Thus, the new international legal order allowed for these nations to be treated in an exceptional way to how the rest of the states would be treated – a fundamental violation of democratic principles of law.

Within the World Federalist Movement two different approaches emerged in terms of how to address these shortcomings:

Those groups who believed the UN was thus too flawed and that peace advocates should call for its dissolution – that the UN Charter should be replaced with a 'World Government' Charter.

Those who believed instead that the best strategy for world peace was to work to strengthen and reform the United Nations system and the Charter to replace the rule of anarchy with the rule of law.

The latter prevailed within the Movement, which I will get back to later in this presentation.

Regional organizations vs. international organization

It is significant to note that this new world peace movement also split at its founding meeting over the issue of regional federation. Most of the European groups within the Movement were convinced that since Europe was the source of the last two world wars and most of the imperialism and colonialism of the past centuries, they must first get their own 'house' in order. Thus, these groups mainly focused on regional European Federalism. They were driven by the philosophy that until the European region was integrated and organized, one could not expect to organize the world community. It was expected that a world federation would grow out of the European federation and other regional federations as they would pursue limited unification sometime in the future.

Other World Federalists were against regional federalism, noting that without global laws nothing would prevent the regions from going to war against each other.

Our Movement struggled with these debates for 40 years.

Now, 60 years later the vote is in:

- Regional and sub-regional organizations are working together and relating to the global institutions.

While the danger of regions going to war against each other still remains – and even more so today in the context of 'war on terrorism' – the serious problem of the 21st century is the lack of international democracy and the rule of law within the regional and sub-regional organizations.

The European Union is the greatest achievement of international democracy in all history. Though it is a weak federation, it has been tremendously successful in preventing wars among its members. Similarly, we are seeing the African continent, with its new charter, strongly seeking to move towards replacing the rule of anarchy and force with the rule of law.

Latin America remains fearful of imperialism and occupation, but this region also has progressed in establishing greater regional and sub-regional economic and political governance, especially for human rights purposes, for example, in the Organization of American States.

Asia and CIS (Commonwealth of Independent States) remain the least willing to develop regional and sub-regional unions based on enforceable democratic rule of law.

United Nations – international democratic deficit

While there has been important progress at the regional level, we meet today as the imbalance in global governance has grown even greater. The Cold War represented a mortal confrontation between the East and the West. The challenge of these times is to avoid a perhaps even more danger-ous clash being drawn between North and South.

In addressing this and in spite of its shortcomings, the UN is still the best mechanism that we have.

WFM believes the UN is not only not irrelevant, but indispensable for pursuing world peace in the 21st century. The UN is at the centre of the international legal order and plays a vital role in bringing all govern-ments together to address the issues of democracy, human rights and rule of law.

The UN's decisions thus confer a unique legitimacy and moral and political authority, having been reached by both North and South, East and West, despite extreme differences. The democratic principle is thus at the core of the UN. It is its purpose and must be its fate.

One of the greatest tragedies, however, remains the impact of perma-nent membership and the veto. Thus, three great national democracies continue to be primary opponents of international democracy. In the last few years, this plague spot has infected other governments – at least ten other powerful nations, most national democracies, have campaigned to be given the same 'P-5' powers, thus undermining the integrity of their national political principles in demanding that they become regional hege-monies in the UN.

Unfortunately, we see it on a daily basis; national democracies behaving undemocratically internationally, resulting in a serious global democratic deficit.

The historic evolvement of international institutions is a similarly grim picture – a picture of destruction and human suffering necessary to force advances in international cooperation. It took World War I to get agreement of many governments to finally create a League of Nations, and the even greater destruction and holocaust of World War II for the United Nations to be created.

Some thus fear that a World War III would be necessary in order to reach the political will for the next generation of global governance: the creation of a limited but world legal union enforcing disarmament, providing basic human rights and sustainability.

However, humanity most likely would not survive such a war, so we must put all our efforts into pursuing this goal through a gradual – and peaceful – reform of the existing system of international institutions.

Security Council and veto

As many know, the last century has been the most violent ever and the first six years of this century are not promising any change. No principle UN organ has failed in its responsibility as much as the Security Council.

One should not underestimate the power of the veto – or rather the power of the threat or even possibility of the veto – both inside the Security Council and in other inter-governmental processes. Thus at the heart of the matter of democratic global governance is the reform of the Security Council: it must be reformed to be a more democratic, accountable, transparent and peace-preserving body. Both in terms of membership but just as importantly reform of working methods.

However, now that the most powerful countries have given themselves constitutional powers to enforce international law on other countries but not on themselves, immediate fundamental reform of the current international legal order is not possible. None of the powerful states will give up these exceptional rights overnight. The only way to achieve a strong and democratic international legal order is to do it piece (peace) by peace by piece (can be with either *ie* or *ea*).

Currently, most of the world's largest arms dealers run the Security Council. It is thus an important factor to create an international structure that does not allow large economic sectors to encourage war for their own economic benefits. Entire sectors of the global economy that do not benefit from arms production or trade must be mobilized against this trend –

sectors such as clothing, food, health, education, housing and tourism, whose economic activities are completely disrupted by war.

Per definition, permanent members are not vulnerable to democratic elective repercussions for failures or misconduct. This imbalanced and unrepresentative structure has allowed for individual national political agendas to influence, and even obstruct, the maintenance of international peace and security. WFM therefore strongly supports the idea of adding more elected members to the Security Council and believe that 20 elected members could allow for a much more democratic and powerful counterpart to the five permanent members.

Veto

The most pressing reform of the Security Council's working methods is to work with many small and middle power nations to encourage the P-5 to limit their use of the veto.

For example, it is of utmost importance to work towards a limited use of the veto and veto abstention in cases of genocide and large-scale human rights abuses, as called for within the principles of Responsibility to Protect (R2P). Indeed, proposals for voluntary restrictions of veto are highly appropriate, just as there needs to be continuous pressure on the permanent members to restrict the misuse of their veto powers, as proscribed in international treaties such as the Rome Statute of the ICC.

The ICC treaty is another way to approach veto reform, for the Rome Statute actually turns the veto on its head – that is, the veto cannot be used to stop the ICC from investigating or prosecuting war crimes, the veto can only be used to prevent the Security Council from interfering with the ICC.

Limited use of the veto could also be achieved through 'indicative voting', by which members of the Security Council could call for a public indication of positions on a proposed action. This would considerably increase not only the Security Council's transparency but also accountability.

The best way to achieve limited use of veto would be to pressure countries to honour democratic principles at national level and force them to act democratically internationally. The EU members on the Council could also agree to subordinate their veto to the EU.

Equal international authority and status

WFM calls for democratic institutions that can help facilitate debate on and implementation of international law, not only within the area of peace and security, human rights, trade, finances and labour, but the global environment as well.

WFM believes that if we are to have a World Trade Organization, World Bank, International Labour Organization, World Health Organization – it is a moral and legal travesty that global environmental protection is only afforded the status of a voluntary funded programme.

WFM has long advocated for a global structure that would give appropriate legal and institutional authority to global environmental issues to counterbalance the powerful trade and financial international institutions.

The UN Environment Programme, for example, should thus be upgraded to the same level as other international organizations, with the same legal status even if it will not have the same level of funding. A World Environment Organization should replace the UNEP, as the essential step towards a more equitable, effective and accountable system of global governance.

Independent funding for democratic global governance

For multilateral institutions to be effective and independent they must have stable and adequate funding. There is a fundamental need for new and innovative financial mechanisms to provide a strengthened and democratized multilateral system. At present the most powerful countries provide the vast majority of funding for international organizations, and exercise an immense and unbalanced control over the political decisions. Many organizations are intentionally massively under-funded to ensure dependency on few donor countries.

To reverse this trend, WFM calls for a mixture of state and independent funding to ensure more fair and democratic decision-making processes in international organizations, less vulnerable to economic power politics. Such independent funding would help overcome key challenges and obstacles for achieving democratic global governance such as the one-dollar-one-vote approach advanced by the US and Japan among others.

Equally important, we must create an international mechanism to regulate Multinational Corporations' increasing power in the global economy. With incomes at the size and even bigger than the GDP of some governments, Corporations must be controlled by appropriate international law. Such policies are ensured by law at national level; hence international law should be used to provide similar regulations at global level.

Closing

Among the least known achievements of the 2005 UN summit was that governments formally recognized that the UN has three pillars: development, human rights, and peace and security. In addition, the world leaders affirmed the need for the world community to continue to work for the advancement of democracy. Seeking national, regional and democratic global governance in the pursuit of the three UN pillars is a vital path to achieving peace and justice and sustainable prosperity for all on our increasingly fragile planet.

In order for the UN's strengths to outweigh its weaknesses, its institutions and decision-making processes must democratize further.

Multilateralism and the reform of international institutions

Juan Eduardo Eguiguren, Deputy Permanent Representative of Chile to the International Organizations in Geneva

The 21st century is seeing the complications ahead, and it is nothing like what was expected at the turn of the century. I will not delve into the main features characterizing the present-day international situation, which look set to become major points of reference in the future. These are difficult times, and yet they are times in which much must be done for peace and security, development and intercultural understanding.

Let us recall how the world's leaders agreed, at the end of a terrible war 60 years ago, to set up international institutions that would help humanity to preserve peace and to achieve development. 'Liberation from poverty' and 'liberation from fear' were the aims which, together, might sum up what all humanity was aspiring to. These aims are more relevant than ever now, as we recall the relationship of interdependence linking the three components of the triad formed by peace, development and human rights.

The relevance of multilateralism in the 21st century

I sincerely believe that multilateral action – multilateralism – is one of the chief tools available to the international community for coping with the problems we have now and those that will come in the future. Chile as a country is firmly convinced that multilateralism can make a substantial contribution in attending to and dealing with the multiple challenges now facing our peoples. We believe that multilateral decisions and actions possess the necessary legitimacy and universality to make them effective, as well as giving us the feeling that we have all made a contribution to them.

Though this assertion may be seen as somewhat unrealistic, in fact it is not. In this respect, I would like to stress how multilateralism can prove effective in times of crisis.

11 September 2001 stands as a watershed marking a profound change in the contemporary international system. However, it is important to bear in

mind that a deep and immediate sense of international solidarity emerged in the aftermath of that tragedy, and for a while – regrettably not for very long – multilateralism began to work with an effectiveness rarely witnessed previously.

Let us recall the actions of the Security Council in the days that followed after 11 September. On 12 September the Security Council approved Resolution 1368 condemning terrorist actions (and doing so with a sense of urgency but without making the mistake of jumping to conclusions about those responsible for the attack, even though there was clear evidence by then); the Resolution voiced feelings of sympathy and condolence for the families of the victims, and for the people and the government of the United States; it called on all States to work together to hold to account those responsible and their sponsors; and it signalled a readiness to do all that was necessary to respond to terrorist actions.

Just 17 days afterwards, on 28 September, the Security Council adopted Resolution 1373 by consensus as the paramount multilateral instrument for fighting terrorism, making major demands of States – demands of a kind that might otherwise, at other times and in other forums, have taken months (or maybe years) to negotiate – as well as creating the Counter-Terrorism Committee. Then came two resolutions concerning Afghanistan, also passed unanimously: Resolution 1378 of 14 November, in which the Council, lending its backing to international actions to root out terrorism, condemned the Taliban regime and supported efforts to establish a transitional administration in Afghanistan; and Resolution 1383 of December, endorsing the Agreement on Provisional Arrangements in Afghanistan.

As we can see, in the months following 11 September, multilateral action proved dynamic and effective, as well as being backed by consensus, and it achieved results that could hardly have been expected in other circumstances. It is nonetheless true that the security agenda and the fight against terrorism became the chief focus, to the detriment of development issues and the attention paid to major conflicts.

Yet there was more still: the Security Council also tackled the Middle East question, which was then going through extremely difficult times.

Accordingly, the Security Council approved Resolution 1397 on 12 March 2002 concerning that conflict, it being perhaps the most important Resolution to have been passed in recent years. Support was given to the notion of a region in which two States, Israel and Palestine, would live side by side, each within secure, officially recognized borders. It also expressed concern over the tragic, violent events that had continued to occur since September 2000; the diplomatic efforts of the Quartet and other contributions were embraced; the immediate cessation of all acts of violence was demanded, while urging the Israeli and Palestinian sides to apply the Tenet work plan and the recommendations of the 'Mitchell Report' with a view to recommencing negotiations on a political arrangement. That same year also brought other resolutions on the Middle East in response to the serious situation prevailing there.

Consequently, it was hoped at that time that these events could mark the beginning of a new stage in the international sphere, one in which, since the political will was there, multilateralism would set to work in the other main bodies, such as the General Assembly and the ECOSOC, on the field of development and on other areas that were of urgent interest to the system. Moreover, it could also be confirmed that the multilateral approach can indeed be positive and effective for all involved, including the great powers.

Regrettably, progress along that new path was frustrated by the way the Iraq issue was handled.

Envisioning the United Nations system in the coming decades

I would like to point out that the United Nations has achieved a great deal over its 60-year history. There have of course been shortfalls, omissions and unfortunate decisions. Moreover, realities change, and international institutions have to adapt to the changes. That is why it is essential to go further with reforming the intergovernmental system. It cannot be denied that change is possible, albeit difficult to achieve. This is demonstrated in achieving the Millennium Development Goals, which are geared towards the action that the international community has taken upon itself and which we must strive to fulfil. For its part, the '2005 World Summit Outcome Document' also shows us that world leaders can take significant steps when there is a will to do so. We may recall here that among the results of that Summit were the creation of the Human Rights Council and the Peacebuilding Commission, two fundamental bodies that must now be implemented in practice. Furthermore, the notion of human security was embraced by the General Assembly, enabling the individual to be highlighted as a focus of attention for the international system.

However, major reforms are still pending; beginning with the reform of the Security Council, a prominent body that was designed with the world as it was 60 years ago in mind, and that must now be adapted to the realities of the 21st century. We must also seek to give the General Assembly a weightier role, since it is the main organ of the United Nations and represents the whole world, and to get the ECOSOC to live up to all that was expected of it when it was created. It has become necessary to go further in updating and adapting our multilateral institutions to the reality we must face. And while we persevere in seeking reform, we must also watch over the Charter of the United Nations, which has room for improvement, and over international law and the institutions of the system as well.

In this connection, the High-Level Panel on System-Wide Coherence within the United Nations, created by the Secretary-General for the spheres of development, humanitarian assistance and the environment, has done important work. As you know, that Panel presented its report to the General Assembly a few days ago under the title 'Delivering as One', it being the result of over six months' work. It was an honour for us to have the former Chilean president Mr. Ricardo Lagos participating in that Panel.

The Panel's report contains a set of recommendations aimed at overcoming the fragmentation now reigning at the United Nations, and seeks a better approach to the system's operation, efficiency, accountability and results. The Panel members portray this new era of the 21st century as one of unprecedented global change in terms of the speed, breadth and scale of change. Now that the world is tending to be increasingly interdependent, we are exposed to growing social and economic inequalities. This report is now in the hands of the General Assembly, and we hope the Assembly will build proactively on its important recommendations.

Factors to take into account in reforming the international system in the 21st century

I think it is important to consider some of the factors – not all of them, of course – that should be taken into account in readying our international institutions for attending to the problems of this century, clearing the way for effective multilateral action.

- **We must all contribute to reforming the international institutions.** When the United Nations was founded, the main contributors were the countries of the West and of Latin America, plus a few non-Western States. In other words, the West set in motion an international institutional model to which scores of new countries were later added through decolonization, countries that now form a majority among the members of the organization, which is thus privileged with the wealth gained by its global cultural diversity.

In the reforms which have come in recently and in those still to come in the future, it is important that all countries make their contribution from the standpoint of their own diverse realities, the central objective in this process being placing the individual and his or her dignity as the focus of attention.

- **Intergovernmental administration needs to be reformed.** The administration of the United Nations system needs to be thoroughly examined. The idea is not just to see what is happening in the various agencies, programmes, funds and mechanisms in the system, but also to get the decisions of the organs of multilateral government to work along the same lines. We are indeed all responsible in this. Decisions involving the use of resources must be properly oriented and there must be coordination and consistency across all those decisions.

Among the High-Level Panel's various recommendations, it is proposed that the Secretary-General set up an independent task force aimed at eradicating duplication, overlapping functions, failures of coordination and any inconsistencies between policies within the United Nations System. This task is fundamental, and I believe that it is hoped thereby to achieve greater transparency in the activities of the international institutions.

The issues of consistency and administration must necessarily be taken into account in reforming the international institutions. And financial resources, which are scarce, must target chiefly those who need them.

- **A prominent role for civil society.** In recent times, civil society has been taking an increasingly weighty role in the sphere of international multilateral institutions. This has proved beneficial for the system. This conference is itself an example of the role that civil society is now playing: taking the lead in putting forward proposals, sounding the alert over particular situations, drawing attention to challenges and problems, attempting to frame a responsible critique, and seeking transparency.

We ought to have moved on by now from the issue often raised in various international forums regarding how non-governmental organizations should be represented and should participate in intergovernmental meetings of all kinds (Conference of the Parties (CoPs), preparatory processes, etc.). There are times when that debate claims more time and even takes precedence over the topic being discussed.

It would be advisable for the participation of civil society to be permanently instituted in the United Nations system and in the various multilateral bodies, and the private sector too. The 'World Summit on the Information Society' was very positive in this respect, in that the NGOs, the private sector and the academic world were able to make contributions of substance to the discussions. Another example of full participation by civil society that should be weighed up is the case of the recent Internet Governance Forum.

Closing words

While there may well be several other important considerations regarding the governance of international institutions in the 21st century, I would like to wind up by reasserting two aspects that I regard as central. Firstly, multilateralism is not only possible, but necessary. When there is a real political will, multilateral action can be effective, and beneficial for us all. Secondly, multilateralism will be all the more effective if it is framed in institutions that are appropriate for the realities of today. Consequently, the need for certain reforms is insisted upon, and we must all contribute to that and feel ourselves to be fully involved in this. In those reforms, the administration of intergovernmental institutions must be thoroughly examined. Lastly, it must be reiterated that the involvement of civil society is fundamental in this process.

11

Proposals on Reforming the General Assembly of the UN and the World Parliament

A system of international institutions, once thoroughly reformed, should, firstly, seek to resolve the problem of its own democratic legitimacy in order to empower itself before both international political players and the world's citizens. In a world in which States are no longer the only international political players and in which many problems have and require a global scale and vision, **how should we understand and apply the concepts of legitimacy, sovereignty, democracy, etc.?**

Could the above problem be resolved by reforming the composition of the General Assembly (for example, a composition similar to that of the international agency hosting this meeting, that is, one formed by many different stakeholders) or by introducing a two-chamber-type system, creating a world parliament formed by representatives?

Some proposals on reforming the General Assembly of the UN and the World Parliament

Improving the functioning of the General Assembly
- Creation of a general UNGA committee and specific work groups.
- Increasing its supervisory capacity over UN organizations and programmes.
- Effective control of UN agencies and all multilateral institutions.
- Joint UNGA and UNSC working group in order to institutionalize consultations and reports.
- Empowerment to consult the ICJ in cases of doubt as to the constitutionality of UNSC resolutions.
- Greater participation in decision-making about intervention and the establishment of rapid response forces to prevent conflicts and maintain peace.

- Creating an Inter-parliamentary Assembly (composed of members of parliament, this being an organism that would coordinate the national parliaments) with follow-up functions on matters pertaining to the UNGA could contribute towards improving democracy in the system.

The UN General Assembly should evolve – substantive reform – with the progressive unification of the other already-existing assemblies and general conferences, until it has a central role in the system, authority to adopt binding resolutions and to exercise effective control over the other organizations, agencies, funds, programmes and institutions of the system.

The creation of an independent Assembly of Representatives (World Parliament) with consultative functions within the UN system, and the holding of World Referendums that would have consultative status, could make a major contribution towards improving the democratic functioning of the system.

A system of international institutions subject to in-depth reforms should be based on:

- A two-chamber system representing the states and citizens of the world.
- Unification of general assemblies and conferences into a single institution with a central role in the system: UNGA.
- Binding authority: capacity to adopt binding resolutions.
- An Assembly of Representatives – World Parliament: direct representation of the world's population by universal suffrage with:
  - Participation in the international legislative process;
  - capacity to make recommendations to other organizations in the system;
  - capacity to exercise parliamentary control over other organizations in the system.

Reforming global institutions: lessons from European experience

Antonio Papisca, Chairholder of the UNESCO Chair in Human Rights, Democracy and Peace at the University of Padua

The difficult transition towards a new, more humane and sustainable world order can be read with the metaphor of the delivery, in our case of a very troubled childbirth. Who should be born, that is the outcome of the transition, is more than a mere wish, it is already a well recognizable map.

I mean that the world order we need does exist as a project whose identity we can actually reconstruct by using parts that are really existing. In other words, we have not to imagine the baby; we have to help him to live and to develop.

A further metaphor is that of the mosaic: we cannot make the mosaic without the tesseras, the tesseras are there but the mosaic will not appear unless somebody arranges the tesseras.

With this twofold metaphor I would emphasize that the key elements of a stable and sustainable world order do really exist – I refer to the moral and juridical paradigm of human rights internationally recognized, to the International Law rooted in the United Nations Charter, multilateral institutions, actors, historical circumstances – but the coherent outcome has not yet appeared because the political actor which has the inherent capacity to arrange the tesseras lacks the courage to cope with that task, firstly by making visible the model of world order.

I urge on the necessity of making visible that project, of making people aware that we are not groping in the dark, that it is possible to resist the ideology of Realpolitik determinism, that in the second half of the 20th century we have some positive achievements (epiphanies of global good governance) that it is unreasonable to give up to.

I would add a third metaphor. In the 1940s a generous and far-sighted sowing of 'universals' took place: especially, the 'UN Charter', the 'Universal Declaration of Human Rights', the United Nations Organization, the UN system of specialized agencies. Then we could say that the planet is like a house with a lot of useful household appliances and sophisticated facilities, that are not properly exploited.

In the middle of the last century a human-centric revolution started and it has already changed the DNA of the world system: today, nobody would say, at least as a matter of principle, that the principle of the respect of human dignity should subordinate to state's sovereignty. Apartheid and colonialism are perceived as taboos, security and development are more and more perceived as people security, and people development, unilateralism, although emphasized by the superpower leadership, is considered unnatural and costly in both moral and economic terms.

Before a situation that is providing not only conflicts and confusion but also a lot of opportunities, we can actually wonder whether the European Union is the very political actor that is capable of collecting and arranging the tesseras of the mosaic, of giving rise to the birth of the baby, of making household appliances working.

The big task is to recapitulate the seeds and the fruits of the fertile sowing of universal values into a coherent strategy of world peace building, that is, to develop and improve that common heritage.

To take over that flag, two kinds of power resources are needed for the candidate actor: moral consistency and appeal, and governance capacities. I mean that the actor is primarily asked to lead by example. Is this the case for the European Union? I shall try to provide a hopefully comprehensive response by articulating it in several 'lessons' drawn by the empirical evidence of more than 50 years of functioning of the European integration system. I envisage those lessons as being significant for the whole international community. I emphasize positive aspects, bearing in mind the huge assumption that the EU should be more consistent and coherent both *ad intra* and *ad extra* of its own system.

First lesson

The European integration process is a convincing example of how it is possible to construct lasting peace among those states and peoples and religious entities that for many centuries were fighting each other. The main independent variable of the overall process is the firm will of a group of far-sighted political leaders sharing the same basket of moral values and the same operational approach.

Second lesson

The European system is a living laboratory of reciprocate learning among different political systems and cultures, which facilitates intercultural dialogue in a very complex historical context.

Third lesson

The European system is a laboratory of multi-and-supra-national governance based on the principle of subsidiarity, both territorial and functional. We could say that the system is proving to be successful in carrying out the twofold task of 'agenda development' and 'institution building', in order to meet in a suitable way the governance needs stemming from the crisis of both the state 'capacities' and the state 'form' (structural crisis of traditional statehood) and of the democratic practice. The crisis is the result of the political impact of globalization that deprives states of the power to decide in many fields and of the space in which meaningful democracy can actually go on. The European Union is the extra-national system in which new and more sophisticated forms of governance – better, of statehood – are actually pursued.

Fourth lesson

The European system is pioneering the experience of international democracy, I mean of genuine transnational democracy as:

- Legitimatization of supranational political institutions through direct election of a parliamentary body.
- Participation of civil society organizations and groups to the decision-making process at the supranational level. In this case we see significant results of the curriculum development.

At the beginning of the European Communities there were neither elections nor physiologic civil society participation. Gradually the European system moved from a 'Parliamentary Assembly' to a real 'Parliament', and from a lobbying practice limited to powerful economic interest groups to the enlargement of access channels for civil society organizations, including local government entities. In particular, as regards participation we have two institutional outcomes: the creation of the Committee of Regions and Local Powers and the starting of the so-called 'civil dialogue', that will complement the already established 'social dialogue'.

Fifth lesson

The European Union is metabolizing the internationally recognized paradigm of human rights inside and outside its own system. EU member states fully comply, at least from a formal point of view, with the requirements of human rights, the rule of law and democratic principles. But this was considered non-sufficient for the holistic institutional architecture of the EU, in which so many heavy decisions are daily taken. Now we havet the EU 'Charter of Fundamental Rights', that successfully advocates for its inclusion in the 'Constitutional Treaty' and then for the full 'constitutionalization' of the overall system. Furthermore, the EU is visibly championing the effectiveness of the International Law rooted in the 'UN Charter', and especially the 'International Law of Human Rights' and the 'international rule of law' as emphasized by the UN Secretary-General. The EU has established the practice of the 'human rights clause' in the treaties with third countries, and it was campaigning – orally and with huge financial support – for the establishment and the entering into function of the International Criminal Court. These are good indicators of the human rights advocacy.

Sixth lesson

The European Union is gradually enlarging both concept and practice of citizenship. The 'Maastricht Treaty' established the 'EU citizenship' as a basket of rights that are additional to those of the only citizens of EU member states: it is an enlarged citizenship, of course, but always *ad excludendum*. The EU 'Charter of Fundamental Rights', proclaimed in Nice in December 2000, regards individuals as 'human beings' (*personnes humaines*), not as 'registry citizens' of a given state. For sure this new outcome – citizenship *ad includendum* – is challenging the discriminatory approach of the original 'EU citizenship'. Also from this point of view, the European integration process shows it to be a laboratory of structural change according to universal ethics requirements, finally an example for the entire world.

Seventh lesson

The 'conventional way' to the institution-building process is strictly linked with the comprehensive democratic lesson stemming from the EU. So far, we had two experiences of 'European Convention', the first on human rights (the EU Charter is the outcome), the second on the EU future. The lesson says that for some important goals to be achieved, the supranational (summit) decision-making needs to be complemented by an enlarged input, including the most significant actors of the subsidiarity game. The intrinsic value of the Convention resides in the magnitude and variety of membership, that allows to gather and build up, through participation of a large typology of actors, both ideas and legitimacy.

For sure we could find out further lessons, but all those mentioned above are enough to make the European integration process an impressive example for all and the European Union a credible actor in world politics. But the actor has not yet the capability to use those lessons as resources of power – very legitimate resources indeed: the lack of an EU 'single voice' in world politics, despite the fact that it has a home single currency, well indicates a persistent, exasperating deficiency. And the lessons could be a boomerang for the EU in the sense that it has to meet external expectations of political effectiveness as well as internal expectations for more coherence and consistency.

In the world system, the European Union is urged to cope with the magnitude of its achievements; it bears a moral duty to act as it is, a power marked by successful human rights mainstreaming, successful peacebuilding and democratization.

In this moment, priority should be given to the arrangement of tesseras of the world order mosaic, bearing in mind that behind economic deregulation there is a strategy of institutional deregulation, that means undermining the system of organized multilateralism, of supranational criminal justice, of collective security, of nonprofit transnationalism. Furthermore, bearing in mind that the destiny of the (new) International Law is strictly linked with the destiny of the United Nations, of multilateralism and of the entire system of international organizations. If we give up to the latter we shall have neither suitable machinery to implement human rights and pursue collective security goals, nor a suitable place for extending the practice of democracy.

Then which task for the EU with regards in particular the UN future? As a priority, the European Union should make, and comply with, what I would call the 'preferential choice for the United Nations'. On the EU international agenda, the first item should read 'Strengthening and democratizing the United Nations', in order to make clear that the democratization of the UN would enhance its capacities.

UN democratization should be conceived as a process that urgently:

- will provide more representativeness to the Security Council, hopefully reorganizing its membership on regional basis;
- will establish a UN Parliamentary Assembly, as a second UN General Assembly, and a permanent Global Civil Society Forum;
- will enhance the role of both non-governmental organizations and local government institutions;
- will reinforce the ECOSOC functions in pursuing social justice goals including the empowerment of the UN human rights machinery;
- will establish a permanent UN police force (both civil and military);
- will enlarge the mandate of the International Criminal Court and further empower it by human and material resources.

Assuming that these are priority items on the operational agenda of the European Union, how to make it credible and actually working, by which means and methods?

Bearing in mind the useless work done by several UN internal 'working groups' on the UN reform in the last decade, I dare to suggest (only) one major initiative aimed at providing healthy, plural inputs and a really constituent dynamism to the overall reform undertaking: the UE should propose to address the UN development with the scheme of the Convention ('We, the Peoples [...]'), then by establishing a 'Universal Convention for strengthening and democratizing the United Nations'.

This ad hoc 'body' would not be a mere 'working group', but a real constituent entity, with the mandate of drafting a coherent set of formal proposals. By this way it should be possible to overcome what until now has proved to be the real obstacle to the reforming process that is a strict, exclusive, self-sufficient, finally sterile inter-governmental approach.

It should be appointed by the UN General Assembly (veto power would be avoided and the 'UN Charter' not affected).

Membership would read as follows:

- UN member states, by regional groupings;
- representatives of the UN system institutions;
- representatives of 'regional' organizations;

- representatives of national parliaments (through the Interparliamentary Union?);
- representatives of local government institutions (International Union of Local Authorities – IULA+ United Cities?);
- representatives of the NGO networks;
- permanent Observers (Holy See, ...).

An ad hoc web-site should be open to inputs from civil society and academic *milieux*. The 'UN Universal Convention' should convey its formal output to the General Assembly.

Institutional architecture for world democracy: the issue of the UN General Assembly and the World Parliament

Heidi Hautala, Euro MP for Finland and Chair of the Finnish Service Centre for Development Cooperation (KEPA)

> As you will see, all that the Secretariat of the World Campaign and the UBUNTU Forum has of Ms Heidi Hautala's talk is her outline of it. Even so, since the outline is self-explanatory and since it is of great interest in our view, we have left it in the form of that original outline in this publication.

I. Towards global democracy
- 'At the national level, there is democracy but no choice. At the global level, there is choice but no democracy' (George Monbiot 2004).
- Every citizen should have a say at all levels which affect his/her life.

II. Democratic deficiency of global government
- United Nations the only truly universal global organization
    - Legitimacy undermined.
- The Bretton Woods institutions
    - Economic power (US) dominance.
    - Large scale resistance of e.g. IMF structural adjustment programmes.
- WTO
    - Undemocratic nature of procedures.
    - Large-scale effects in Member States.

III. Presented solutions
- Enhancing participation in preparation of decision-making.
- Multi-stakeholder processes.
- Increasing direct democracy.
- Referendums.
- 'Citizens' veto', e.g. Denmark, Ireland.
- Citizens' initiatives.
- New EU Constitution Art I-47.
- Renationalization.
- More democratic global institutions.
- What would it be?

IV. Civil society – parliaments
- Common interests:
  - Global decision-making is intergovernmental
  - BOTH excluded from executive power
- Wider participation increases demands for transparency
- Parliaments as LINKS with civil society
- Common representation in delegations to UN conferences now frequent

V. Comparing CSO/NGOs and parliaments
- CSO/NGOs
  - Better networks on international level
  - Often higher level of expertise
  - Well organized global coalitions
- Parliaments
  - Legitimate status in decision-making
  - Conventions ratified in the parliaments
  - International networks of the parliamentarians improving

VI. Elements of civic democracy – three pillars of 'Århus Convention'
- Access to information
  - Open institutions – good governance
  - Active information policies
  - Public space (media, internet)
- Participation in decision-making
  - Hearings
  - Referendums, initiatives
- Right to appeal
  - Courts
  - Ombudsmen
  - Committees of Petition

VII. Global governance institutions should...
- Open up for the public
- Become democratically accountable
  - Better parliamentary control in nation states' early action and follow up
  - Hearings of NGOs and Civil Society Movements
  - Parliamentary networks proliferating

VIII. UN General Assembly
- PROs
  - Every nation has a vote
  - Equitable geographical representation
  - 'Moral authority'
- CONs
  - Weak compared to Security Council
  - Decreased power?
  - Unfair for e.g. Chinese and Indian people
  - No weighting of the votes
  - Ineffective

IX. Suggestions for stronger global parliamentarian action
- ILO report: To establish a global group of parliaments for coherence of global economic and social policy and integrated control of the UN, WB, IMF and WTO (IPU?)
- 'Cardoso Panel': global parliamentarian public policy committees
- Could it be linked with MDGs?

X. Towards World Parliament (WP)
- Operating by means of its 'moral authority', to:
  - Draw up principles of good global governance
  - Assess the performance of other international bodies + make them accountable
  - Act as a forum for negotiations between governments
- Bicameral parliament – directly (WP) and indirectly elected (UNGA) assemblies – or
  - Combination of partially overlapping functional and territorial systems of governance as a starting point? (Network Institute for Global Democratization – NIGD)
- Regional integration: EU, African Union, MERCOSUR (Southern Common Market) ...?

Towards a Global Parliament
Richard Falk and Andrew Strauss

> The close cooperative links between the Secretariat of the World Campaign and Professor Richard Falk having already been mentioned, we asked him and also Professor Andrew Strauss (Professor of International Law at the Widener University School of Law) to grant us their permission to republish the following in this book. We are most grateful to them, and to Foreign Affairs, in which it was first published (Falk, Richard and Strauss, Andrew, 'Towards a Global Parliament', *Foreign Affairs*, 2001, v. 80, no 1), for giving their consent. This surely stands as one of the books of reference on the issue concerned.

Challenging the democratic deficit

One crucial aspect of the rising disaffection with globalization is the lack of citizen participation in the global institutions that shape people's daily lives. This public frustration is deeper and broader than the recent street demonstrations in Seattle and Prague. Social commentators and leaders of citizens' and intergovernmental organizations are increasingly taking heed. Over the past 18 months, President Clinton has joined with the secretary-general of the United Nations, the director-general of the World Trade Organization (WTO), the managing director of the International Monetary Fund (IMF), and the president of the World Bank to call for greater citizen participation in the international order.

But to date, these parties have not clearly articulated a general vision of how best to integrate a public role into international institutions. So in the absence of a planned design, attempts to democratize the international system have been ad hoc, as citizen organizations and economic elites create their own mechanisms of influence. In domestic politics, interest group pluralism flourishes within a parliamentary system of representation. In global politics, interest-group pluralism is growing, but no unifying parliament represents the public interest. This state of affairs cannot last in a world where the prevailing understanding of democracy does not accept the fact that unelected interest groups can speak for the citizenry as a whole. Any serious attempt to challenge the democratic deficit must therefore consider creating some type of popularly elected global body. Before globalization, such an idea would have been considered utopian. Now, the clamour of citizens to participate internationally can no longer be ignored. The only question is what form this participation will take.

Decision-making goes global

Behind this clamour lies a profound shift in power. Thanks to trade, foreign direct investment, and capital flows, globalization is dispersing political authority throughout the international order. International governance is no longer limited to such traditional fare as defining international borders, protecting diplomats, and proscribing the use of force. Many issues of global policy that directly affect citizens are now being shaped by the international system. Workers can lose their jobs as a result of decisions made at the WTO or within regional trade regimes. Consumers must contend with a market in which state-prescribed protections such as the European ban on hormone-fed beef can be overridden by WTO regulations. Patients who need medicines pay prices influenced by WTO-enforced patent rules, which allow pharmaceutical companies to monopolize drug pricing. Most of the 23 million sub-Saharan Africans who have tested positive for the HIV/AIDS virus cannot afford the drugs most effective in treating their illness. They will die much sooner as a consequence.

For the half of the world's population that lives on less than $2 a day, governmental social safety nets have been weakened by IMF decisions. The globalized economy has not meaningfully reduced poverty despite a long period of sustained growth. Economic inequality is on the rise, as is the marginalization of regions not perceived as attractive trading partners or 'efficient' recipients of investment. Furthermore, environmental trends pose severe dangers that can be successfully dealt with only through global action and treaties. Against such a background, it is little wonder that people who believe they possess a democratic entitlement to participate in decisions that affect their lives are now starting to demand their say in the international system. And global civil society has thus far been their voice as they attempt to have this say.

Civil society's global presence

Civil society, made up of nonprofit organizations and voluntary associations dedicated to civic, cultural, humanitarian, and social causes, has begun to act as an independent international force. The largest and most prominent of these organizations include Amnesty International, Greenpeace, Oxfam, and the International Committee of the Red Cross; in addition, the UN now lists more than 3,000 civil society groups.

During the 1990s, these transnational forces effectively promoted treaties to limit global warming, establish an international criminal court, and outlaw antipersonnel land mines. These same actors also helped persuade the International Court of Justice to render an advisory opinion on the legality of nuclear weapons and defeat a multilateral investment agreement. More recently, civil groups mounted a drive to cancel the foreign debts of the world's poorest countries. Although these efforts remain works in progress, civil society to date has been indispensable in furthering them.

During the early 1990s, civil society's organizations began visibly cooperating at large international conferences of states. When conservative political pressures forced an end to these conferences, civil society began to coalesce to act cohesively and independently in the international arena. For example, 8,000 individuals representing civil society organizations met in May 1999 at the Hague Appeal for Peace to shape strategy and agree on a common agenda. Among those attending were such luminaries as Nobel Peace Prize winners Desmond Tutu, Jose Ramos-Horta, and Jody Williams. Similar smaller meetings in South Korea, Canada, Germany, and elsewhere followed.

These meetings were a prelude to the Millennium NGO Forum held at the United Nations in May 2000, to which UN Secretary-General Kofi Annan invited 1,400 individuals representing international civil society groups to present views on global issues and citizen participation in decision-making. The forum agreed to establish a permanent assembly of civil society organizations, mandated to meet at least every two to three years, before the UN General Assembly annual session. Although it is still to be realized, such a forum might earn recognition over time as an important barometer of world public opinion – and a preliminary step towards creating a global parliament. Regardless of how this specific forum develops, civil society will continue to institutionalize itself into an independent and cohesive force within the international system.

The corporate movers

Through expanding trade and investment, business and banking leaders have also exercised extraordinary influence on global policy. Even in formerly exclusive arenas of state action, these private-sector actors are making a mark. For example, Secretary-General Annan has made 'partnering' with the business community a major hallmark of his leadership. The United Nations has now established a formal business advisory council to formalize a permanent relationship between the corporate community and the UN.

As with citizen groups, elite business participation in the international system is becoming institutionalized. The best example is the World Economic Forum (WEF) in Davos, Switzerland. In the 1980s, the WEF transformed itself from an organization devoted to humdrum management issues into a dynamic political forum. Once a year, a thousand of the world's most powerful business executives get together with another thousand of the world's senior policymakers to participate in a week of roundtables and presentations. The WEF also provides ongoing arenas for discussion and recommendations on shaping global policy. It is notable that Annan's ideas about a UN partnership with the business community have been put forward and endorsed during his frequent appearances at Davos. In addition, the WEF also conducts and disseminates its own research, which not surprisingly shows a consistently neoliberal outlook. For example, it produces a well-publicized annual index ranking the relative economic competitiveness of all countries in the world. The Davos assembly and overlapping networks of corporate elites, such as the International Chamber of Commerce, have been successful in shaping compatible global policies. Their success has come in the expansion of international trade regimes, the modest regulation of capital markets, the dominance of neoliberal market philosophy, and the supportive collaboration of most governments, especially those of rich countries.

Pondering a global parliament

Global civil society still cannot match the resources and power linkages of the corporate and banking communities. But many civil society groups have carved out niches within the international order from which to influence decision-making by relying on imagination and information. The evolution of these two networks – civil and business – has been largely uncoordinated, and it remains unclear how they could fit together in a functionally coherent and representative form of global governance. Neither can claim to represent citizenry as a whole. As global civil society acquires a greater international presence, its critics are already challenging its claims to represent the public interest. The charge of illegitimacy has even greater resonance when levelled at corporate and banking elites, who do not speak for organizations.

Now that the global system is increasingly held up to democratic standards – and often comes up short – those people who find their policy preferences rejected are unlikely to accept the system's determination as legitimate, and the democratic deficit will remain a problem. Only when citizen and business interests work together within an overarching representative body can they achieve policy accommodations that will be seen as legitimate.

For the first time, a widely recognized global democratic forum could consider environmental and labour standards and deliberate on economic justice from the perspectives of both North and South. Even an initially weak assembly could offer some democratic oversight of international organizations such as the IMF, the WTO, and the World Bank.

Unlike the United Nations, this assembly would not be constituted by states. Because its authority would come directly from the global citizenry, it could refute the claim that states are bound only by laws to which they give their consent. Henceforth, the ability to opt out of collective efforts to protect the environment, control or eliminate weapons, safeguard human rights, or otherwise protect the global community, could be challenged.

In addition, the assembly could encourage compliance with established international norms and standards, especially in human rights. The international system currently lacks reliable mechanisms to implement many of its laws. Organizations such as Amnesty International, Human Rights Watch, and even the International Labor Organization, attempt to hold states accountable by exposing their failures of compliance, relying on a process often referred to as the 'mobilization of shame'. In exercising such oversight, a popularly elected global assembly would be more visible and credible than are existing watchdogs who expose corporate and governmental wrongdoing.

The assembly's very existence would also help promote the peaceful resolution of international conflicts. Because elected delegates would represent individuals and society instead of states, they would not have to vote along national lines. Coalitions would likely form on other bases, such as world-view, political orientation, and interests. Compromises among such competing but non-militarized coalitions might eventually undermine reliance on the current war system, in which international decisions are still made by heavily armed nations that are poised to destroy one another. In due course, international relations might more closely resemble policymaking within the most democratic societies of the world.

All those in favour

In spite of its advantages, would the formation of such an assembly threaten established state and business interests so much that its creation would become politically untenable? The European Union's experience suggests otherwise. Established by states – and with little initial authority – the transnationally elected European Parliament has now become powerful enough to help close a regional democratic deficit.

As with the early European parliament, a relatively weak assembly initially equipped with largely advisory powers could begin to address concerns about the democratic deficit while posing only a long-term threat to the realities of state power. Systemic transformation of world order that would largely affect successors would not significantly threaten those political leaders who are inclined to embrace democratic ideals. Indeed, it might even appeal to them.

Despite these humble origins, the assembly would have the potential to become an extremely important fixture of the global architecture. Upon the assembly's inception, civil society organizations would almost certainly lobby it to issue supportive resolutions. Groups who opposed such resolutions could shun the process, but that is not likely: they would concede the support of the world's only elected democratic body. Over time, as the assembly became the practical place for clashing interests to resolve differences, formal powers would likely follow.

Some business leaders would certainly oppose a global parliament because it would broaden popular decision-making and likely press for transnational regulations. But others are coming to believe that the democratic deficit must be closed by some sort of stakeholder accommodation. After all, many members of the managerial class who were initially hostile to such reform came to realize that the New Deal – or its social-democratic equivalent in Europe – was necessary to save capitalism. Many business leaders today similarly agree that democratization is necessary to make globalization politically acceptable throughout the world.

As the recent large street protests suggested, globalization has yet to achieve grassroots acceptance and legitimacy. To date, its main claim to popular support is not political but economic: it has either delivered or convincingly promised to deliver the economic goods to enough people to keep the antiglobalization forces from mounting an effective challenge. But economic legitimacy alone can rarely stabilize a political system for long. Market-based economic systems have historically undergone ups and downs, particularly when first forming. The financial crisis that almost triggered a world financial meltdown a few years ago will not be the last crisis to emerge out of globalization. Future economic failures are certain to generate political responses. Standing in the wings in the United States and elsewhere are politicians, ultranationalists, and an array of opportunists on both the left and the right who, if given an opening, would seek to dismantle the global system. A global parliament is therefore likely to serve as an attractive alternative to those people who, out of enlightened self-interest or even public spiritedness, wish to see the international system become more open and democratic.

Making it happen

Although the raw political potential for a global assembly may exist, it is not enough. Some viable way needs to be found for this potential to be realized, and it can most likely be found in the new diplomacy. Unlike traditional diplomacy, which has been solely an affair among states, new diplomacy makes room for flexible and innovative coalitions between civil society and receptive states. The major success stories of global civil society in the 1990s – the Kyoto global warming treaty, the convention banning land mines, and the International Criminal Court – were produced in this manner.

Civil society, aided by receptive states, could create the assembly without resorting to a formal treaty process. Under this approach, the assembly would not be formally sanctioned by states, so governments would probably contest its legitimacy at the outset. But this opposition could be neutralized to some extent by widespread grassroots and media endorsement. Citizens in favour could make their voices heard through popular, fair, and serious elections.

Another approach would rely on a treaty, using what is often called the 'single negotiating text method'. After consultations with sympathetic parties from civil society, business, and nation-states, an organizing committee could generate the text of a proposed treaty establishing an assembly. This text could serve as the basis for negotiations. Civil society could then organize a public relations campaign and persuade states (through compromise if necessary) to sign the treaty. As in the process that ultimately led to the land mines convention, a small core group of supportive states could lead the way. But unlike that treaty, which required 40 countries to ratify it before taking effect, a relatively small number of countries (say, 20) could provide the founding basis for such an assembly. This number is only a fraction of what would be needed for the assembly to have some claim to global democratic legitimacy. But once the assembly became operational, the task of gaining additional state members would likely become easier. A concrete organization would then exist that citizens could urge their governments to join. As more states joined, pressure would grow on non-member states to participate. The assembly would be incorporated into the evolving international constitutional order. If it gained members and influence over time, as expected, its formal powers would have to be redefined. It would also have to work out its relationship with the UN. One possibility would be to associate with the General Assembly to form a bicameral world legislature.

The pressures to democratize the international system are part of an evolutionary social process that will persist and intensify. The two dominant themes of the post-Cold War years are globalization and democratization. It is often said that the world is rapidly creating an integrated global political economy, and that national governments that are not freely elected lack political legitimacy. It is paradoxical, then, that a global debate has not emerged on resolving the contradiction between a commitment to democracy and an undemocratic global order.

This tension may be the result of political inertia or a residual belief that ambitious world governance proposals are utopian. But whatever the explanation, this contradiction is spurring citizen groups and business and financial elites to take direct actions to realize their aspirations. Their initiatives have created an autonomous dynamic of ad hoc democratization. As this process continues to move along with globalization, pressures for a coherent democratic system of global governance will intensify. Political leaders will find it more difficult to win citizen acquiescence to unaccountable policies that extend globalization's reach into peoples' lives. To all those concerned about social justice and the creation of a humane global order, a democratic alternative to an ossified, state-centred system is becoming ever more compelling.

12

Proposals on Institutional Reforms for Peace, Disarmament, Security for People, Global Justice and Human Rights

---

The present system of international institutions came into being more than 50 years ago, their original design responding to the desire to prevent any more wars like those that occurred in the first half of the 20th century. To a large extent, they reflect the situation at the time and in the domain of peace and security, the victors of World War II obtained a privileged position within the institutional design of the United Nations.

The establishment of the UN in order to preserve world peace and the adoption shortly afterwards of the Universal Declaration of Human Rights are crucial events in the 20th century. They are one of the great success stories of human history. However, the original design of current international institutions has a number of shortcomings. The restricted number of permanent members of the Security Council and the UN body with binding authority weakens the chances of the UN having greater legitimacy and enforcement capacity, in particular with regard to its role in maintaining world peace and security.

Over time, some of the democratic deficiencies and imbalances of the system have been highlighted by the erosion of the original mandates governing certain organizations. The UNGA, which was very active in the 1960s and 1970s, when the Security Council was paralysed due to rivalry between the superpowers, began to play an increasingly minor role after the late 1980s when, with the end of the Cold War, the UNSC was reactivated.

The war in Iraq and other serious recent events of worldwide concern have revealed the divorce between certain decisions at the level of world politics and the opinion of citizens around the world, as well as the inability of the nation states to find peaceful, collective and enduring solutions to the grave problems affecting all of us.

The international institutions must substantially improve their capacity for conflict prevention and the maintenance of peace. This means that the organizations responsible for the domains of peace and security should collect all viewpoints in a balanced fashion, accept them universally as legitimate, as well as being empowered to implement their decisions.

Global justice should be empowered in order to contribute towards eradicating international impunity, not only with respect to criminal law, but also in the civil, economic, social and environmental spheres. To make all this possible, steps must be taken towards a worldwide juridical framework that would ensure the proper application of the present system of international treaties, reinforce the already-existing international legal institutions, and create the necessary institutions in other spheres with all the appropriate and necessary mechanisms.

Some proposals on the reform of the Security Council

Is the current composition of the Security Council legitimate? Should the General Assembly exercise controls of any type over the Security Council to effectively ensure world security and non-violent conflict resolution?

Improving present functioning
- Guaranteeing transparency in decision-making procedures.
- Discouraging the use of the power of veto in all cases except those pertaining to Chapter VII of the UN Charter ('Action with respect to threats to the peace, breaches of the peace, and acts of aggression').
- Implementation of the SC Resolution 1325 calling for the presence of women and their active participation in peace processes and conflict resolution.

Substantive reforms
- Limiting the right of veto to certain specific issues (Chapter VII of the UN Charter) and introducing the requisite of two simultaneous vetoes to exercise this right.
- Establishing permanent and transparent procedural norms.
- Resolutions to be subject to ICJ review.
- Guaranteeing coherent and effective regional representation.
- The extant Security Council should be reformed so that, duly supervised by the UNGA, it would have a composition representing all the regions of the world. The use of the power of veto should be limited to specific issues and steps should be taken towards its abolition in favour of a system of qualified majorities in issues of major importance.

In-depth reforms
- Supervision by the UNGA.

- Representative composition by regions.
- Review/abolition of the category of permanent member.
- Abolition of the power of veto.
- Voting by direct majority, with a two-thirds majority in very significant issues (to ensure a regional balance and to prevent the sidelining of less powerful nations and regions).

In any case, all reforms should be undertaken in order to:
- Improve the mechanisms of conflict prevention and maintenance of peace.
- Ensure the effective resolution of endemic conflicts that are responsible for a large part of the world's tension.
- Real and effective development of mechanisms for conflict prevention, with the participation of regional organizations.

Some proposals on the role of the General Assembly and the peacekeeping forces

Improving current operations
- Increased availability of financial and human resources for peace missions (including the reaching of agreements under Article 43 of the Charter) and the reinstigation of the activities of the Military Staff Committee (Article 47).
- Increased usage of UNGA Resolution 377: 'Uniting for Peace'.
- Increased resources in the field of conflict prevention (creation of regional observatories, etc.).
- Revitalization of the Disarmament Conference.

Substantive reforms
- Rules to be drawn up for the 'Uniting for Peace' resolution and a permanent working group of the UNGA to be set up on the issues of peace and security.
- A permanent multinational force that the UN can call on directly to be set up.
- Specific accords on cooperation between the UN and regional peace and security agencies.

In-depth reforms
- The UNSC to be supervised by the UNGA.
- Permanent UN peacekeeping forces to be set up.
- Collective security system with strong regionalization.

Some proposals on the world justice; making human rights universal

Improving present functioning
- Providing greater powers of appeal to the ICJ in the case of constitutionally doubtful UNSC actions.
- Working for the universal ratification of the Treaty of Rome and advancing towards universal recognition of the ICC.
- First steps towards creating international tribunals with specific jurisdictions.

Substantive reforms
- Creating a chamber with the capacity to advise on the constitutionality of actions of UN organizations, including the UNSC.
- Universal reach of the ICJ.
- Advancing towards the creation of a Council of World Justice, a new international human rights tribunal, a new international tribunal dealing with economic and financial crimes, and a new international tribunal for environmental crimes.

In-depth reforms
- Interconnected world legal order covering civil and criminal law, with mechanisms for implementation from local through to worldwide levels.
- Enabling the ICJ to determine the constitutionality of decisions taken by the organizations of the system.
- Full integration of the ICJ into the UN system.
- Effective creation and implementation of specific international tribunals within the UN system.
- Creation and implementation of a World Legal Police Force.

Vision for the reform of the United Nations Security Council

Poul Nyrup Rasmussen, former Prime Minister of Denmark; Global Progressive Forum (GPF)

As you will see, all that the Secretariat of the World Campaign and the UBUNTU Forum has of Mr. Poul Nyrup Rasmussen's talk is his outline of it. Even so, since the outline is self-explanatory and since it is of great interest in our view, we have left it in the form of that original outline in this publication. This address and also the next one by Mr. Edoardo Greppi were given in the 'Conference on Reform of United Nations and Other International Institutions' in 2004. By contrast, the other two speeches – by Mr. Tomas Magnusson and Mr. Luis Alfonso de Alba, respectively – that compose this chapter belong to the 'International Conference for the Reform of International Institutions', in 2006.

A renewed United Nations Security Council (UNSC)

This Council could be renamed Human Security Council:

- To improve the role of the UN on Security and Peace issues: to tackle 'hard threats' (wars, weapons of mass destruction, terrorism ...).

A renewed United Nations Economic and Social Council

This Council could be renamed the Human Development Council:

- To improve the role of the UN on Development, Social, Environmental and Economic issues to tackle 'soft threats' (poverty, hunger, diseases ...).

Why do we propose two councils rather than just one to oversee both the political and security domain and the economic and social domain?

Because the 'relative importance' or the most desirable 'weights' of different nations or grouping of nations in the top level governance of the international system may not be the same for the security and the economic spheres.

For both operational reasons (the ability to act) and because of the realities of power, military capability will have to be a determining factor in the governance of the security domain.

The situation is somewhat different, however, when it comes to economic and social matters. It would be entirely desirable that if a country or a group of countries is ready to spend large amounts of resources on funding global public goods, the weights in the top-level governance council should reflect that effort.

A new UN Security Council

A. In terms of institutional changes

- The P5 (five permanent seats) is outdated: we need to enlarge the Security Council to strengthen its legitimacy.
- Joint seat for the EU.

- Larger representation on the base of regional integration.
- To abolish the right of veto – idea of double veto or qualified majority.

If every one of the old P5 retains their veto in its current form, many decisions could, again, simply be blocked by a single country – even if it is not a very large country, and even if it is isolated in international public opinion.

If new permanent members also were to acquire veto power, the chances of paralysis would increase further. If new important countries such as Japan and India are added as permanent members without giving them the veto power, while countries that are by any reasonable measure smaller, such as the UK and France, retain their individual veto power, such a new council may be perceived as *less* legitimate than the old one.

Instead, the reform should be based on moving towards a system of weighted votes and universal participation, where everyone can be involved, but where the weights in the voting scheme also reflect the actual size, ability to act and importance of the participating nation states.

Instead of individual veto rights, supermajorities would be required for the most important decisions:

- For cross border military interventions, the supermajority required could be four/fifths of the weighted votes.
- For other matters, the required majority for a binding decision could be three/fifths.
- To dispose of permanent military force at the sole disposition of the Secretary-General. By example: EU – Eurocorps or Rapid Reaction Force.

It has to be completed by Civil Observers, with mandate to take care of good governance programme, fair elections, good justice administration ...

- Balance the responsibilities between the UNSC (25 per cent of the world population) and the UNGA.
- Push the UN Secretary-General to use more systematically Article 99 of the Charter that gives him the right to hold the UNSC for worrying situations for peace and international security.
- Call for extraordinary urgent sessions of the UNGA (resolution 377(V) – called resolution Acheson or 'Uniting for Peace' – proposed by the secretary of state, Dean Acheson).

B. In terms of policies
- Taking into account that the nature of conflicts has changed: conflicts are internal to states more than between states. The United Nations

remains poorly prepared to detect or anticipate these types of conflicts, and also lacks the tools to intervene in what is generally considered to be a member state's internal affairs. Serious reflection should begin on the way that the United Nations (in addition to any potential politicians, diplomats, military personnel and legal professionals) might be assisted by certain elements of civil society (religious or spiritual leaders, traditional chiefs, women's associations, etc.) to help it to adapt towards solving these types of crises.

- Real priority on the fight against international terrorism and the main causes of terrorism.
- Contrary to the current practice: names of countries, leaders, companies that break morals, ethics, use of corruption, violation of human rights and terrorism financing should be pointed out in UN official reports and transferred in front of competent international jurisdictions.

A new UN Human Development Council

- The UN Human Development Council should replace both the G8 and the UN ECOSOC:
  - Continuously assessing the state of the world economy and ensuring macro-economic coordination.
  - Providing a long-term strategic framework for sustainable development.
  - Securing consistency between the policy goals and actions of the international economic, social and environmental institutions.
  - Producing common guidelines on the priorities of the global agenda, monitoring their follow-up, and acting as a coordinating body for trade-offs between commerce, employment and environment.
  - In the case of partial financing of global policies through international taxation, monitoring and surveillance of the use and allocation of funds.
- Pre-emptive policies instead of pre-emptive wars.
- It would fall to this Council, for example, to ensure that all international organizations' policies and programmes are consistent with the Millennium Development Goals and the Johannesburg and Monterrey declarations.
- This would include building the WTO and the Bretton Woods Institutions into the UN System.
- Support for the case of a World Financial Authority.

Some reflections on reforming the UN, the General Assembly and the maintenance of peace
Edoardo Greppi, Professor at the University of Turin;
World Political Forum (WPF)

The World Political Forum

The World Political Forum's mission is to promote meetings of politicians, scientists, outstanding religious and cultural personalities from all continents, of different faiths, languages and cultures. The Forum is based on cultural diversity and interdependence.

Its goals are to identify the ways to construct a network of governance bodies capable of finding the critical points and to bridge the gaps within politics, and tackling the major topics affecting the international community at the beginning of the Third Millennium.

President Mikhail Gorbachev promoted this initiative together with President Bill Clinton and the President of Brazil, Fernando Henrique Cardoso. Giulio Andreotti, Jaques Attali, Benazir Bhutto, Luigi Guidobono Cavalchini, Emilio Colombo, Andrea Comba, Francesco Cossiga, Ralf Dahrendorf, Jacques Delors, Hans Dietrich Genscher, Boutros Boutros Ghali, Toshiki Kaifu, Jack Matlock, Tadeusz Mazowiecki, Keba Mbaye, Oscar L. Scalfaro, Cardinal Achille Silvestrini, Robert Skidelsky, Mario Soares, Hubert Vedrine, Federico Mayor Zaragoza, Milos Zeman are among the Forum's founding members. A Scientific Committee is chaired by Andrei Gratchev and co-chaired by Carlo Ossola.

The need for a forum to seek out new institutional know-how able to identify methods and ways of creating innovative world governance arises from the fact that, with the sudden and uncontrolled growth of globalization, the old international political bodies sometimes seem unable to face the new problems of the 21st century.

The World Political Forum's activities adopt a cross-disciplinary approach through the interaction of culture, science, economics, politics, sociology, law and religion. The Forum will provide constructive input on all issues that today concern the international community.

The WPF stands out from other initiatives for being open to representatives of all cultures, for dealing with issues such as equal cooperation on economic, financial, social and cultural problems, and for interacting not only with politicians but also with scientists, writers, researchers and political commentators. It is a meeting place to share cultures and experience, because only the mutual understanding, without ideological or religious prejudice, can lead to common values and prospects.

Here, today, I represent the World Political Forum, as a member of its Scientific Committee. However, I will not present the Forum's official views on the issues of reform of the UN and the other international institutions.

The World Political Forum has not yet discussed them in one of its sessions. I will therefore make some reflections on my individual capacity, and the WPF is not to be held responsible for what I'm going to tell you now.

United Nations reform issues: the role of the General Assembly, peace-keeping forces and regional organizations

The debate on the issue of reform has been going on since a long time. The creation of the UN was a response to the great demand of peace and security since World War II. The organization is the result of the combination of two basic principles: universal equality and oligarchy power. In other words, world peace and security should have been granted by a dualistic institution, composed of a General Assembly – in which States should have been represented on an equality basis – and a Security Council, with a primary competence in the field of security and crisis management – in which a special position would be granted to States having a major responsibility in international affairs. Those were essentially identified in the States which had won the war and in those which still had a widespread colonial power (such as the United Kingdom, already belonging to the first category, and such as France, who had lost the war, but was on the 'right side' and had still a colonial 'empire'). The five permanent members were conceived as a sort of 'directorate' of world affairs. As we all know, the system didn't work because of the Cold War, of the impossibility of keeping the necessary harmony among the directorate members. But it didn't collapse. The Security Council was paralysed by the abuse of the so-called right of veto, but the General Assembly was capable of playing a role. It focused on economic and social issues and, moreover, it concentrated on the adoption of declarations of principles and on the fundamental transformation of the enlarged international community which was the result of decolonization.

The emerging developing countries quickly became the majority in the General Assembly. And they became very active in demanding reforms. They wanted to discuss the main political, economic and legal issues of the international community. From the very beginning, they seemed to refuse acceptance of an order with rules they hadn't contributed to form. One essential 'leitmotiv' was that of democratization of the UN, basically through an increase of the powers of the General Assembly and an increment of the Security Council members with parallel elimination of the right of veto or its extension to new countries.

Today, after 60 years, the issue of reform has become essential. The end of the Cold War, the reunification of Germany, the progressive integration and enlargement of Europe, the challenge of development, the difficulties of keeping a multilateral institutional approach in a world in which there is only one superpower left; the challenges of globalization: these are elements which have deeply modified the general framework and which therefore complicated the debate.

I'll try and summarize a few elements to contribute to the discussion.

In the UN Charter, primary responsibility in the field of peace and security was given to the Security Council. Attempts to move the focus from this oligarchic body to the General Assembly failed. The main question was: how can the organization put in place an effective action in the typical Cold War situation of a Security Council paralysed by a veto? According to the Charter, there is no place for a General Assembly competence in the field of actions falling within the scope of Chapter VII. The 'Uniting for Peace' Resolution and the creation of the United Nations Emergency Force – UNEF in 1956 were strongly opposed by the Soviet Union and the Eastern European block. Moreover, no major State or group of States recognized the existence of a customary international law rule in international practice.

If this is the situation under the Charter and under customary international law, what about the possibility (or desirability) of a modification of the Charter in order to shift the competence from the Security Council to the General Assembly? In my opinion, the major point remains in the UN Charter principles. Charter provisions can be modified; basic principles still belong to customary international law, and some of them are of a peremptory character. Principles like peace, security and respect for human rights are not – and cannot be – a matter of discussion or negotiation. Does democracy belong to these principles? When the General Assembly was envisaged, there is no doubt that (at least some) States had in mind to apply the principle 'one State one vote', as a parallel to the one traditionally underlying democracies ('one man one vote'). If this is true, a relevant problem arises. Is it possible to imagine the shifting of competence and power to a General Assembly in which decision making would be based on the participation in an international democratic process of countries which lack democratic legitimacy in their national constitution?

This is clearly true if we enlarge the scope of the discussion to subsidiary bodies. The Commission on Human Rights – a General Assembly subsidiary body – has currently Cuba, Saudi Arabia, Sudan and Zimbabwe among its members, and in 2003 it has been chaired by Libya. If international bodies are not composed of States strongly committed to the respect of human rights and fundamental freedoms, they are lacking the necessary moral authority.

So, the question is: can we consider scarcely acceptable that the major decision-making power is given to an oligarchic Security Council and at the same time increase the role of the General Assembly without solving this problem of a lack of democracy in a broad sense? We cannot close our eyes and accept that democracy does not belong to the fundamental heritage of human rights. On the contrary, it belongs to the original 'first generation' civil and political rights. And we should always remember that democracy plays an essential role in conflict prevention, both in an internal and in an international perspective. Moreover, democracy is a crucial issue in peace-building situations.

If there is the will to strengthen the General Assembly by recognizing some decision-making power, we should imagine that we introduce some kind of weighted voting. A plenary body which can only adopt recommendations could be shaped in strict respect of the principle of sovereign equality of States (Article 2, § 1 of the Charter). If the General Assembly is to be given the power to adopt legally binding acts ('decisions'), it would probably make sense to introduce mechanisms which would grant a different weight to the People's Republic of China and to the Republic of San Marino, to the USA and to Palau, to India and to the Seychelles, to Germany and to Vanuatu, to the United Kingdom and to Tonga.

The European Union decision making-mechanisms provide us with a useful model. It is a multilateral organization, whose member States have different size, different population, different political, military and economic 'power'. Both the European Parliament and the Council of the Union have a representation of peoples and States respecting their different dimensions. Seats in the European Parliament are linked to the population of each State. In the Council, on the other hand, when a qualified majority is required, each government is given a different amount of votes. The Treaty which will be signed 29 October in Rome introduces an even more sophisticated system, based on a combination of a double qualified majority of States and population. The solution is therefore practical. It works, it respects high democratic standards and the request of a representation based on principles of equity and balanced power.

Along with the cases of the World Trade Organization and the Food and Agriculture Organization (FAO), the European Union should be represented in the UN as a single subject, provided, of course, that its member States ratify the new 'Treaty adopting a Constitution for Europe' (including, in the first place, the provisions on the common foreign policy of the Union and its related legal personality).

Another issue which should be taken into account is that of efficacy. Are we sure that a representative body, composed of 191 States, is the ideal actor to face international crisis and conflicts? One of the reasons which had pushed the founding members towards the creation of a Security Council with a limited membership was that a plenary assembly is generally considered inadequate for an efficient decision-making mechanism.

Therefore, competence in the field of peace and security should be left – as it is currently occurring with the Security Council – to a body with a restricted membership, in order to guarantee a quick and efficient response to threats to world order. The General Assembly could be given a global political supervision responsibility, provided with – as I said – respect for genuine democracy.

In addition to this, a useful instrument to the improvement of democratic methods is the involvement of non-governmental organizations. NGOs are often the true voice of individuals, peoples, and their basic needs. An institutional representation of NGOs appears therefore necessary.

As far as the proposals to set up permanent UN peace-keeping forces are concerned, I strongly support this vision. There is no doubt that the failure in the creation of bodies such as the Military Staff Committee has greatly contributed to the lack of success of the UN.

Last but not least, regional organizations should be given clear responsibility, provided that they comply with that general obligation to respect human rights and accept to introduce democratic mechanisms. There is no doubt that a collective security system based on a strong regionalization would be much more effective than a universal one. Regional conflicts, peculiar local situations could be much more effectively approached and dealt with through the action of regional organizations. That was also the approach in 1945, and should be re-launched. Chapter VIII of the Charter is still an unexplored world of opportunities.

Concluding remarks

One of the key elements of the UN and of the whole of the United Nations system is multilateralism combined with institutionalization. In particular, in order to guarantee peace and security, the Charter was conceived as an instrument to provide the international community (which is typically an-organic) with an institutional framework. Negotiations and agreements – and, in general – the law of treaties, were considered an essential but not exhaustive method to approach and solve international problems. Rules should be established among States, but they should be placed in hand of international institutions. These would have the responsibility to manage the rules, to apply them, to improve their effectiveness, to modify them when they become inadequate or obsolete.

The world has changed since the establishment of the UN and of all the main international organizations. But the need for multilateralism and universal institutions is still strong. International order needs a generally shared acceptance of the rule of law. Institutions were more than 60 years ago called to offer the general framework for international cooperation.

There is no alternative to the strengthening of the UN and of all other relevant international organizations. But all mechanisms' changes and 'technical' provisions should be based on the full acceptance of basic principles such as respect for human rights, democracy, rule of law and justice.

International institutions are often accused of being inadequate or ineffective. But there is no alternative to multilateralism and institutionalization. The international community is still heavily influenced by the Westphalian principle of sovereignty. International organizations are the only answer to a system based on the individual attitude of States to act on their own, to take unilateral decisions, to use force in the framework of international relations built around power and equilibrium.

Only through a patient dialogue among nations, through daily negotiations among governments, can the international community hope to achieve world peace and security, world justice, an efficient fight against terrorism and a real development. Only international institutions can grant global governance.

As the great Dag Hammarskjöld used to say, the UN has not been created to grant Paradise to mankind, but to save it from Hell.

Peace, disarmament and the reform of international institutions

Tomas Magnusson, International Peace Bureau (IPB)

I came directly here to Geneva from another gathering in the field of peace and disarmament, the Seventh World Summit of Nobel peace laureates and Nobel laureate organizations, which took place over the weekend in Rome, Italy.

It so happens that the International Peace Bureau, which I represent, having been elected President two months ago, won the Nobel Peace Prize in 1910. It was long ago, but we still have a portion of the prize money invested in banks here in Switzerland, which helps us to survive and keep an office working at no. 41 rue de Zürich.

IPB was established to be the permanent Bureau to organize international peace conferences. This was long before the UN and today's institutions, so some of the pioneers felt the need to get people and nations together in the cause of peace.

Today IPB represents some 282 organizations in 70 different countries, and we are not only arranging conferences but working through internet and all modern means (you know WWW means World Without War!) to inspire and mobilize for peace and disarmament, and for sustainable development.

In Rome, one of the key ideas was to organize a world summit for civil society on nuclear disarmament. And I am pretty excited about this idea, so I would like to talk about it within the framework of reform of international institutions.

In Rome, among those Nobel personalities, and also a number of experts on nuclear weapons, we felt that this is the moment in history to re-invent, re-organize, re-activate a mass movement against nuclear weapons, weapons of terror as they are called by the Weapons of Mass Destruction Commission.

Nowadays we have a very dangerous situation in terms of the nuclear threat. But it is not because North Korea has managed to conduct a nuclear weapons test recently; it is because there is a modernization of nuclear arsenals under way in the established nuclear weapon states. They are devising smaller nuclear weapons (mini-nukes) in order not to have nuclear weapons as a separate strategic arsenal, but rather to integrate them into conventional war-fighting plans – this is a US-led development. Meanwhile, we know, for example, that the UK is heading for a new Trident system.

This renewal of the nuclear arsenals is taking place while the stock of some 27,000 nuclear warheads, with an enormous amount of TNT, remains, mostly in Russia and the US, with more in Britain, France, China, Israel, Pakistan and India. And now also North Korea. None of these nuclear weapon states is intending to completely eliminate its nuclear weapons.

If we recognize the nuclear policies of the superpowers and the new trends of renewal as a crucial danger (in some ways even more dangerous than it was during the Cold War), what can we do about it? Will the UN disarmament system take care of this problem? What can we expect from the Conference on Disarmament here in Geneva? What can we expect from the next meeting of the Non-Proliferation Treaty Review? What can we expect from the General Assembly? Or from the Security Council?

The truth is – we cannot expect anything. You may have heard the US President describe North Korea as an 'evil' state. But in a recent vote in the UN General Assembly, the United States joined forces with just that North Korea: two states alone blocking progress on a treaty banning nuclear weapons testing. The Security Council is capable of issuing Resolution no. 1718 on the North Korean nuclear test, because that resolution singles out just one small country, which anyhow is isolated. But we cannot of course expect the five permanent members of the Security Council to impose sanctions on themselves because of their nuclear policies. So right now, we need to find new and innovative ways to tackle the threat of nuclear arms. Here we go:

When the UN Under-Secretary General for Disarmament, Jayantha Dhanapala, proposed in 2003 that there should be an International Commission on Weapons of Mass Destruction, the Secretary-General Kofi Annan was not willing or able to host such a commission within the UN. Instead it was set up by the Swedish Foreign Minister, the late Anna Lindh, as an independent Commission under the chairmanship of Hans Blix. In June the Commission presented its final report, with 60 recommendations on how to get rid of Weapons of Mass Destruction, and the report has now been tabled as a UN document.

But what will happen with the 60 recommendations? I think the best we can try to do is to take care of them outside the UN disarmament mechanisms. One of those 60 recommendations is to hold a World Summit on Disarmament, Non-Proliferation and Terrorist Use of Weapons of Mass Destruction (Recommendation no. 59).

This is the Summit that I talked about earlier – well, it is, and it is not. Because the Nobel laureates in Rome suggested and even committed themselves to try to mobilize civil society, peace movements, artists, independent leaders, the business community and so on – to organize a Civil Society Summit on Nuclear Disarmament in the coming two or three years. With the purpose of leading up to a UN-run, inter-governmental Summit in the way that the Commission on Weapons of Mass Destruction proposed.

That would be a similar strategy to the one that brought about the Landmine Ban Convention, as an initiative driven forward by civil society, until the way was paved, and the door was opened – and it finally could get incorporated in the institutional system.

We need to do that inspiring work again, in order to get rid of nuclear and all other weapons of mass destruction. Let us use the mighty force that is civil society – with all its energy and massive support! Let us not wait until the institutions are reformed – but reform them through action!

The Human Rights Council into the United Nations reform process

Luis Alfonso de Alba, President of the UN Human Rights Council

Many would agree with me that the creation of the Human Rights Council is the most important achievement so far in the process of reforming the United Nations. The creation of the Council is only one part of that process, and a recently launched one at that, and so it must be allowed some leeway to become consolidated.

The approach taken in New York and approved by the heads of State and government last year went far beyond creating a new institution: it aimed at creating a new culture so that human rights could be given a new dimension, a new space for itself within the system of international relations as a whole. It means placing human rights on a level with objectives such as the quest for peace and international security, or promoting development. In this respect it implies a fundamental change in international life, a change that leads to human rights promotion and protection becoming firmly established as a shared aim of the international community. The Council, as a UN body responsible for this issue, is just one instrument to meet that goal. Many other pre-existing ones will have to be used to support and promote vigilance in human-rights issues, for indeed the General Assembly itself, the Security Council and many other bodies have a very important role to play in this and can complete the Council's task.

Even so, within this priority focus accorded to human rights from the political standpoint, the issue had to be given added solidity from the institutional standpoint, and that is where the Council comes in.

What is the Council essentially seeking? I would say that it is seeking first and foremost to give all rights a balanced treatment. That is something necessary and that has long been called for: that the treatment given to civil rights and political rights, as opposed to economic, social and cultural rights, and of course the right to development, must be the same, because it is this whole that essentially forms the edifice of human rights; there is no order of precedence among those rights, for they are all interdependent. And while this was a step that had been recognized as necessary to some extent back in 1993 at the World Conference on Human Rights, it had not previously been set down so clearly in a commitment to action as it was when the Resolution creating the Council was adopted.

Secondly, the new institution has the aim of applying those rights equally in all countries, and it is important for this to be stressed as well. The starting point is the recognition that today there is not a single State anywhere that is complying in full with its duties and commitments in the sphere of human rights or able to claim that human rights are fully respected. There are indeed some situations that are more pressing than others, and more pronounced institutional deficiencies in some countries than in others; yet all without exception have a duty to make greater efforts, and they all have in particular the right to be treated on a fair basis by the international mechanisms.

'All human rights of all people in all countries' is the underlying premise for the functioning of the Council. To this is added a clear readiness to start treating or to continue to treat these issues from a standpoint that I would call 'the gradual approach' – that is, one in which cooperation, dialogue and transparency are highlighted in the first instance, while work proceeds on identifying emergency situations requiring firmer action by the Council. However, the aim a priori is not to judge, and still less to condemn, particular human-rights situations. Rather, the aim is to strengthen the capacity of each and every state to fulfil its commitments. All this is evidently something we must reflect in practice, in the everyday work of the Council, and it will be seen more clearly when we finally have the periodic universal revision mechanism designed for that purpose.

The fundamental aim of the Council is to achieve greater capacity for action, in terms of agility and response, in order to safeguard rights rather than just singling out infringements or seeking penalties for them where appropriate. That is why it is very important to complete the building of the structure and the mechanisms, making sure that there are neither unnecessary duplications nor gaps in the protection provided, and maintaining the valuable legacy of the Commission in its entirety – that is, the system of mechanisms and special procedures, Rapporteurs and Working Groups. If this is not strengthened and extended, it will scarcely be possible to claim that progress is being made. On the one hand we have a general approach, and on the other the means through which the work is tackled.

Lastly, the Council has another key component that I feel is particularly appropriate to point out here: the fact that the Council is no longer working strictly among States: rather, it seeks to get members of civil society, national human-rights institutions, and regional and inter-governmental organizations much more directly involved in its institutional life. This opening-up of the Council is the most important component in the new culture, because it is the one that will give it the impetus needed in the long run for making the changes a reality.

In the absence of fresh stimuli, it is no easy matter to carry on tackling the same issues with the same States maintaining the same old stances. And these fresh stimuli must come from civil society, and from the pressure exerted by the international community to achieve the transformation and opening-up of these institutions, with the aim of achieving direct benefits for the victims of human-rights violations, rather than just seeking to spark off a worldwide conceptual debate, or even making use of these issues for political ends. Real change will have come when we have managed to move on beyond the strictly political debate and the political manipulation of human rights to achieve a pro-human-rights culture at State level and in conjunction with society.

13

Proposals on Institutional Reforms for World Social, Environmental and Economic Well-being; or the Dialectics of Development, the Environment, Finance and Trade

The Bretton Woods Institutions are seriously marred by their lack of legitimacy and undemocratic functioning because of their decision-making system that clearly benefits the more powerful industrialized countries to the detriment of the developing countries. This situation has permitted the introduction of policies without consensus and without the support of all member states.

When the demands of the developing countries finally began to be heard in the UNGA in the 1960s, the developed countries tended to turn to the BWI for decisions because their decision-making process was much more favourable to their interests. With the collapse of the Eastern Bloc, the neoliberal policies enshrined in the Washington Consensus began to gain ground.

The BWI and the WTO – established in 1994 as a new multilateral organization outside of the United Nations system – have helped to spread the neoliberal economic policies applied in many parts of the world in recent years. In contrast, the declarations and plans of action resulting from UN summits of the 1990s and the new millennium have not been implemented due to a lack of political will and failure to deliver the resources that are necessary to put them into effect.

Is it possible to promote development through implementing neo-liberal policies? Have these not increased poverty in the global South? How can we put an end to the shocking contradictions between the UN's declarations and action plans and the constant, clear failure to implement them?

The capacity of international institutions for global macroeconomic management should be increased through financial, economic, trade, social and environmental policies that take into account the interests of all, and most significantly of those who are most vulnerable and excluded from the international system. To resolve the serious problems of poverty and inequality in the world, all of these policies should be approached in an integrated and coordinated fashion that recognizes the primacy of human rights. Economic policy should be coherent with social and environmental priorities and human rights, and should be properly integrated into effective and democratic structures of coordination and accountability towards those who are subject to this policy.

All of this requires the implementation of mechanisms for the coordination of world financial, economic, social and environmental policies. One proposal that has received wide-ranging support from a number of sectors is that of reforming ECOSOC (Economic and Social Council) so that it becomes an Economic, Social and Environmental Security Council with effective authority over UN agencies, funds and programmes, the Bretton Woods Institutions and the World Trade Organization.

Some proposals on the in-depth reform of the BWI and of its relations with the UN; in-depth reform of world financial and economic policies

Improving the functioning of the BWI
- Improving coordination between the UN and the BWI through ECOSOC.
- With regard to the BWI:
- Reviewing their policies and powers bestowed in the original mandate.
- Reviewing practices and procedures.
- Reforming the voting system to ensure a balanced representation of all members: raising basic votes to the original levels.
- Greater transparency in procedures and decision-making.
- Improving coordination and coherence of policy with other economic, financial or trade organizations and with Human Rights declarations.
- Renegotiating agreements on relations with the UN.

Substantive reforms (including the above)
- Effective control and real coordination by ECOSOC of the BWI.
- Reviewing decision-making and selection mechanisms used by the governing bodies.
- Greater accountability.
- Answering to the UNGA through ECOSOC.

In-depth reforms
- The International Monetary Fund and the World Bank should go back to their original mandates (world monetary and macroeconomic balance – IMF; reconstruction and development – WB), establish a democratic

decision-making process and be effectively integrated within UN auspices.
- These reforms should lead to a definitive solution to the problem of foreign debt, eliminate tax heavens, and set up mechanisms for world-wide financial cooperation and a global taxation system, as well as favouring increased levels of Official Development Aid. All these measures should make it possible to cofinance the functioning of international institutions and to set up funds of worldwide contributions for development. Only in this way will it be possible to ensure that the Millennium Development Goals come into effect and to promote truly sustainable human development that will conserve our cultural heritage, and the environmental and cultural diversity of the planet. In this context, the UN must urgently confront the task of establishing a framework for regulating the flow of finance capital around the world.

Some proposals on the in-depth reform of the WTO and of its relations with the UN; in-depth reform of world trade policies

Improving the functioning of the WTO
- Improving coordination between the UN and the WTO through UNCTAD and ECOSOC.
- With regard to the WTO:
- Reviewing practices and procedures to ensure the democratic participation of all its members.
- Greater transparency of procedures and decision making and, in general, of all its processes.
- Improved coordination and coherence of policy with other economic, financial and trade organizations and with Human Rights declarations.

Substantive reforms (including the above)
- Reviewing decision-making mechanisms and democratizing negotiation practices.
- Contributing funds to ensure the permanent presence and participation in Geneva of delegations from countries with fewer resources.
- Establishment of an agreement binding the WTO to the UN, obliging it to report on a regular basis to ECOSOC.
- The Consultative Organ for Resolving Differences should, in the last instance, come under ICJ jurisdiction.
- Answering to the UNGA through ECOSOC.

In-depth reforms

- The World Trade Organization must go back to being based within the UN and, along with UNCTAD, design world trade policies that are amenable to promoting a truly sustainable human development, conserving both our cultural heritage and the environmental and cultural diversity of the planet, and in compliance with human rights and world social and environmental regulations. Only in this way will it be possible to contribute towards fulfilment of the Millennium Development Goals.
- Bringing the WTO back into the UN must also entail a redefinition of the role of world trade and the setting of a clear framework for its effective regulation.
- Trade in raw materials and manufactured goods (presently under regulation by the General Agreement on Tariffs and Trade – GATT) must not continue to extend freely into Agriculture (Agreement on Agriculture) or Services or essential spheres such as education, health, biodiversity, culture, etc. (GATS and Agreement on Trade-Related Aspects of Intellectual Property Rights – TRIPS).
- It is essential to develop the concept of 'global public welfare' and, as part of the process, to redefine the concept of 'public service'.

Some proposals on the transformation from ECOSOC to an Economic, Social and Environmental Security Council

Improving the functioning of ECOSOC

- Improving the mechanisms for coordination with the programmes, funds and, in particular, the agencies, and also with the BWI and the WTO.
- Creating an executive committee with greatest regional representation.
- Improving working methods.

Substantive reforms to ECOSOC

- Effective control and real coordination of UN agencies and programmes and of all multilateral institutions with mandates in the pertinent fields, which would then answer to the UNGA through ECOSOC.
- Increasing the prerogatives and capacities of the Executive Committee.

In-depth reforms

- Evolving from ECOSOC to an Economic, Social and Environmental Security Council with effective control of the BWI (IMF and WB), the WTO, along with the relevant UN agencies, funds and programmes, which, once appropriately reformed, would become specialized technical agencies that are fully integrated into the system.

International institutions to address the environment

Martha Chouchena-Rojas, International Union for Conservation of Nature (IUCN)

I will focus today on the area of the international governance system in which my organization works, that is, the environment. It is important to look first at the challenges and the nature of the environmental problems that need to be addressed to then try to identify possible short-term responses.

The nature of the environmental problems and the measures that need to be taken

I will start by mentioning very briefly three points that I think are important when considering the environment.

First, it is important to stress that the current problems are unprecedented. In the many years in which we have had environmental institutions the problems have never been of the magnitude that we see today. If we take biodiversity loss, for example, we are losing species at more than 1,000 times the background rate of natural extinctions; one in four mammals are endangered and trends for other groups are also alarming. If we take climate change, we are seeing an unprecedented increase in the volume of greenhouse emissions with predictions, not any longer contested, of increasing temperatures in the years to come.

The second point is 'so what': we are losing biodiversity and we are in an environmental crisis, but what are the implications of these trends? This is a very important point when thinking about which institutions we need. The fact is that environmental degradation has consequences in the economy, in the social life, and in the possibilities of growth and development of all peoples. And, actually, if you take biodiversity it is now also uncontested that biodiversity is the basis for many of our economic activities and especially for the poor that live in rural areas. If we take climate change, the recently published 'Stern Report' argues in economic terms that climate change is going to have an impact on the economy and that if we don't act now the consequences on the economy are going to be comparable to those after the great wars and the economic depression of the first half of the 20th century.

The third point that I would like to mention is that the environmental problems are global and thus they need action by all. Governments have been traditionally the main actors, but there is an increasing need to engage more and more civil society, the private sector and local communities. But it is important to take into account that if action is needed by all, it cannot be done in the same way by everybody. Action needs to be taken in an equitable way, taking into account that responsibilities are differentiated across countries, and that the principle of national sovereignty needs to be respected.

I would like to touch very briefly in this respect on the specific case of the Kyoto Protocol and the ongoing negotiations on climate change, as requested by the organizers. There are considerable hopes and expectations in terms of the outcomes of the meeting of the last two weeks. The 'UN Framework Convention on Climate Change' and the Kyoto Protocol are indeed the main multilateral instruments to address the unprecedented climate change. It is important to note, however, that the Kyoto Protocol includes 35 industrialized countries that have committed to cut emissions to 5 per cent below 1990 levels in the five-year period between 2008 and 2012. The Kyoto protocol countries thus account for only 30 per cent of the emissions from power plants, factories and cars. The United States alone, which is not a Party to the Protocol, is responsible for 25 per cent. Also, the Protocol only covers the period until 2012 and thus negotiations are ongoing to develop a post-2012 agreement.

Taking climate change as an example, multilateral work under the Convention and the Kyoto Protocol are essential and provide the basis for international cooperation. But more ambitious and longer term action is now required. Interestingly, the 'Stern Report', mentioned earlier on, proposed that a future international framework needed to include emissions trading and thus to have market mechanisms working to address climate change. It also proposed to have technology cooperation thus involving the private sector and actors outside of the environmental sphere. It also identified the need to address deforestation as an important source of emissions, and to work on adaptation measures, taking into account that developing countries and poor communities are likely to suffer most from the impacts of climate change.

The main weaknesses of the current system and possible responses

The unprecedented nature of the environmental problems, their implications in human well-being and prosperity and their global dimension show that the challenges that we are dealing with are of a new dimension, but the institutions that we have to address them were created when the situation was very different. The fact is that our institutions are not any longer suitable for the challenges that we have before us.

I am going to focus now on some possible responses to address the weaknesses of the international governance system. It is important to start by mentioning the outcome of the United Nations World Summit of 2005, in which there is a specific reference to the need to look at the environmental aspects of the governance system. Heads of State recognized the need for more efficient environmental activities in the United Nations system with enhanced coordination, strengthened scientific knowledge, better treaty compliance and better integration of environmental activities in the broader sustainable development agenda and operations. The mandate of the Summit also asks to look at a more coherent institutional framework. Thus, in terms of short-term responses, it is important to take into account that there is a mandate and there is an ongoing process looking at this.

Actually, international environmental governance is being discussed in two tracks: first, the President of the 61st session of the United Nations General Assembly launched consultations under the cochairmanship of Mexico and Switzerland to identify current challenges and proposed options; and secondly, the United Nations Secretary-General formed a High-Level Panel on System-wide Coherence looking at the areas of development, human assistance and environment. The report of the latter process was issued on 9 November and it contains very positive recommendations that could allow putting in place short-term responses on the environmental governance system.

The possible responses need to address the weaknesses of the environmental governance system, so I am going to refer to four main weaknesses and some concrete measures which I think could help us move forward.

Limitations of the environmental governance system and institutions

- The first main weakness relates to the environmental governance system itself and its institutions. Anybody working on the environmental field knows that one of the challenges is the proliferation of agreements. We have more than 600 different agreements both at global and regional levels addressing environmental issues. These agreements are independent legal treaties and they also have different requirements which result in a heavy burden to countries to implement and to report on their progress.
- A second problem is the way in which science informs the decision-making process. Climate change is unique in that there is one scientific panel and a decision-making process under one convention and its protocol. On biodiversity we have many organizations, including the technical bodies of the biodiversity-related conventions doing assessments, but without a coordinated and strategic approach that could provide the necessary information to decision-makers.
- Another problem is the lack of cooperation and coordination among international organizations. Many United Nations organizations

have a mandate on the environment, including UNEP, UNDP, the Commission on Sustainable Development (CSD), WHO, FAO, and the biodiversity-related conventions. UNEP's leadership is not enabled in this context. Special attention is required on existing mechanisms and in particular the Environmental Management Group and the UN Development Group.

- Also, there is a clear lack of implementation, enforcement and effectiveness in the international environmental governance system. Moving from negotiation to implementation has proved extremely difficult due in part to the lack of appropriate instruments and capacities at national level.

So what kind of proposals could be made to try to have institutions and a governance system to address these limitations? Basically, what is needed is a system that allows more coordination and coherence of United Nations' actors and agencies within the environmental sphere, as well as enhanced monitoring, provision of knowledge and capacities to follow up environmental trends, and to respond with more effective decision-making and policy formulation processes. What type of institution could do all that?

As you know, several countries have been proposing to have a United Nations Environmental Organization – UNEO. France and other countries as well as some NGOs have been pushing for this with the idea that such a proposal would result in giving a higher weight to the environment in terms of the international decision-making system; providing a more secure funding base; and establishing universal membership for the governance of the organization. However, there are very divergent views on this proposal with a considerable gap between the positions of those that support a UNEO and those that are totally opposed to this idea.

In this context, we need perhaps to think about some incremental process, starting to see how to strengthen UNEP, which is the environmental body of the United Nations. The Panel on System-wide Coherence actually made this proposal in order to have 'real authority as an environmental pillar in the UN system', including enhanced normative and analytical capacities and broad responsibility to review progress towards improving the global environment. The report does not mention a possible UNEO, but it recognizes the need to upgrade UNEP with a renewed mandate and improved funding. It also recommends that some more work needs to be done in terms of looking at the institutional form and coordination.

Concerning the need to enhance coordination, this is perhaps one of the areas in which I find that the panel did not go far enough. This is a very difficult issue in which even a UN environmental organization would face limitations because each agreement has its own governance structure and they don't have the same parties. It is thus very difficult to think about one umbrella that would cover everything. Having said that, and this is a short-term proposal, there are experiences in which treaties under a particular issue can work together. There are interesting experiences in the area of chemicals. For example, a joint Secretariat has been established for two agreements, that is, the Rotterdam and the Stockholm Conventions. Together with the Basel Conventions these agreements are also identifying areas for common work. It would be thus possible to have some cluster-issues under which more synergistic work could be found. The Environmental Management Group could have an important role in this regard.

Concerning the lack of implementation and enforcement, it is unlikely from a political point of view to think about an enforcement mechanism that would sanction countries not complying with their commitments. The key is to build greater capacities and to get appropriate resources so that all countries are able to achieve their commitments. It is also important to reduce the burden imposed on countries by the lack of coordination among different agreements and to promote regional approaches to implementation.

Insufficient resources

In addition to the weakness of the environmental governance system itself, a major problem is the lack of sufficient financial resources. We can look at this in two ways:

There is of course the need to consider the financial needs of UNEP. One of the constraints of UNEP is that it depends on voluntary contributions provided by some willing governments creating uncertainties in its operations in the longer term.

But we also need to look more broadly at the resources available to respond to the environmental challenges and to protect the environment in all countries. The Panel on System-wide Coherence recommended strengthening the Global Environment Facility as a major financial mechanism for the environment, to review its contributions and to significantly increase its resources.

The other important point, which is very relevant to this panel, is the need to mainstream environment in development cooperation and to ensure that environment is not seen as a 'side' issue, but as the foundation upon which many of the development activities currently funded depend.

International governance outside of the environmental arena not always supportive of environmental objectives

This leads me to the third main weakness which I think is perhaps the most difficult one, that is, the need to address the international governance system outside of the environmental arena. We can do as many efforts as we can in the context of the environmental international agreements, but when the WTO takes a decision that does not support environmental objectives, or when development cooperation decides that the environment is not a priority, or when policies are developed in other sectors that have negative impacts on the environment, there is not much progress that can be achieved even with the best environmental governance system.

We thus need to have some type of institutional arrangement that ensures that environmental sustainability is mainstreamed across the norms and operations of the United Nations system but also outside, including the WTO and the Bretton Woods Institutions. A key message here is that a strong environmental agency like a UNEO would not be sufficient if measures are not taken also outside of the environmental sphere.

Concrete measures are needed first at country level: it is important to ensure that the work of the United Nations at national country level integrates environment in its operations. The Panel on System-wide Coherence proposed a One UN country programme. If this proposal is to be put in practice, it would be critical to ensure that environmental expertise is built in country teams and that environment is integrated in national development planning efforts. Governments need to mainstream environment within their policies, as this is a requirement to ensure sustainability at national level.

At international level, it is important to think about mainstreaming sustainable development in the United Nations system, including through guidance, safeguards and standards. ECOSOC has a very important role to play in this regard. One of the proposals of the Panel is to have a Sustainable Development Board to oversee the work of One UN country programmes. It also proposes to have a sustainable development segment in ECOSOC and to reinforce the partnership between UNEP and UNDP.

The Commission on Sustainable Development (CSD) also needs to be looked at in this context. One of the weaknesses of the Panel results is that it did not make any specific recommendations on the role of CSD, which clearly has some weaknesses as it has not succeeded in terms of linking environment and development. There is also a need to build coherence and mutual supportiveness between environmental policies and those of the WTO, the Bretton Woods Institutions and other non-UN organizations. The challenge here is that all the systems need to work together to achieve sustainable development.

Insufficient recognition of non-state actors in a state-centric system
The final aspect that I would like to address is the increasingly important role played by non-state actors in the international environmental

governance system. These include organizations like my own – IUCN, NGOs, local associations, and increasingly, the private sector. They play an important role in areas like the provision of scientific information and assessments (e.g. IUCN), influencing political behaviour, catalysing action, building capacity, providing funding, greening corporate practices, holding accountability of different actors, and contributing to technology transfer and the implementation of international commitments. The current system does not engage these actors in an appropriate way and this constitutes an important weakness that needs to be addressed.

It is thus important to engage non-state actors in the international institutions and processes and to use their contributions in the areas mentioned to enhance the effectiveness and performance of the system.

Way forward

The challenges before us are unprecedented and thus need unprecedented solutions. The ongoing processes in the United Nations provide a very important opportunity to engage in and to promote the needed reforms to get appropriate institutions and processes for the current times. These reforms need to address and reinforce institutions in the environmental sphere at international and national levels. Importantly, they also need to integrate environment in institutions in other sectors and to engage non-state actors in order to build an international governance system that effectively contributes to achieving sustainable development.

Two scenarios for action for change: financing for development, and innovative financing

John Foster, North-South Institute and Social Watch

I wish to highlight two theatres of activity which, depending on peoples' objectives, may be relevant to achieving change, over the next months, the next two years or so.

Financing for development

The United Nations has agreed that there will be a review or 'follow-up' conference of the 'Monterrey Conference on Financing for Development'. It will occur in Qatar, in the second half of 2008.

- Civil society did not endorse the Monterrey Consensus; some of us said it was the 'Washington Consensus in a sombrero'. In our message to the official conference we challenged the results.

- However, there were elements in the agenda and in the process of the Conference that were positive. The agenda included many of the themes and items of preoccupation to CSOs, particularly those concerned with development. The process was relatively open, both to CSOs and the private sector. Further, it brought together representatives of all, or at least most, of the major multilateral actors – the UN, the BWIs and WTO and UNCTAD – as well as governments into one tent, a UN tent. Most importantly, in terms of this dialogue, the purview of the Monterrey process includes systemic issues, opening the door to governance reform and, I would hope, to discussions of substantive factors like gender, and of how the whole system operates. I don't see why the sorts of issues that were raised yesterday, regarding UN and potentially ECOSOC accountability for the BWIs, and potentially the WTO, cannot be addressed under this item.

The preparatory process which is to begin soon in 2007 is an opportunity to engage with governments and multilateral institutions. The resolution just passed in the General Assembly speaks of consultations which will be 'open, inclusive and transparent', and which will engage the 'full involvement of all relevant stakeholders' and involve 'modalities used in the preparation' of the original conference.

Several organizations represented here were instrumental in creating an NGO follow-up group, after Monterrey, the International NGO Facilitating Group on Financing for Development or IFG. It will be important to clarify the terms of participation as soon as possible. It will also be key to collaborate both within whatever formal stages of preparation are created, but also in national capitals, with ministries.

There are a couple of events already announced which will be formal opportunities to engage. Civil Society has participated in the past and the IFG has facilitated nominations.

- The annual High Level meeting between ECOSOC, the Bretton Woods Institutions, the WTO and UNCTAD, which will normally follow the Bank/Fund meetings in April.
- The High Level dialogue on Financing for Development (FfD), organized by the General Assembly, which will be held in the fourth quarter of 2007.

Leading group on innovative financing

One of the most important initiatives in recent years was the joint Chirac/Lula declaration against poverty and hunger, which has led to the formation of an ongoing 'leading group' or 'groupe pilote' in innovative financing, originally chaired by Brazil and currently chaired by Norway.

This relatively informal formation has more than 40 members and has a series of potential and actual innovative projects under review.

- Many will be familiar with the airlines solidarity levy initiated in July by France and taken up by several other countries, and with the UNITAID (International Drug Purchase Facility) fund which will administer funds raised dedicated to the provision of treatment for HIV/AIDS and other diseases. This project has moved beyond research, negotiation into action.
- The currency transaction tax, long taboo in international conversations, is the subject of a focused seminar in Oslo in a couple of weeks. It is to be hoped that the Norwegian government picks up the initiative and carries it forward, and further, that networks like those at this conference support an initiative if it occurs.
- The International Finance Facility, proposed by the UK, has been discussed as the IFF (Intermediate Financing Facility) for immunization. There is a considerable list of other initiatives under study, including a further issue of Special Drawing Rights, other forms of international taxation including carbon taxes, and remittances. Of particular interest to many CSOs is the issue of 'leakage' in international flows, tax havens and tax evasion.

As mentioned, the Leading Group will sponsor a one day seminar in Oslo on 5 December, and a full meeting with workshops on a variety of initiatives in February 2007.

There are some clear positives to this initiative

- It has broken the US imposed five-year taboo on official discussion of global taxes.
- It has moved that from debate into a form of implementation through the formula of convenience: international taxes, nationally delivered.
- It has elaborated a diverse list of potential initiatives with the expectation that as France implemented one, other member countries would initiate others.
- It mobilized support for an initiative by wedding a desirable health objective, the provision of consistent funding for AIDS treatment, to the introduction of a new tax.
- It is eclectic, in that you may find finance, foreign, development and health ministers at group meetings, breaking through some of the silos or stove pipes of international debate.
- It welcomes NGO participation.

There are also some concerns

- The solidarity levy/UNITAID effort moved into operation quite quickly, with engaged NGOs arguing that it should be used as a means of collective pressure to gain lower prices and break the stranglehold of the patent system on key pharmaceuticals. The constitution of UNITAID, however, was approved without adequate opportunity for the consideration and possible approval of substantive amendments submitted by NGOs.

- The solidarity levy/UNITAID initiative brought together at least two communities of CSOs who did not normally deal with each other – AIDS Service and campaigning organizations like ACT UP Paris, and health action groups like MSF Brazil (Doctors Without Borders Brazil), together with groups focused on Tax Justice, debt abolition and financing for development. This has been a very dynamic alliance, but a lot of work was needed to be done to keep it together, as groups essentially spoke different languages.

- The engagement of NGOs is extremely informal, and there is nothing like NGLS or an effective international process to assist participation of marginalized groups, so it's rather catch as catch can. Further, decision-making among the NGOs has been quite informal and not particularly transparent. Although there was probably a measure on consensus about the criteria for selection of NGO nominees to the Board of the new UNITAID, there was not an inclusive process of nomination or election.

- The seminars/workshops held by the Leading Group are a positive advance, but unless other concrete initiatives, for example on a currency transaction tax (CTT), are undertaken by member governments it will decline into a short-lived talk shop.

- There is also the fear that those governments engaging in the extra-budgetary initiative of an airlines tax may simply be attempting to top up regular budgets, and that the distinction of additionality to existing aid commitments will be lost.

Conclusion

Whatever the limitations, I personally would argue that the Leading Group has been an important breakthrough.

- It is a locale for precisely what we are advancing at this event, dialogue between governments and other actors including civil society about substantive reform of key aspects of the system.

- It has been the locale for advancing at least one project from conception to implementation.

- It exists, in good part, due to political leadership on the part of a small but Southern as well as Northern group of governments, something we have repeatedly called for.
- But I would also remind us that breaking the taboo on global taxes is also due, in part, to the continued pressure of international coalitions, like Social Watch and others who campaigned throughout the Geneva 2000 UN Conference reviewing the Copenhagen agreements on social development, getting Canada and Norway to facilitate continued study of the CTT by the UN, and by national campaigns by groups like ATTAC in countries like Belgium and France.
- Finally, and picking up on the various calls at this event for independent financing, tax justice, etc., the airlines tax is a useful initiative, which can be considered a form of carbon tax as well. If it was adopted universally, it would raise significant funds. However, the potential revenue from a tiny Currency Transaction Tax is several multiples of even that amount. The strategic importance of having even a small group of countries which will take the leadership on this issue can hardly be overstated. The fact that one progressively led country is considering it offers an opportunity which civil society advocates should not miss. It might not come again.
- Both the Financing for Development process and the continued work of the Leading Group on Innovative Financing present opportunities for engagement on issues of substantive reform. In both cases feet are already in the door. The challenge is to open it fuller and redecorate the room inside.

Refounding and reform of the International Monetary Fund (IMF), the World Bank (WB) and the world financial and economic architecture

Marta Garrich and Josep Xercavins

Now, five years after the beginning of the World Campaign, the propositional work of the Secretariat of the World Campaign and the UBUNTU Forum has greatly intensified. The two sections that bring this Part 4 of the book to a close are a sample of the most recent fruits of the project. In this case they take the form of texts produced when hard at work on one of the main challenges for 2008: the Review of the Monterrey Consensus on Financing for Development (FfD) (Doha, 29 November–2 December 2008).

Initial design brief

Is the current model of world financial and economic architecture the right one for development? Are the current Bretton Woods Institutions suited for leading it?

According to the UN Charter of 1945, the ECOSOC should have reached agreements with the WB and the IMF laying down the conditions under which said bodies would be linked with the United Nations. In this case, under article 57 of the Charter the WB and the IMF should have been linked as 'specialized bodies'.

While the agreement that was actually adopted by the ECOSOC (13 votes in favour, 3 against and 2 abstentions), however, and later ratified by the Bank's Council of Governors (with one abstention) and approved by the UN General Assembly in November 1947, does state their nature to be specialized bodies of the UN, they were at the request of the Bretton Woods Institutions allowed to operate as 'independent international organizations'. Accordingly, they themselves decide what information might usefully be communicated to the ECOSOC, thereby involving a derogation of article 17 paragraph 3 and article 64 of the UN Charter (article 64 authorizes the ECOSOC to request and obtain regular reports from the specialized bodies). There is likewise a derogation of article 70 that provides for reciprocal representation at each deliberation: the Bank and the Fund reserved the right to invite UN representatives only to the meeting of the Council of Governors. And this independence not only has not diminished with time, but has in fact clearly increased radically and definitively down to our days.

Thus, and especially since the 1980s, this organizational and political independence has slanted world economic policy and international economic and financial cooperation, as well as the social and economic development of the developing countries, in favour of the small group of the world's chief industrialized countries, who have acted as and exercised the role of majority shareholders thereof. But it was from the 1980s that these institutions became the instruments with which this club of the world's richest and most powerful countries promoted and executed their well-known, damaging neoliberal structural-adjustment policies.

The Bank's incursion into loans for development policies and sectoral-reform programmes has boosted the liberalization of markets, the privatization of essential services such as health, education and water supply, the removal of subsidies and other forms of government protection for budding industries and agriculture, and land reforms based on market forces. This policy based on liberalization has moved in a direction opposed to the original mandate to provide capital and resources for reconstruction and development.

The IMF, for its part, is no longer a guarantor of international financial and monetary stability, although the need for a multilateral organization of this type has never been greater, given the globalization of financial capital and the volatility of today's financial movements. The institution no longer exercises the least discipline over its member states' exchange policies and lacks authority over the most industrialized countries (its 'principal share-holders', in the last analysis, and the main players in the world financial system), whose domestic policies affect the stability of the international financial architecture very much more than do those of the developing countries upon which the IMF rules have been most frequently imposed. What is more, its role in promoting development in the borrower countries has been pernicious, to say the least.

The recent report from the Secretary-General of the United Nations on the international financial system and development furnishes revealing information and offers fundamental reflections concerning the present role of these institutions:

- Net financial flows from the Bretton Woods institutions have tended to be negative, in some years significantly, in the last ten years. Since, in the current context, their financial operations are directed at developing countries, this pattern raises profound questions about the role of these institutions in financing for development. This trend has raised many questions about their continued relevance and effectiveness.
- The effectiveness and legitimacy of these institutions in pursuing their assigned objectives can be attained only if their agenda and decisions better reflect the needs and concerns of the majority of countries affected by their operations. The need for changes in voice and repre-sentation, to reflect the economic importance of many emerging market economies and to ensure that low-income countries are adequately represented, has been recognized.

Document A/62/119, 6 July 2007; International financial system and
development; Report of the Secretary-General

More specifically, article 11 and its reference table show that not only are the Bretton Woods Institutions currently incapable of fostering develop-ment, but are in fact a clear added handicap to development in many countries.

This inability to foster development was in fact already acknowledged in the Monterrey Consensus, which came down in favour of a greater United Nations role in the coordination and management of development:

- In order to complement national development efforts, we recognize the urgent need to enhance coherence, governance, and consistency of the international monetary, financial and trading systems. To contribute to that end, we underline the importance of continuing to improve global economic governance and to strengthen the United Nations leadership role in promoting development. With the same purpose, efforts should be strengthened at the national level to enhance coordination among all relevant ministries and institutions. Similarly, we should encourage policy and programme coordination of international institutions and coherence at the operational and international levels to meet the Millennium Declaration development goals of sustained economic growth, poverty eradication and sustainable development.
- We attach priority to reinvigorating the United Nations system as fundamental to the promotion of international cooperation for development and to a global economic system that works for all. We reaffirm our commitment to enabling the General Assembly to play effectively its central role as the chief deliberative, policy-making and representative organ of the United Nations, and to further strengthening the Economic and Social Council to enable it to fulfil the role ascribed to it in the Charter of the United Nations.

> Document A/CONF.198/11, March 2002; Monterrey Consensus,
> Final Document of the 'International Conference on Financing for
> Development'

What reforms are being discussed over the short term?

The power structure: votes and government
This is in fact a debate that is already common within both the IMF and the WB:

- If the reform process is to be consistent with its overall goal of redressing inequities in voting weights, the final outcome should ensure that the consolidated share of developing countries is not reduced. A reduction in the total developing country share will mean that the increase in the share of some emerging markets would be at the expense of all other developing countries. Furthermore, if the shares of low-income countries are preserved as a result of an increase in basic votes, such a reduction in the total developing country share could also be at the expense of a selected group of middle-income countries.

> Document A/62/119, 6 July 2007; International financial system and
> development; Report of the Secretary-General

• The international community should close ranks and make substantial progress towards governance reform in the IMF and World Bank in the next two years. At a minimum, the final outcome of the voting realloca- tions should result in a significant increase in the voting power of developing countries as a group. Strong and effective governance in all global institutions must be built on the basis of the accountability of their management and governing boards. Global economic decision-making should, as much as possible, be consolidated in international institutions of a universal nature – those that are part of the United Nations system – rather than in limited, ad hoc groups.

> Document A/62/217, 10 August 2007; Follow-up to and implementation of the Monterrey Consensus of the 'International Conference on Financing for Development'; Report of the United Nations Secretary-General

And some reforms have indeed already been approved. But they are of the type that is more akin to 'minor changes to ensure that nothing changes' – that is, they are not changes that involve any real alteration in the power structure. The Fund, for example, is now trying to restore its credibility by granting slightly more speaking rights and some increase (though less still) in voting rights to the developing countries. But approving an increase in quotas (and with it, of the vote that goes with them) for China, Mexico, South Korea and Turkey only means continuing to associate the Fund's power distribution with the economic weight of the member countries. Any more ambitious proposal only meets with rejection, thereby demonstrating a lack of real intent to change anything substantial. That is what happened to the proposal made by the civil society organizations that most closely monitor the ups-and-downs of the UN bodies, for example, the proposal for a 'double majority' (i.e. adding one vote per country to the current sys- tem of proportional voting according to the quotas of the member States). Furthermore, the recent changes of director in both institutions were in line with well-known pacts reached in the past, whereby the WB would be headed by an American and the IMF by a European.

Removing the regulatory function of the Bretton Woods Iinstitutions: putting an end to attached conditions, cancelling external debt
The attaching of political conditions as a means of achieving internationally agreed social and development objectives must be thoroughly overhauled. Along the lines of what was later to become known as the Washington Consensus, the content of the Bank's and the IMF's attached conditions has been based on policies postulated on a foundation of fiscal austerity and

restrictive monetary policies, liberalization of movements of capital, trade liberalization, deregulation of markets and the privatization of public or State sectors.

What is more, such policies generally followed a pattern that imposed uniformity, with a range of policies being applied to the great majority of countries without due consideration for the particular situations they found themselves in. The practice of attaching conditions has thus also undermined the national political arena of the borrowing governments and limited those countries' right to regulate their own economies. Indeed, the use of attached conditions runs counter to the Bank's own constitutional prohibition preventing it interfering politically in borrower member States.

Furthermore, the scope of conditionality of loans from the Bank or the IMF encompasses a great number of conditions that are neither pertinent nor fundamental to the purposes of the financing in question. There have even been cases where the conditions were in spheres in which neither institution had sufficient experience to offer an assurance that its advice would be sound, as has been amply revealed by cases in which their poor recipes gave rise to mistakes and the incurring of externalities.

The Bretton Woods Institutions must not become de facto organizations of governance in spheres for which they have no competence. Rather, these institutions must be subject to principles agreed by the international community, including the rules of international law that govern international economic relations, environmental protection measures, the protection of minorities and indigenous communities, etc. As international organizations, they will have to be accountable if their loan granting or withholding policies are in breach of these internationally agreed rules, for the conditions of the loans must reflect nothing other than their fiduciary role. On this whole issue, the following citations from reference documents speak for themselves:

- An April 2007 study by the IMF Independent Evaluation Office, on programmes drawing on the Poverty Reduction and Growth Facility for 29 African sub-Saharan countries, indicates that the conceptual and policy challenges in IMF's role in low-income countries continue to be daunting. The report finds that IMF staff focus too narrowly on macroeconomic stability and have severely restricted the utilization by countries of increases they have received in aid flows. Because of this narrow focus, Poverty Reduction and Growth Facility programmed the absorption, on average, of only two-thirds of the additional aid, the rest being applied to increasing international reserves. For countries whose reserves were below the threshold minimum, the study finds that 95 per cent of the additional aid was programmed for increases in reserves. For households in countries that are not only attempting to reduce widespread poverty but are also fighting significant HIV/AIDS epidemics, this stance has profound life-and-death consequences. For donors, the non-arrival of aid disbursements because IMF Poverty Reduction and Growth Facility ceilings could not be breached is unforeseen.

> Document A/62/119, 6 July 2007; International financial system and development; Report of the Secretary-General

- To promote fair burden-sharing and minimize moral hazard, we would welcome consideration by all relevant stakeholders of an international debt workout mechanism, in the appropriate forums, that will engage debtors and creditors to come together to restructure unsustainable debts in a timely and efficient manner. Adoption of such a mechanism should not preclude emergency financing in times of crisis.

> Document A/CONF.198/11, March 2002 (chapter I, resolution 1, annex); Monterrey Consensus, Final Document of the 'International Conference on Financing for Development'

Return to the original mandate

It is important to stress that, while these institutions have with the passing of years taken on mandates that did not lie within their remit, they have almost entirely relinquished the roles for which they were indeed created, and this at a time in which the need for institutions that play such a role has never been more pressing. This is a point made insistently in the following quotes from the various reference documents. In the case of the IMF, this concerns its supervisory function in a world that is more globalized than ever, in which balance of payments instability and the risk of macroeconomic crises are greater than in the past:

- The multilateral financial institutions, in particular the International Monetary Fund, need to continue to give high priority to the identification and prevention of potential crises and to strengthening the underpinnings of international financial stability. In that regard, we stress the need for the Fund to further strengthen its surveillance activities of all economies, with particular attention to short-term capital flows and their impact. We encourage the International Monetary Fund to facilitate the timely detection of external vulnerability through well designed surveillance and early warning systems and to coordinate closely with relevant regional institutions or organizations, including the regional commissions.

> Document A/CONF.198/11, March 2002 (chapter I, resolution 1, annex); Monterrey Consensus, Final Document of the 'International Conference on Financing for Development'

- Surveillance is a key IMF tool in its assigned responsibility of preventing crises and promoting macroeconomic stability. Looming over the surveillance reform currently under way at the IMF is the recent insufficiency of the Fund's influence in alleviating the exploding global financial imbalances through policy adjustments of large economies.

> Document A/62/119, 6 July 2007; International financial system and development; Report of the Secretary-General

In this respect, the report from the Secretary-General insists:

- Current account imbalances and exchange rates are economic variables shared among nations, and not fully determined unilaterally. If given the tools of economic surveillance, the IMF has the potential to become the lead institution in attending to global imbalances. But the Fund's influence has not been sufficient in getting the needed policy adjustments in the systemically important economies. The Fund's effectiveness depends, in the first place, on the quality of its surveillance activities; however, in the final analysis, its effectiveness ultimately depends on each country's willingness to compromise in the interest of multilateral cooperation. It is important that surveillance activities be perceived as even-handed to avoid the perception that these are targeted at specific countries.

> Document A/62/217, 10 August 2007; Follow-up to and implementation of the Monterrey Consensus of the 'International Conference on Financing for Development'; Report of the United Nations Secretary-General

And there is stress on a call for impartiality in the supervisory function of the IMF:

- If the proposed reform of the surveillance process is to succeed at restoring the effectiveness of surveillance by the IMF, the new mechanism should enhance focus and even-handedness; otherwise, the IMF will be seen as a player which is partisan to specific interests unable to play the role of an honest broker. Whatever the quality of the Fund's surveillance, its effectiveness will ultimately depend on each country's willingness to adhere to the principles of multilateral cooperation.

Document A/62/119, 6 July 2007; International financial system and development; Report of the Secretary-General

What world financial and economic architecture for the medium and long term?

The Bretton Woods Institutions must be refounded within the United Nations, such that they become truly specialized bodies (but not independent ones as they have so far been) of the UN system, and, on the basis of a return to the way they were conceived in their original mandates, take on the competences that the United Nations does really confer upon them.

Refounding the IMF within the United Nations system
In the case of an IMF refounded as a specialized body of the United Nations for sound governance of the world financial and economic architecture, its powers would be:

- Multilaterally correcting world current-account and exchange-rate imbalances, thereby ensuring worldwide macroeconomic and monetary stability.
- Supervising, controlling and regulating global movements of finance capital in order to prevent financial crises and ensure world macroeconomic stability – in general, stemming potential financial crises and strengthening the foundations of international financial stability.
- Undertaking ongoing surveillance activities over all economies, paying special attention to short-term capital flows and their consequences, in order to ensure timely detection of signs of external vulnerability.
- Offsetting the dizzying growth of world financial imbalances by means of policy adjustments in the large economies.
- Supervising, controlling and regulating tax havens, with a view to their ultimate disappearance, as an assurance of moving towards a steady and effective reduction of tax fraud and, in general, of corruption connected with the world of financial capital.
- Undertaking new functions in line with its refounded role, such as collector and manager of revenues from new and innovative mechanisms of financing for development and, in particular, of potential new levies on global financial capital.

Refounding of the WB within the United Nations system

If we compare the WB and its IDA (International Development Association) with the UNDP and its UNDCP (UN Development Capital Programme), we will see that the essential difference between them (stated in comparable terms at all times) is that the former manages some 1,000 times more funds than the latter. But the difference does not stop there by any means, for the former carries out its management within the paradigmatic framework of the Bretton Woods Institutions, while the latter does so within that of the UN. Refounding of the WB as a specialized body of the UN involves all that we have said for the IMF, except as relates to its powers, which in so far as they would then be practically the same as those of the UNDP would involve the two bodies being merged. It would thus become the UN body charged with best fulfilment of the Development Agendas throughout the world and, in cases of catastrophes of all kinds, also of the Reconstruction Agendas.

Central role of the United Nations financial, economic and development bodies in world development

As noted earlier, the solution does not lie in increasing the authority of the WB and IMF as they presently stand, in granting these institutions greater control over social and economic development aspects, but in having their working remits refocused back onto their core responsibilities, the tasks for which they were conceived during their creation: providing a stable and orderly international trade and financial system, and facilitating reconstruction and development.

And it is then a matter of revitalizing the United Nations bodies (UNDP, UNCTAD) that have the necessary mandate and competence to take social and economic development upon themselves in a more democratic manner very much more closely in accordance with international legislation based on the development of rights, to recover the role of the United Nations' economic and development bodies. These bodies are the forums that must take the lead on matters of human, social and economic development in the international field and that must achieve significantly greater influence over key economic policy decisions for the borrowing member States, as against the influence so far exercised by the IMF and WB.

These refounded institutions would thus become part of a coherent world institutional architecture, which with a stronger, appropriately reformed and democratized United Nations would represent a solid and genuine example of global democratic governance. And these are the forums from which to undertake a thoroughgoing review of the direction of development assistance, in which donors and recipients, lenders and borrowers share in taking decisions, making commitments and allocating responsibilities.

While we have not expressly considered in this document matters concerning trade and its more characteristic institutions, our proposals regarding the WTO and the UNCTAD are structurally identical to those made for the WB in relation to the UNDP.

Reforming the Economic and Social Council (ECOSOC)
Marta Garrich and Josep Xercavins

Initial design brief

To start off this section, let us return to these words from the Secretary-General's Report:

> The 'United Nations Millennium Declaration' (General Assembly resolution 55/2), the Monterrey Consensus, the São Paulo Consensus, adopted by the United Nations Conference on Trade and Development (UNCTAD) at its 11th session (TD/412, part II), the 2005 World Summit Outcome and other internationally agreed decisions have emphasized that trade, development and finance should be treated in an integrated and coherent manner to create and sustain an enabling environment for maximizing development gains for all countries, and minimizing attendant costs.

Document A/62/217, 10 August 2007; Follow-up to and implementation of the Monterrey Consensus of the International Conference on Financing for Development; Report of the Secretary-General

Let us note immediately that, from our standpoint, the ECOSOC would seem to be the essential multilateral body for turning that idea into a reality. This would in fact endow it with a contemporary mission for its work.

Moreover, coming on top of the exceptional importance of development issues in the present-day world is their close relationship, particularly nowadays, with another key issue: development must be compatible with the capacity of the earth's ecosystem to sustain it (environmentally sustainable economic, social and development). Though this is not the right time to go into this matter at length, particularly in its environmental aspects, we are seeing the need for a new conception of the role to be played now and in the future by the ECOSOC, a role that is broader and more closely geared to our present-day reality. What would be involved is a substantive internal refounding of the ECOSOC, along with a significantly reinforced role and major new powers for it, as a new **council for financial, economic, commercial, social and environmental security.**

The ECOSOC after the 'reform' process of 2005

On a more specific level, this quotation is appropriate for this session:

- We reaffirm the role that the Charter and the General Assembly have vested in the Economic and Social Council and recognize the need for a more effective Economic and Social Council as a principal body for coordination, policy review, policy dialogue and recommendations on issues of economic and social development, as well as for implementation of the international development goals agreed at the major United Nations conferences and summits, including the Millennium Development Goals. To achieve these objectives, the Council should:
- Promote global dialogue and partnership on global policies and trends in the economic, social, environmental and humanitarian fields. For this purpose, the Council should serve as a quality platform for high-level engagement among Member States and with the international financial institutions, the private sector and civil society on emerging global trends, policies and action, and develop its ability to respond better and more rapidly to developments in the international economic, environmental and social fields.
- Hold a biennial high-level Development Cooperation Forum to review trends in international development cooperation, including strategies, policies and financing, promote greater coherence among the development activities of different development partners and strengthen the links between the normative and operational work of the United Nations.
- Ensure follow-up of the outcomes of the major United Nations conferences and summits, including the internationally agreed development goals, and hold annual ministerial-level substantive reviews to assess progress, drawing on its functional and regional commissions and other international institutions, in accordance with their respective mandates.
- A point to note here is that during the last ECOSOC meeting, in July 2007, the first Annual Ministerial Review (AMR) was held. The AMR, which was already envisaged in this Outcome document from the 2005 World Summit and in Resolution 61/16 of the General Assembly, was seeking to review progress in implementing all the Internationally-Agreed Development Goals, including the Millennium Goals, and to provide guidance in this respect for countries, international organizations and other actors.

- Play a major role in the overall coordination of funds, programmes and agencies, ensuring coherence among them and avoiding duplication of mandates and activities.
- We stress that in order to fully perform the above functions, the organization of work, the agenda and the current methods of work of the Economic and Social Council should be adapted.

Document A/RES/60/1, 24 October 2005; Resolution adopted by the General Assembly; 2005 World Summit Outcome

Here a possible weakness emerges from initial thoughts/proposals: this framework may fall short of what is required (and we think it falls well short). There is also the risk of setting up more and more sub-bodies working on various levels within the institutional system, when what would be more appropriate and effective would be to delegate normative powers in the relevant spheres, even if express ratification was then required from the General Assembly. That same document in fact endorses the UNGA holding such power:

- We reaffirm the central position of the General Assembly as the chief deliberative, policymaking and representative organ of the United Nations, as well as the role of the Assembly in the process of standard-setting and the codification of international law.

The ECOSOC after a potential refoundation of the Bretton Woods Institutions and the World Trade Organization within the United Nations

Our second line of thought, complementing the above, is embraced in the World Campaign for In-depth Reform of the System of International Institutions. The grave political problem constituted by the abyss between what was agreed in the action plans emerging from the United Nations' Summits in the 1990s and what was actually implemented afterwards certainly does not stem from any 'manifest incapacity' of the United Nations in matters of implementation: rather, the inability to implement the agreements stems chiefly for the way the richest and most powerful countries have persevered in applying the neoliberal structural-adjustment paradigm, acting through the Bretton Woods Institutions – Institutions in which the decision-making power lies, let us remember, almost solely with those countries. And that is a paradigm, as everyone has seen by now, that not only fails to facilitate but often actually prevents the implementation of action plans rooted in the idea that responsibilities for development lie in the public sphere.

Since this is a systemic structural issue, we continue to insist that only a refounding of those BWIs within the United Nations – and thus with the associated decision-making, statutory and normative powers – can definitively resolve both the institutional conflicts and the implementation difficulties involved. For indeed the problem lies in the differing conceptions and outlooks held by the BWIs and the United Nations, and that is where the emphasis must be placed, rather than jumping to the mistaken conclusion that the problems lie in the coordination system for the final application of particular policies.

Although this stance may be regarded as utopian, as we see it both the clear crisis now affecting the BWIs and statements such as those found in the quotations presented herein from the Secretary-General of the United Nations amount to developments that surely point to a new, deeply reformed framework for our multilateral financial, economic and commercial international institutions.

See also this passage:

> *For its part, the General Assembly might consider it timely to decide on a fundamental strengthening of the institutional arrangements for intergovernmental follow-up of the financing for development process. It has been suggested on previous occasions that Member States could, for example, consider setting up a committee on financing for development or a similar mechanism to serve as a more dynamic and permanent forum to address issues related to the follow-up of both the Monterrey Conference and Doha Follow-up Conference. Such a committee could also serve as a continuing interface, at the intergovernmental level, with relevant bodies of the Bretton Woods Institutions, the World Trade Organization and other stakeholders.*

Document A/62/217, 10 August 2007; Follow-up to and implementation of the Monterrey Consensus of the International Conference on Financing for Development; Report of the Secretary-General

Nevertheless, we must insist here on our proposal: that this permanent-liaison level should fall to the ECOSOC rather than being an affair to be dealt with 'among equals'. Competence for dealing with all this could be conferred on the embryonic Development Cooperation Forum (DCF), for example, which would avoid any need to spawn still more bodies.

The ECOSOC's new Development Cooperation Forum

The official launch of the Development Cooperation Forum (DCF) came on 5 July 2007 in Geneva, and its first biennial meeting will be held in New York in July 2008 in the framework of the High-Level Segment of the ECOSOC's annual meeting:

- It seems to be that for the moment the new key that is intended to improve the ECOSOC's functioning, particularly in the issues that are of concern to us in this document, is to be this Development Cooperation Forum (DCF). Its nature and functions have been defined by the General Assembly.
- Review trends and progress in international development cooperation and give policy guidance and recommendations to promote more effective international development cooperation.
- Identify gaps and obstacles with a view to making recommendations on practical measures and policy options to enhance coherence and effectiveness and to promote development cooperation for the realization of the internationally agreed development goals, including the Millennium Development Goals.
- Provide a platform for Member States to exchange lessons learned and share experiences in formulating, supporting and implementing national development strategies.
- In accordance with the rules of procedure, be open to participation by all stakeholders, including the organizations of the United Nations, the international financial and trade institutions, the regional organizations, civil society and private sector representatives.

> Article 4, Document A/RES/61/16, 9 January 2007; Resolution adopted by the General Assembly; Strengthening of the Economic and Social Council

We now have more 'official' quotations proposing possible powers for this body:

- The launch of the Development Cooperation Forum under the Economic and Social Council has the potential of expanding participation in and building political accountability for the effort to improve aid effectiveness.
- There continues to be an urgent need to increase the overall volume of aid flows net of debt relief, technical assistance and emergency relief to meet the internationally agreed development objectives, including the

Millennium Development Goals. Donor countries should meet all of their aid commitments.

In the spirit of Monterrey, discussions between both donors and recipients need to be rekindled, in the new Economic and Social Council Development Cooperation Forum, on what kinds of flows should really be counted as 'aid'.

- There is increasing recognition among the parties directly involved in the Paris Declaration that, in order to accelerate progress, intensifying and regularizing the participation of developing countries in both the conceptual and operational aspects of the aid effectiveness discussion is indispensable. The new Economic and Social Council Development Cooperation Forum can play a crucial role in this regard.

- The Economic and Social Council Development Cooperation Forum could become the regular venue where the concepts of donor and recipient partnership – based on solidarity, effectiveness and mutual accountability – can be advanced. In the same vein, the governance structure of the International Development Association of the World Bank window needs to be reformed to include recipient countries.

Document A/62/217, 10 August 2007; Follow-up to and implementation of the Monterrey Consensus of the International Conference on Financing for Development; Report of the Secretary-General

The launch of the DCF might in theory bring an opportunity for effective control over international development cooperation, with this body attending to all aspects of that cooperation, including its governance, financing, effectiveness and impact. Its mission would thus initially have points in common with the mission of the OECD's Development Assistance Committee (DAC), and particularly with the mission of the Development Committee: the Joint Ministerial Committee of the Boards of Governors of the Bank and the Fund on the Transfer of Real Resources to Developing Countries (plus of course points in common with other bodies of those institutions).

In this context, we would stress that the creation of this new instrument, whether or not it is accompanied by in-depth reforms to the system such as those cited in this document, may conceivably lead to an increase in the complexity and inefficiency of the system as a whole rather than contributing to the system's coherence and effectiveness. For example, it will increase the complexity of coordination within the system, particularly insofar as the creation of the DCF may not be accompanied by any assurances regarding its real capacity to coordinate the above-mentioned institutions and bodies effectively.

This brings us to the Proposals section in this session: we will start with the areas in which we think the ECOSOC should hold competence – for example, through this new DCF (though not necessarily exclusively through it); and we will end by stressing once more the very important matter of the systemic-level role we feel it should end up playing.

ECOSOC competences in the field of development
- The ultimate definer, with normative powers rather than just the power to make proposals, for rethinking FfD, and the ultimate coordinator regarding the predictability, collection and stability of those Funds, for:
- The World Solidarity Fund.
- Multilateral ODA (helping to increase it by boosting the above Fund);
- Bilateral ODA (helping to reduce it, or at least providing much better coordination).
- nFfD – New and Innovative Mechanisms in Financing for Development – schemes (particularly those concerning regulating and controlling tax havens, and setting up levies on the global economy aimed at redistributing wealth), as a new fundamental source for feeding the above-mentioned Fund.
- The ultimate effective coordinator – normative rather than merely proposal-making – for international agencies, programmes, funds and bodies connected with capital flows (whether of the debt kind or FDI schemes and other private flows), with the aim, among others, of creating and maintaining a world macroeconomic environment that is conducive to development, and of pursuing and guaranteeing the stable existence of net flows for aid and development.
- The ultimate effective coordinator – normative rather than merely proposal-making – for international agencies, programmes, funds and bodies connected with trade flows in the world, with the same ultimate aim as in the previous case.
- The ultimate effective coordinator – normative rather than merely proposal-making – for international agencies, programmes, funds and bodies connected with efforts relating to assistance, cooperation and aid for development, with the aim of designing and beginning to implement the operational side of the Development Cooperation Forum as the right ultimate coordination instrument for these purposes.
- Taking precedence in status over the equivalent bodies in the BWIs and the donor countries in general – the OECD's Development Assistance Committee (DAC).
- Taking over as the driving force behind, and the ultimate multilateral body for effectively coordinating, present and future efforts concerning the efficacy of aid.

- As the ultimate guarantor for permanently defining and implementing the world's development agendas.

- The ultimate effective coordinator – normative rather than merely proposal-making – for international agencies, programmes, funds and bodies connected with worldwide financial, economic and commercial flows.
- In short, turning into the world's SECURITY COUNCIL for these issues.

In-depth reforms related to the ECOSOC

It is important in our view to highlight here this assertion:

> *We reaffirm the role that the Charter and the General Assembly have vested in the Economic and Social Council and recognize the need for a more effective Economic and Social Council as a principal body for coordination, policy review, policy dialogue and recommendations on issues of economic and social development, as well as for implementation of the international development goals agreed at the major United Nations conferences and summits, including the Millennium Development Goals.*

> Document A/RES/60/1, 24 October 2005; Resolution adopted by the
> General Assembly; 2005 World Summit Outcome

We can only conclude that this status as the chief body is unattainable within the present-day frameworks and with its current capacities. Consequently, both in-depth reforms in competences (e.g. those outlined in the previous sub-section) and structural reforms in the system to enable those competences to be pursued in practice are indispensable. What is involved is defining and coordinating policies, and taking on all necessary responsibilities to make sure that those policies are implemented and fulfilled.

In this, in return to the context of the World Campaign for In-depth Reform of the System of International Institutions, in our view it is essential that the Bretton Woods Institutions and the World Trade Organization be refounded within the United Nations in the way explained above. Equally necessary, however, are in-depth reforms concerning the powers and the democratic nature of the United Nations itself, as well as the various structural levels within it, so that the ECOSOC may one day become the kind of body that nearly everyone has called for and is still calling for.

An Open Letter to the New Secretary-General of the UN: Mr. Ban Ki-moon;[1] and the Three Broad Issues in a Process of In-depth Reform of the System of International Institutions

In order to make another world possible, let us make the UN more democratic and stronger

We the signatories have over the last seven years, at the initiative of UBUNTU – World Forum of Civil Society Networks, issued a number of statements to world public opinion detailing various common issues, important among them the fact that **'the democratization, strengthening and primacy of the UN in international politics are essential in order to make a better world possible'**. Some of these statements have been launched at the various World Social Forum gatherings, which, in our view, represent one of the most important expressions of **the will and determination of worldwide civil society to participate actively and responsibly in the construction of a better world.**

At this, **the start of Mr. Ban Ki-moon's term of office as the new UN Secretary-General,** to whom we wish every success in his work for the benefit of humankind, we want, in this open letter, to stress the following considerations and proposals:

I. In view of the problems of poverty and of development in general, there is a need to:

- Achieve the **Millennium Development Goals** (which we regard as minimum standards) and the **Plans of Action drawn up at UN summits in the 1990s** (which are far from being implemented), to which end **external debt must be truly cancelled without further delay.**

- Move towards a **fair world trade system oriented towards sustainable human development**, unlike the system that would be brought in by the Doha Round of the WTO, which, following the failure of its last meeting in Hong Kong, is still insisting on a neoliberal model of world trade that would continue to benefit the rich and powerful of the world only.
- A worldwide commitment to tackle **global warming**, in keeping with the principles of the Rio and Johannesburg summits, that would see countries responsible for their own emissions – first and foremost the USA, which must, as a minimum, sign and comply with the Kyoto Protocol – and, beginning with rich countries, would **develop and implement alternatives to the existing unsustainable trends in production, consumption and energy model.**

II. In view of the problems of peace, security and human rights, there is a need for:

- **Compliance with democratic international law based on universal human rights.** Consequently, we unreservedly criticize, as we always have, terrorist acts, as well as the illegal 'preventive' use of force (the most serious unilateral and persistent example of which is the war in Iraq). We once again declare that the deadlock, militarization and employment of all kinds of illegal mechanisms ('clandestine' prisons, walls of shame and 'selective' assassinations with collateral damage) in Afghanistan, Iraq, Lebanon, Palestine, Sudan and more recently Somalia merely lead to widespread and indiscriminate suffering among the civil society in these places. **We call for an immediate end to all these ignominious situations and acts** and above all urge that, in deadlocked conflicts, the armed forces should act as 'blue helmets' under the UN flag and command.
- **The essential reform of the UN Security Council** (removal of the power of veto, enlargement of the number of seats on the council to reflect the regional reality of the world, and effective control by the General Assembly) as a necessary step leading to the recovery of international confidence in the body that should be the guarantor of world peace and security. Its action, together with that of the General Assembly and other UN councils, should focus on the following areas: the peaceful resolution of conflicts (by promoting a culture of peace, the strengthening of the Alliance of Civilizations, etc.), disarmament and non-proliferation, R2P (Responsibility to Protect) and the use of violence as a last resort and only under the provisions of the UN Charter.

III. In view of the essential reform of international institutions, including the democratization and strengthening of the UN, we note that:

- The UN reforms on peace, security, disarmament and human rights proposed at the 60th session of the General Assembly have not materialized, with the sole exception of the Peacebuilding Commission and Human Rights Council.
- The capability and possibilities open to the UN on issues to do with development are being 'hijacked' and 'transferred' to the 'market', above all through the Bretton Woods Institutions and the World Trade Organization.
- Consequently, as the manifesto of the **World Campaign for In-depth Reform of the System of International Institutions** asserts, there is a need for '**a stronger, more democratic UN, placed at the centre of a consistent, democratic, responsible, effective system of international institutions. More specifically, we need to democratize the composition and decision-making procedures of UN bodies and agencies to ensure that they are effective and democratic. And we need to refound and integrate within the UN all other global multilateral organisations (IMF, WB, WTO, etc.).**'
- **These reforms, each of which are necessary in themselves, will at last make it possible to approve and implement the policies required to tackle and put an end to the grave problems that humanity faces at the start of this century.**

We the signatories urge the new UN Secretary-General, Mr. Ban Ki-moon, to press forward with the debate and work on these issues to enable us **once and for all to move from reports and resolutions to reforms and their implementation**, with the participation not only of member states but every other stakeholder in the world arena, especially civil society. **The democratization of international institutions is one of the priorities in the process of reform**. Consequently, international institutions ought to act in accordance with the various interests, needs and aspirations of all the world's citizens, **which involves setting in motion new and effective opportunities for citizens, civil society, the various tiers of government, etc. to enjoy representation and to participate in international institutions**. We will support every effort made to achieve the above.

PART 5

HOW CAN PROGRESS BE MADE TOWARDS GLOBAL DEMOCRATIC GOVERNANCE?

Part 5

A Multi-actor Socio-political, Global Movement for Global Democratic Governance

With regard to international – and also national and local – policies, there is growing agreement among very different political and social sectors that there is a need to change current global policies with a view to meeting the great challenges (social, environmental and economic) that humanity faces; and that in order to do this we need to advance together towards truly global democratic governance based on in-depth reform of the system of international institution.

Who are, in this case, the stakeholders that should and/or want to organize themselves into a socio-political movement to help put in motion these processes of reform, governance, policies, etc.? How can more players be involved in these processes, with a view to ensuring that they are as wide-ranging and diverse as possible? What form should the two-way reflection towards/from public opinion and towards/from global citizenry take?

We need to find a way to relate action carried out by different players with a view to setting in motion specific short-term reform processes, to mid- and long-term processes towards global democratic governance. It is necessary to achieve maximum visibility, clarity and transparency for all reform processes, ensuring that we take full advantage of all possible synergies.

> The dialogues held between different levels of governance and civil society actors in Geneva during the international conference organized by the UBUNTU Forum began the road towards shaping, articulating, defining ... a global social and political alliance of many actors able to promote advances towards the goal of real reform of the multilateral international institutions.

Towards a multi-actor political will coalition
Josep Xercavins

I think it is more or less accepted at this stage that when, as now, we are facing great problems and challenges, it must be possible to decide upon and implement major policies to settle those problems and to take on those challenges. And while not everyone sees it all the same way, I would nonetheless like to stress that major reforms are no doubt essential in this.

Why? To begin with, it has been ascertained – or at least posited – that we have seen that some international institutions pursuing certain policies have created certain problems. Thus if we wish to solve those problems – such as the issue of neoliberal globalization or structural-adjustment policies – we must adopt institutional reforms to put an end to those policies once and for all, and to bring change to those policies.

Yet there is more: there is another reality. A new reality in which we find new problems and new challenges, ones which our present institutions were not designed to tackle, not even the United Nations.

One example that is very apparent and also important at present is the issue of the environment: while CO_2 emissions cross state frontiers and know no borders, we have institutions in which ultimate sovereignty falls to the states. That was decided in the past, and it was natural to do so. And so when the United States does not sign or comply with the Kyoto Protocol, that is perfectly in accordance with international legality. Consequently, in my view, a number of reforms are needed to change this so that environmental policies, for example, are binding on all parties; for if not, in the end, the planet will not understand that even though we had the United Nations, each member state could ultimately do as it pleased.

Civil society should have an agenda of in-depth reforms. An agenda of in-depth reforms in the sense that responding to the challenges and problems now facing us as we are doing now is most probably neither efficient nor what is most needed at present. We must set ourselves a goal, a future to head towards. In this respect, we have tried from the World Campaign for In-depth Reform of the System of International Institutions to define a goal, and while we do not say that the goal is this one in particular, we do believe that civil society needs to begin to discuss what this agenda is, what the goal is.

I would like, if I may, to bring out what I see as three aspects of this goal we should be heading towards, at least in the medium and long term. On the one hand we have the challenge of making the system of international institutions more legitimate, and better able to face the realities of our present-day world. The General Assembly of States – a vitally important body that must continue to play the role it now plays – should be given a parliamentary body representing the world's citizens, for that would greatly boost the legitimacy of those institutions.

I believe that only by giving real power to this more legitimate United Nations and setting about a thorough refounding of the BWIs and WTO within the United Nations, with their policies being placed in the sphere of the United Nations, and defined and controlled by the ECOSOC, can we achieve an assurance that these institutions will not leave us, in 20 or 25 years' time, under the sway of policies that will be given a name in a few years' time and that will create an array of problems that will prove very difficult to solve.

The issues of peace, security and disarmament have come to a standstill, that no serious discussion on world disarmament has taken place for ten years, and that there is no current drive towards disarmament. Among other considerations, I think that if we also ultimately fail to achieve an in-depth reform of the Security Council, we will find those issues extremely difficult to solve.

Regarding the discussion of having a long-term agenda, from the stand-point of those of us who work in this field, it is important to recognize that there are urgent problems that need reforms in the short term, and that we must thus combine the two agendas, those two strategies. One I have just stressed, concerning the issues of peace, human security and disarmament, particularly this issue of disarmament. In the run-up to the Monterrey +5 Summit, the topics of Financing for Development and global levies must be specifically on the agenda over the next few months and, at least, the next few years as well. And as for environmental issues, as I have said before – and besides the newspapers are hardly talking about anything else these days – if we do not make a start on doing something soon, the planet will not forgive us.

How can these two agendas be pursued now? Who should be driving them?

How? Through political will. In the absence of political will, neither process would exist. Political will on the part of whom? Well, in the first place, the political will of civil society. There is a very great deal of political will and it has been shown over the course of many years' work by civil society. There is a strong political will to take on these two agendas, to do this work, and thus to undertake the reforms needed in the system of institutions in order to achieve those policy changes and to solve the problems confronting us.

We can highlight the fact – a fact that pleases me at least – that there are also political wills at work in some very important governmental levels, and I would like to spotlight them. For example, in connection with Financing for Development issues (FfD), there are governments working on and seeking ways of implementing new financing aspects, even independently from the United Nations to some extent. We could also highlight the fact that the General Assembly explicitly expressed its opposition last week to the latest attack by Israel on Palestine, though the Security Council did not, on account of the United States' veto.

We can see in this how political wills can also be found in governmental sectors. Roberto Bissio used an expression this morning that struck me as very interesting when he said that we should work towards 'coalitions of political wills'. We spoke of civil-society coalitions, since civil-society organizations do not all see things the same way, but when we do feel sure about particular projects we should form coalitions. And we should also join up whenever it is possible to do so – and it certainly is – with governmental actors, governments, regional-government levels, etc., in order to achieve these reforms, these transformations.

I do think that we should move towards some kind of forum for dialogue, one that could be part of this World Campaign or that could be set in some other framework. Because if we do in the end manage to bring about a scenario for reform – and I am convinced that we will get there through those 'coalitions of political wills' we were talking about – then we must work shoulder to shoulder with like-minded governmental sectors favourable to wills. To that end, a start must be made now on building these political coalitions with these actors: we will be living together as we move towards this near future.

To wind up, I would just like to add that what we will not give up is our work, at least the work done from the UBUNTU Forum and from the World Campaign. We will not cease in our endeavours to spread that campaign, reaching out still further to public opinion, creating a climate of opinion that is aware of and favourable to those changes. For without that climate of opinion, without that mobilization of citizens everywhere, we would fail to complete the building of a scenario conducive to unleashing those reforms, reforms which, I insist, are fundamental for changing the policies that are to improve our world.

Reform or transformation? The end of one era and the start of another

Yash Tandon, South Centre

Beginning of the end of an epoch

Listening to the debates on this floor and talking to many of you here, I get the strong sense that we live in tumultuous times, the beginning of the end of one epoch in transition to an unborn other epoch. There is complete erosion of the legitimacy of the system we live in. The demand for the reform of the institutions of global governance is only an aspect of it.

Looking back at our times, historians might call this epoch the 'period of Neoliberal Globalization' under Anglo-Saxon hegemony. Its approximate dates will be marked as from the mid-1980s (with the rise to power of Thatcher in the UK and Reagan in the US) to about 2010 – a span of about 25–30 years, or roughly a generation. In other words, we are witnessing the beginning of the end of this epoch, but it has not yet ended.

Four cardinal characteristics of the near demise of the US–UK driven neoliberal globalization may be briefly described.

One is the end, for all practical purposes, of US military hegemony. The superpower has military power unparalleled in the annals of military history. No power on earth has ever accumulated as much military power as the US today. And yet, apart from fighting small wars such as in Grenada or Haiti or Panama, the US military power has reached its nadir, its denouement. Time does not allow further expansion of this point, except to point out that when Donald Rumsfeld, the US Secretary of Defence, said at his resignation that we have not even begun to understand the nature of contemporary war, he was right. At least on this occasion he was right. Before the Iraq war, he had thought that he could use technologically superior precision weapons to target the enemy, and minimize the use of personnel in combat. He was wrong. Both Afghanistan and Iraq have shown that technology cannot displace people, and the military cannot take the place of politics or diplomacy. When women and men provide a human protective shield to Palestinian fighters against Israeli bombardment, we have entered a new era of peoples' war the like of which, in its magnitude and daring, we have not seen in the recent past.

The second reason the neoliberal globalization is nearing its end is its total and complete failure to bring jobs (in the case of the countries of the South, any jobs, let alone 'decent' jobs), and basic means of survival to the bulk of humanity. Never in history has science reached such enormous potential for servicing the needs of people, and yet so little of it is used to uplift the lives of ordinary people from misery and destitution. It is a historically unparalleled scandal. Neoliberal globalization has been driven mainly by corporate greed. The result is that we have on the one side the super-rich counted in their hundreds or maybe thousands, and on the other the absolute poor counted in their millions. The rhetoric of poverty reduction or poverty elimination is just that – rhetoric. It needs no rocket scientist to predict that MDG goal number one on poverty reduction will NOT be met by 2015.

A third reason that the neoliberal agenda is coming to an end has to do with the health of this planet and the environment. Corporate greed continues to pillage the earth, but there is increasing consciousness that something has to be done about it, that the 1972 Rio agenda needs to be revisited, and that serious action is called for at the global as well as local level. We are not there yet, but maybe by 2010, we might see some real movement on this matter.

And a fourth reason why the US–UK led neoliberal agenda is coming to an end is that the specific gravity of economic action is steadily shifting to the South, especially to countries like China, India and Brazil. It is too early to understand the full implications of this development. But one thing is sure: the United States and Europe are likely to become protectionist on the one hand, and on the other hand very aggressive in trying to open the doors of the countries of the South for investments and the services sector for their corporations.

Where do we go from here and how?

Three sets of ideas appear to me to have come from this multi-stake dialogue.

One is to work within the system; the second is to reform the system; and the third is to transform the system so that an alternative paradigm directs the course of future history.

Those who have advocated working within the system hope that the Millennium Development Goals are met by 2015, and in that optimism they have suggested how to try to meet those goals, for example, in poverty reduction or education. Still within this genre of thinkers are those who are working to control the damage caused by the present system. Among them are those that seek to limit the power of such institutions as the IMF, the World Bank, the WTO and the Security Council of the United Nations, so that nations of the South, and the peoples of the North as well as of the South, have a say in the shaping of their destinies, rather than institutions that have become the agents of the powerful and the rich.

Those who take a reformist road are arguing that the problem lies with the manner in which decisions are taken in these institutions, and that what needs to be done is to democratize them and ensure that they take into account the hopes and aspirations of the world's peoples, and those governments of the South that are responsible and sensitive to the needs of their people.

Then there are those among you who are advocating a total systemic overhaul, a transformative strategy, a strategy that would bring into discussion and then implementation of alternative strategies to the neoliberal globalization. In other words, a paradigm shift.

My own view is that we need to work at all three levels. Let me put it somewhat simply, and say that we work in the future towards a three-pronged strategy, and put our time and energy into these proportionately. Here is a rough tabular illustration of the three strategies, and how much time and energy we need to put into these over the next decade:

	2007	2010	2015
Strategy One: Damage control	60%	40%	25%
Strategy Two: Reform the system	25%	40%	25%
Strategy Three: Paradigmatic shift	15%	20%	50%

How do we go about this?

I suggest this assembly gives mandate to UBUNTU to contact all those who are here and those not here, but who can join this effort later in order to do three things:

- Disseminate the ideas of this multi-stake dialogue widely.
- Create a Task Force that would organize another such meeting every two years.
- Create a website and maybe a quarterly publication (with articles in all major languages) that would pool together ideas and suggestions while we collectively think on how to move from the epoch that is dying to one that is still to be born. Federico Mayor Zaragoza is the President of the UBUNTU Foundation, the President of the Culture of Peace Foundation, and former Director General of UNESCO. He acts as the mentor of the UBUNTU Forum initiative. The UBUNTU Foundation is a legal body responsible for the legal activity of the UBUNTU Forum Secretariat.

Notes and References

Chapter 1

1 Markets and liberal reason were proclaimed as the sole agents of progress and freedom, the final stage in human history. See Fukuyama, F. (1989) *The End of History and the Last Man*, Hamish Hamilton, London.

2 We take as understood as the background to this debate the process by which a specific type of power – political power – became expressed in the State, and why democracy became associated with this sphere of power and not with others – economic power, for example. Held, D. (1995) *Democracy and the Global Order: From the Modern State to Cosmopolitan Governance*, Stanford University Press, Stanford.

3 Kant, E. (1995) *La paz perpetua*, Editorial Porrua, Mexico.

4 Although the concept of governance is much criticized due to its conservative origins, it is used here with the same meaning as Dror assigns it: 'the political and institutional conditions to intermediate between interests and political support to govern'. Dror, Y. (1996) *The Capacity to Govern: A Report to the Club of Rome*, Frank Cass, London and Portland.

5 Valaskakis, K. (2001) 'Westfalia II: Por un nuevo orden mundial', *Futuribles,* no. 265, June.

6 It is not necessary here to enter into the debate on globalization which has occupied so much time over the last decade. Ulrich Beck has demonstrated its broad, complex nature. Beck, U. (1999) *What Is Globalization?*, Polity Press, Cambridge. The term is used here in the sense employed by Beck. See also, for an overview of interpretations of the concept of globalization, the definition of globalization in the Oxford Companion to Politics: www.oxfordreference.com/views/BOOK_SEARCH.html? book=t121&subject=s20

7 This thesis was expounded in DEMOS-UNESCO (1997) *Gobernar la Globalización. La política de la inclusión: el cambio de responsabilidad compartida.* DEMOS-UNESCO, Mexico.

8 Prera, Anaisabel (1999) 'El poder sin rostro', working document, France.

9 It should be remembered that of the 100 most powerful bodies economically, 51 are transnational companies. And that the agendas of all the UN's world summits were put to international debate by nongovernmental organizations, not to mention organized trafficking organizations or non-state networks of violence, or code societies.

10 As Held powerfully puts it: 'At the heart of this turn resides a conflict between demands in favour of individual states and demands in favour of an alternative organized principle for world affairs: in the final instance, a global democratic community.' Held, D. (1995) *Democracy and the Global Order: From the Modern State to Cosmopolitan Governance*, Stanford University Press, Stanford.

11 Some isolationist elements in US politics call for the abolition of the UN. This is the view offered by William Norman Grigg in the John Birch Society publication The New American, written in October 2001: 'The UN long ago defined itself as an ally of terrorism and an enemy of the American way of life [...] The UN is a haven for foreign thugs, tyrants, and terrorists ... a vehicle through which corrupt, powerseeking elites in this country and elsewhere intend to acquire power over the entire world.' http://www.thenewamerican.com. Such comments may be more extreme than most, but they are not qualitatively different from those made by many critics popular in the US.

12 In his overview of 'The Historical Development of Efforts to Reform the UN', Maurice Bertrand draws a parallel distinction between 'American and more generally North (including East and West) understanding of the problem' regarding 'reform of the structure of the Secretariat', 'suppressing obsolete programmes' and 'reorganizing the intergovernmental machinery to make it more efficient or more representative of the international community ... without reforming the Charter'; and 'representatives of developing countries who generally insist on enlarging membership of committees' and who increasingly stress the UN's obligations with regard to UN development. See Adam Roberts and Benedict Kingsbury, eds. (1993) *United Nations, Divided World: The UN's Roles in International Relations* (Oxford University Press, Oxford, pp. 420–421). James Paul of the Global Policy Forum also affirms that 'The UN needs reform. On that everyone agrees. But people disagree sharply on what kind of reform is needed and for what purpose. NGO leaders aim for a more democratic UN, with greater openness and accountability. Technocrats seek more productivity and efficiency from the UN's staff. Delegates favour reforms that conform to national interests and promote national power. Idealists offer plans for a greatly expanded body, that would reduce states' sovereignty. While conservatives push for a downsized UN with sharply reduced powers. Agreement is exceedingly hard to come by.' Paul, J. (1996) 'UN Reform: An Analysis', Global Policy Forum. www.globalpolicy.org/reform/analysis.htm; see also, for specific initiatives: www.earthaction.org

13 The Commission for Global Governance, for example, calls for the creation of an Annual Civil Society Forum with representatives from NGOs accredited before the General Assembly to inform and take part in the Assembly on relevant issues. The Commission calls for the establishment of the 'right of petition' for international society, expressed through a Council of Petitions appointed by the Secretary-General with the approval of the General Assembly. This Council would be able to make recommendations to the Secretary-General, the Assembly and the Security Council.

14 Strong, M. (1995) '"The United Nations at 50"'. Speech at Saskatoon', 3 March.

15 George, S. (2000) 'Fixing or nixing the WTO', *Le Monde Diplomatique* (English edition), January, pp 8–9.

16 Mayor, F. (2000) *Un mundo nuevo*, UNESCO Eds., Barcelona.

17 Mayor, F. (1994) *La nueva página*, Galaxia Gutenberg, Barcelona.

Chapter 4

1 See the UN's official website on the Summit, www. johannesburgsummit.org
2 Chomsky, N. and Dieterich, H. (1998) *La Aldea Global* Txalaparta, Tafalla; Beck, Ulrick (1999) *What Is Globalization?*, Polity Press, Cambridge.
3 'Open letter to President Bush: War on Iraq? The worst remedy for the world's grave problems', UBUNTU Forum statement, 4 February 2003. See www.ubuntu.upc. edu/index.php?lg=eng&pg=2&ncom=11
4 Xercavins, J., 'Diez años de desgobierno mundial', *La Vanguardia*, 4 July 2002, pp 34.
5 See the UBUNTU Forum's press release on Environment Day 2001; www.ubuntu.upc.es/comuni.php?id=ambient&lg=eng
6 See www.infoshop.org/inews/f15antiwar_news.html
7 See Held, D. and McGrew, A. (2002) *Globalization/Anti-Globalization*, Polity Press, Cambridge.

Chapter 6

1 The Commission on Global Governance issued its report 'Our Global Neighbourhood' in 1995.
2 For more information on initiatives on democratization of global governance, please see Helsinki Process: 'Survey of Global Commissions and Processes', Helsinki, 2003, www.helsinkiprocess.fi/Documents; and visit the bank of resources set up by the Ad Hoc Secretariat of the World Campaign for In-depth Reform of the System of International Institutions: www.reformwatch.net

Chapter 7

1 In line with a widely-supported proposal, work could move towards creating a par-liamentary assembly, which could play a role in establishing international law, put forward recommendations and exercise control over the other institutions forming part of the system.
2 Following the example of one of the oldest multilateral institutions – the International Labour Organization – specific assemblies could be established to guarantee partici-pation by different government levels and actors from civil society, in the broadest sense of the term, within the appropriate institutions.

Chapter 10

1 See Amin, S. (1979) *Classe et nation dans l'histoire et la crise contemporaine*, Editions de Minuit, Paris.
2 See Amin, S. and el Kenz, A. (2003) *Le monde arabe enjeux sociaux et perspectives méditerranéennes*, Editions L'Harmattan, Paris, pp 6–12.

3 See Amin, S. (2002) *Au delà du capitalisme sénile, pour un XXIe siècle non américain,* PUF, Paris.

4 See Amin, S. (2002) *Au delà du capitalisme sénile, pour un XXIe siècle non américain,* PUF, Paris, Chapter I.

5 Interview with Samir Amin by Yves Berthelot, 'U.N. intellectual history', UN, New York, April 2002.

6 See Amin, S. (2002) *Au delà du capitalisme sénile, pour un XXIe siècle non américain,* PUF, Paris.

7 See Amin, S. (2001) *Alternatives du Sud,* vol. VIII, no. 3, 2001; Amin, Samir (2002) *Au delà du capitalisme sénile, pour un XXIe siècle non américain,* PUF, Paris, pp.105.

8 See Amin, S. (2003) 'WTO recipe for world hunger', in *Ahram Weekly,* no. 657, September 2003, El Cairo.

9 See Vercelone, C. 'La question du développement à l'âge du capitalisme cognitif', www.forumtiersmonde.net/fren/index.php?view=article&catid=60%3Aetudes-studies&id=164%3Ale-developpement-a-lage-du-capitalisme-cognitif&option=com_content&Itemid=129

10 See Amin, S. (2002) *Au delà du capitalisme sénile, pour un XXIe siècle non américain,* PUF, Paris, Chapter III.

11 Arrighi, G. (ed.) (2003) *The resurgence of East Asia,* Routledge.

12 André Gunder, F. (1998) *Re Orient,* University of California Press, California.

13 Lin Chun (2005) 'What is China's comparative advantage?', *The Chinese model of modern development,* Routledge, London, pp. 264–276.

14 Samir Amin, Le virus liberal, Le temps des cerises, 2003, pp. 32–50.

15 See World Summit Outcome, www. reformtheun.org/index.php/united_nations/ 1433

Chapter 14

1 'Open letter to the new General Secretary of the UN: Mr Ban Ki-moon: To make another world possible, make the UN more democratic and stronger', is the statement no. 23 of the UBUNTU Forum; it was launched on 16 February 2007 and published in the International Herald Tribune bearing the signatures included in the text, and it was subsequently signed by over 1,000 individuals and organizations from all over the world.

Index